Restoring our Hearts

A seed sown for
24/7 prayer

Paul Collett

Paul Collett

More copies available via
New Community West End = Church
Office

Onwards and Upwards Publications, Berkeley House,
11 Nightingale Crescent, West Horsley, Surrey KT24 6PD

www.onwardsandupwards.org

ISBN: 978-1-907509-16-2
Cover design: Guilherme Gustavo Condeixa

Printed in the UK

Dedication

This book is dedicated to my mother, in memory of my father, and it written with gratitude to my wife and for my children.

Acknowledgements

There are so many people that I would want to thank. No one can succeed alone but many fail in isolation. Firstly, I would like to thank my wife, Carol Ann, and my children, Abigail, Jemimah, Keziah and Daniel, for their encouragement, allowing me to include their stories and tolerating my frequent disappearances to write. I would particularly thank Abigail and Daniel for their ideas for the cover design. I would also like to give my special thanks to Carla, Rachel and Chris for their permission to include their stories.

Next I would like to pass abundant thanks to the whole congregation of New Community Church West End; from our friends there, although I could mention everyone, I pick out Clive and Jane Wiseman, Roy and the late Gillian Pearson, Chris and Irene Stacey, and Peter and Shirley Porter. I would like to thank my friend David Payne for reading and making helpful comments on an early draft of this book. I would also like to thank Linda Irvine for reading, correcting and commenting on a later draft. I am grateful to Tom and Kate Hess, Martin Scott and Pulipaka Sukumar for taking time to read what proved to be an earlier draft of book which they still felt able to endorse. I want to give particular thanks to Peter Butt and Stewart Keiller for their comments and help in improving the finished book. I would like to thank the late Jonathan Wallis and his widow Sylvia for their invaluable support in writing. Jonathan had taken the trouble to read through the almost finished manuscript not once but twice and gave invaluable advice on editing and presenting the final book. His wisdom is sorely missed. As a friend put it, heaven's gain is our loss.

I honour Pastor Marion Daniel of Sozo Ministries International for her invaluable wisdom on the chapter that deals with 'Blessings and Curses'. Thanks to Faith Allen for allowing me to pre-launch the book at the Arise Warrior Bride conference in June 2011. I am indebted to the love and support of our friends Steve and Storm Drew, David Muyiwa Adeola, John Duff, Richard Swift, Jeremy and Melanie Douglas, Pete and Wendy Churchill and the team at the London Synagogue Church of All Nations. I have to mention with gratitude the prayer warriors at the

Southampton Half Night of Prayer, particularly Alex Bailey, Ann Hutchinson, Iain and Pat Anderson, Carolyn Vanstone and Katie Coles who have helped birth this book in prayer.

Endorsement by Clive Wiseman

In this book Paul tells his personal story openly and honestly, providing deep insight into his own experience of God working in every detail of his life. He candidly exposes his intimate thoughts and feelings along with his testimony of how his own heart, having suffered emotional pain and damage, is being healed and restored through his relationship with God the Father.

Paul is a man wildly passionate about and deeply devoted to God's word, the Bible. He refers to scripture throughout this book to illustrate and explain the points made and stories told. He also provides opportunities to put in to practise the learning through Action Plans and Prayer Points; expect to be challenged to do more than just read!

I have had the privilege of knowing Paul for several years and have seen his heart of love shown towards many others as a faithful husband, father, colleague and friend. I hope that through reading this book you too will discover something more of God's heart of restoration and experience it for yourself.

CLIVE WISEMAN
Team Leader, New Community Church West End
Southampton
England

Endorsement by Pulipaka Sukumar

I want to thank dear Brother Paul Collett in Christ, fondly known to me. He has a *kind heart* and a big vision. My dear brother, you are truly a blessing.

I pray that our God will propel his word and ministry to new heights in the days to come. I praise God for his book 'Restoring the Hearts', and I praise God for Paul's hard work of three years; all glory to be God.

Writing a book can be a humbling process and also a difficult one. We need to learn more about the word of God and the works of God. We need revelation from Heaven.

I hope this book will ignite a spark among the people of God, a spark that will eventually become a raging, unquenchable fire. The end time church needs to read this book. This timely book will certainly illuminate and restore your heart.

PULIPAKA SUKUMAR
President, Devokthi Ministries
Vuyyuru A.P state
South India

Endorsement by Martin Scott

As you read this book you will encounter a writer with a passion and faithfulness to his convictions. This is not a book with some ideas to be considered; rather it is a piece of writing that has come from Paul's own journey. He shares from his own past the healing he has experienced, his responses to God, his observation on what he sees, and above all the light that Scripture shines into all of that.

Having read the book, I asked myself, "What do I think Paul would want to see happen in society?" My conclusion? Restoration. For example, restoration at the macro level as he writes about Jew/Gentile issues and restoration at a family level are certainly two of aspects of this. Yet his heart expression is not addressing such issues without a context. The context is of a restoration to God and Father of our Lord Jesus as our Father. As you read the book be open to new levels of reconciliation to the Father, and be ready to stand in the gap with others as agents of reconciliation and carriers of hope.

MARTIN SCOTT
Author, Gaining Ground and Impacting the City
http://3generations.eu/blog/?page_id=2791

Contents

Restoring our Hearts

Foreword by Tom and Kate Hess

We know we are in the end-times, even the last days; the signs are everywhere. Consequently, it is time for the **restoration** of all things (Acts 3:21), as it is written, before Jesus' soon coming return. This book is about exactly that!

In Malachi 4:5-6, we are told that "before the coming of the great and dreadful day of the Lord" He will turn the hearts of the fathers to the children and the children to the fathers, lest He curse the earth. How is God glorified without the full manifestation of reconciliation and restoration that His very own Son came to purchase, by taking the curse upon Him and dying on a cross?! God is determined to do this: bless His Son! The turning of the hearts is a full embodiment of the eternal, perfect love of the Father for His Son and the Son for His Father. Therefore, restoration of the fundamental relationship that the universe is based on, the Father/Son relationship, is of supreme importance!

Historical events must happen as well, in this process known as "the restoration of all things". Luke 21 speaks of signs of the end of the age before the coming of the Son of Man, one of which is Jerusalem. In verse 24, we discover that there is a point in history when the "time of the Gentiles" will be fulfilled, signifying not only the return of Jesus to the planet but also His heart turning to the Jewish people. (Again, we see the heart of the Father turning to His children.) This all somehow corresponds with the restoration of Jerusalem, i.e. "no longer being trampled under" but becoming the City of the Great King (Ps. 48:2, Matt. 5:35) in all of His majesty. We are in this time: in 1948, Israel began to be restored, and in 1967, Jerusalem became reunited under Jewish sovereignty. In summary, the King of Kings could not come back to a city that was not prepared for His final triumphal entry!

Another critical restoration that is taking place, in these very moments of history, is the restoration of the Tabernacle of David, spoken of in Amos 9 and Acts 15. This speaks of the glorious restoration of Israel, the Land and the People, and the whole human race, whosoever will seek His face. These are the "living stones" in His "spiritual house," of which we are a part (1 Peter 2:5). As the living stones are restored, so the fallen tabernacle of David is being resurrected. God says, "My House shall be called a house of prayer for all nations." (Isaiah 56:7) God is restoring His House and His family from every tribe, tongue and nation. We are those "living stones" that make up His House, His dwelling place forevermore!

Isaiah 58:12 says: "Those from among you shall build the old waste places; you shall raise up the foundations of many generations; and you shall be called the Repairer of the Breach, the Restorer of Streets to Dwell in." How can we be the repairers of the breach if we are not repaired? How can be the restorer of streets to dwell in if we are not restored? These are the days of restoration, and it begins with us, in us. The restoration we gain, individually and corporately, is the restoration we give to the hopeless, perishing world around us.

In this volume, Paul Collett, a Spirit-filled social worker, minister of reconciliation and intercessor, unpacks the Father heart of God in these last days: restoring the hearts of the Father-Son relationship upon which the whole universe exists and resounds. He is another voice crying out in the wilderness, born to proclaim and see the restoration of all things, preparing the way for the Lord's second coming. He shares freely from a rich wealth of scripture, history, poetry, anecdotes and his own powerful, life-giving testimony. We admire his courage to tell his story with such profound honesty and sensitivity, as one who has been set free. May your heart also be restored to fullness as you partake of this book!

Shalom in Messiah's Love,

TOM AND KATE HESS
Jerusalem House of Prayer for All Nations
Jerusalem, Israel

http://www.jerusalemhouseofprayer.org/index.html

email: ancj@jhopfan.org
Tel: +972 2626 1518
Fax: +972 2626 4239

Prologue

Carla's story

Carla was 10 years old when I first met her. She had a warm, funny and, above all, very loud personality. I found her very engaging. Yet she had suffered the most awful experiences of abuse, neglect and rejection. I was her social worker for two years and found her difficult to help. For one thing, she seemed to run from wherever she was placed, and her family showed little concern or interest in her. All of my training and skills appeared of limited use. Nothing I did seemed to work.

Instead of being able to make her life any better, I watched it get worse. Word came back to me that Carla was using drugs including 'Crack' (the slang name for freebase cocaine) and being drawn into prostitution. The poor in the western world may not be dying of physical malnutrition, but their case is as hopeless as those who are. There is a famine of love - real love - in the land, particularly the love of a father. Within the constraints of my work, 'all' that I could do was to pray for her when she was absent. This I did frequently; it felt as if my heart was breaking as I wept for her. I knew that God had heard me, but nothing outwardly changed.

We can lose confidence when we wait for an answer to prayer. This is particularly the case when we have a clear predetermined view of how and when that prayer should be answered. Solomon once wrote:

Proverbs 13:12
Hope deferred makes the heart sick, but a longing fulfilled is a tree of life.

I have known times of sadness when my hopes were deferred and other seasons of joy when my longings have been fulfilled. However, we cannot and must not draw our information about God, His character and faithfulness from our having bad or even good days. He is the same yesterday, today and forever.

I believe that God is good all the time, regardless of our perception or experience. We need, like Paul, to learn the secret of being content in all our circumstances (Philippians 4:12). For many Christians the dashing of hopes has resulted in disappointment and the development of a 'sick heart'. We cannot dwell in this place, for disappointment is the seedbed of unbelief. We need to learn to hope again. We must use the word of God to challenge our experience rather than allow our experience to defy the word of God. God wants to heal and restore our sick hearts.

The Dream

This book is born out of a passion. I have always wanted to write. When I was a teenager I wrote poetry. I did an English degree with a view to becoming a writer. At college I even started writing a book but had to stop. My difficulty was that I had nothing to say. I needed to live before I could write. I let the dream die, but God did not. In the words of Habakkuk:

Habakkuk 2:3
For the revelation awaits an appointed time; it speaks of the end and will not prove false. Though it linger, wait for it; it will certainly come and will not delay.

God needed to work on my heart.

Over the years, reminders have come. The only time I ever met David Bulnois, who for many years supported the work of Crusade for World Revival as an intercessor, he asked me if I had any difficulty in filling a plain sheet of paper with writing. I honestly answered, "No." I never had done. He then told me that I needed to write. I took it to heart.

In spring 1992, my wife, Carol Ann, and I were on holiday in Corfu. It looked like our last opportunity to take a break before we plunged into parenthood. Our reason for choosing this destination was that Carol Ann's sister was working there for the Christian holiday firm Mastersun, and we could enjoy a 'friends and family' discount! To our great surprise, when we arrived at the hotel we discovered that a Christian writers' conference was taking place during the same week. Hosting the event were Adrian and Bridget Plass and Jennifer Rees Larcombe. It was an even greater surprise when we were invited to join in with the conference. We were made to feel very welcome. The point was reinforced; I felt that I needed to write, but what?

From 1998 until 2008 I worked as an independent social worker and produced countless large and very detailed reports. During this time I could honestly say I made a living from writing. That made me a writer – well, sort of. I even wrote a chapter of someone else's book during this time [1]. To be honest, I knew that this was not my dream, but it was the path to it.

Milton

I am reminded of the story of a great English writer from another age, John Milton, who lived from 1608 to 1674. He was a man who carried impossible dreams for decades. His path to their fulfilment appears to have been tortuous. Milton dreamt of crafting the greatest Christian epic poem ever written that would surpass the classical epics of antiquity. He started well. As a young man he envisaged writing an epic of the Arthurian legend. He became the youngest contributor to the English Hymnal, writing 'Let us with a gladsome mind, praise the Lord for He is kind' when he was just fifteen.

Milton studied hard, and it was said that from the age of twelve he did not leave off reading until past midnight. He became, by common consent, the most learned English poet ever to hold a pen. He gained a command of Latin, Greek, Hebrew, French, Spanish, Italian, Old English and Dutch but at a high price. He went blind before he was forty. His dreams began to crumble. Two of his wives and a number of his children died. The cause of the English Republic to which he gave his life, having served as Oliver Cromwell's Latin Secretary, came to an end with the restoration of the monarchy in 1660. For a time he was imprisoned. He knew what it was to be broken-hearted and disappointed.

I find Milton's 'Sonnet on His blindness', written at this time, one of the most moving poems written. He described how he tried to reconcile his strong sense of vocation with his inability to achieve his dreams as he lost his sight. This is an extract from the end of the poem:

God doth not need
Either mans work or his own gifts, who best
Bear his milde yoke, they serve him best, his State
Is Kingly. Thousands at his bidding speed
And post o'r Land and Ocean without rest:
They also serve who only stand and waite.

The death of all of Milton's dreams and vision proved to be the doorway to the fulfilment of God's vision and purpose for his life. The epic Christian poems that he finally wrote - 'Paradise Lost' and its sequel 'Paradise Regained' - are now recognised as the finest in the English language. These were not published until near the end of his life in 1667 and 1671 respectively. In them he tells the story of man's fall and restoration through the work of Christ's death and resurrection. All of the pain of disappointment from his experience and the consolation of his Christian hope find voice in these lyrics. When writing, it is recorded that Milton woke up each morning with the words of 'Paradise Lost' filling his mind, which he then dictated to his daughters.

For centuries Milton stood just behind William Shakespeare as one of England's greatest poets. Whereas Shakespeare was silent about the things of God, this was Milton's theme. In his words, his intention was to "assert Eternal Providence, and justifie the wayes of God to men" (from his prologue to Paradise Lost).

It is not too dramatic to say that Milton was a father of the writers of our land. At one time, every English home was said to possess a copy of the Bible, John Bunyan's 'Pilgrim's Progress' and Milton's 'Paradise Lost'. Now, sadly, he is part of our forgotten Christian heritage. We need to turn back to our fathers. We forfeit our destiny if we forget our history. It is time to allow God to resurrect our dreams and the dreams of our land.

Fulfilment

One Sunday morning, some twelve years after I had handed Carla over to another social worker, she walked into our church. I had seen very little of her in the intervening years, but we recognised each other immediately. She was as demonstrative as ever and threw her arms around me, and we both wept. My longings for her life had begun to be fulfilled, my prayers answered. She had become a Christian some months before and was experiencing God's help in leaving her old life of drugs and prostitution. I had the joy of seeing her baptised early in the following year when members of her family witnessed her making her commitment public. The transformation in her life was nothing short of miraculous. I praise God for the many people that he used in bringing about her miracle, including my small part.

I wonder, when you think of revival, what does it look like to you? When I think of the revival that we desperately need, I think of answered prayers - lots of them. I am convinced that the more prayers that are uttered in faith, the more will be answered. I see friends and family coming to Christ. I see many, many love-starved Carlas discovering the love of Father God for themselves.

Study of the scriptures reveals God's bias to the poor. In these days the church needs to pick up the mantle of Elijah. We must ask for a double portion of his spirit. I have the conviction that God is coming for the poor, and He is coming whether we are ready or not. We need to get ready. Jesus is coming.

My heart in writing this book is that it should be a catalyst for prayer in general and prayer for revival in particular. It has been written with prayer, and my hope is that it will be read in the same way. I believe that the gospel of Christ, and not social work, is the only hope for our nation.

Therefore let us pray together for a revival that continues until the return of Christ. Pray that as you read it begins to be birthed in your heart.

REFERENCES

1. McMahon, Linnet, Ward, Adrian (editors), *Helping Families in Family Centres:* Chapter 7; Collett, Paul, "Working with men in Family Centres"; published by Jessica Kingsley in 2001; ISBN 1853028355, 9781853028359.

Surely the day is coming

Malachi 4:1

Surely the day is coming...

Joseph's story

It was a bad day, and it was about to get worse. The car glided to a halt at the side of the A3; it had run out of petrol. I pulled in as far as I could but noticed that there was no hard shoulder on this stretch of road. I put on the hazard warning lights and began to walk along the side of the road to get some petrol. It looked like I had a long walk.

Less than fifteen minutes before, I had finished my last visit to the last child that I represented as a Children's Guardian. I did not want to leave my work and, unusually in any sphere of social work, his family did not want to say goodbye to me. Both of us had our fears for the future. His parents, Rob and Rachel, were concerned because of Joseph's life-limiting condition and the continued court proceedings that surrounded him and me because I had no job.

Joseph suffered from a cruel condition called West Syndrome that meant he had epileptic seizures many times a day. These had started (or were first noticed) when he was four months old. He then lost the abilities that he had acquired and eventually even lost the sucking reflex that he had been born with. He was totally dependent on the care that was provided for him. He also had a range of secondary conditions arising from his primary problem; these included scoliosis (curvature of the spine) and breathing difficulties.

I had not walked very far down the road when the flow of traffic stopped. I did not hear the sound of the impact that took place behind me. The first driver through the crash site pulled alongside and told me what had happened. A coach had ploughed into the back of my car, and debris was scattered all over the carriageway. I turned back to face the wreck. It felt like I had just lost everything. It was hard to see how anything good could come out of this.

The contrast with when I had first met Joseph and his family over a year before could not be more vivid. I entered their lives as one of the countless 'professionals' that Joseph attracted but remained as a friend. In walking into complicated family disputes, the emotional equivalent to a car crash, you need wisdom. In praying for this I have been heartened that the supreme expression of Solomon's wisdom was found in resolving the mystery of a child death and the competing claims of two women over the custody of a surviving child (1 Kings 3:16-28).

Joseph's family disagreements made the situation faced by Solomon appear straightforward! No one person could meet his needs so social workers were involved to *help*; although if you asked his parents it did not always feel like it. Rachel had been adopted and was in the process of contacting her birth family. She was in dispute with her adoptive family, and her adoptive father was being investigated for child abuse. In this context there was little agreement about what was best for Joseph. Whilst initially all the competing claims to care for him appeared equal, his mother and father's tender love for him shone through. Not a cry of his went unheeded. If Rob had ever allowed Joseph to stay in hospital on his own overnight, during one of his numerous admissions, it had not been for several years.

Standing at a distance people might have wondered what meaning, if any, Joseph's life had. Love is the only thing that gives real meaning to any of our lives. Rob and Rachel really loved their son. Caring for a child with a condition like West Syndrome has been described as a living bereavement. You know that your child will never run, kick a football or even be able to talk to you.

In the midst of an already complicated situation my main employer started the process of terminating my contract. In short this was because of the way in which I had allowed my Christian faith to intrude on work I had undertaken. Very ironically in their endeavours to get rid of me they warned Rob and Rachel of my previous 'crimes', which had the effect of arousing their curiosity. We had a number of long conversations about faith that I would never have initiated otherwise. I remember Rachel, who had been repelled by the religion she had previously encountered, telling me that she could see herself becoming a Christian at some future point.

In the end I felt that the best way that I could help Rob, Rachel and Joseph was to pray for them and hand their case on to a successor. This I was allowed to do if I promised to leave quietly. Reluctantly I did just that with tears in my eyes. I had just said goodbye when I ran out of petrol.

In the months after the crash I tried to pick up the pieces of my life and remained in touch with Rob and Rachel. There was a possibility that I might have been needed to give evidence on Joseph's behalf. Thankfully that was not necessary. I claimed the insurance from the car crash and signed on and applied unsuccessfully for numerous jobs. In fact I was a year without work. When I had given up hope of ever returning to social work a door unexpectedly swung open for me to do just that. At that time I was first given the use of a car and then given a car. Some months later in November I dropped in on Joseph and his family one Sunday morning after speaking at a church near their home. We were delighted to see each other although I could see Joseph's condition had deteriorated.

At the end of the following January I received a call from a distraught Rachel telling me that her beloved Joseph had passed away. He was only nine. That evening I drove to visit her and Rob, and together we went to visit the room in the children's hospice where Joseph's body was finally at rest. In the face of such pain and grief I did not feel that I had very much to say. However, before leaving home I had looked up the meaning of Joseph's name. In Hebrew Joseph means, "He adds." I shared that Joseph had added something to the lives of those he had touched including mine.

On a bright but bitterly cold day in February Joseph's body was laid to rest. I was honoured, among others, to have been asked to speak at his funeral. As I told of the meaning of his name I also read part of an ancient love song written by Solomon:

Song of Solomon 8:6-7
Place me like a seal over your heart, like a seal on your arm; for love is as strong as death, its jealousy unyielding as the grave. It burns like blazing fire, like a mighty flame. Many waters cannot quench love; rivers cannot wash it away. If one were to give all the wealth of his house for love, it would be utterly scorned.

Love makes no sense to the outsider; it looks crazy and unreasonable. You have to experience love for it to mean anything. Love hurts. If you don't want to hurt, don't love. Rob and Rachel loved Joseph very well. I shared that I was convinced that Joseph was free from the body that had imprisoned him and was now with Jesus. God loves us and wants us to know that he is with us now.

In the year after Joseph's funeral Rachel's adoptive father was convicted of the child abuse charges that had been brought against him and was given a twelve year prison sentence. It grieves the heart of God the Father that too many of those who have borne the title of father have dishonoured and cheapened that name. My desire in writing has been to see the wounded hearts of many in the nations restored to the true Father of us all.

Intercession

As a nineteen year old student I read Norman Grubb's classic biography 'Rees Howells: Intercessor' [1]. It deeply impacted me. Shortly after this I was asked to talk to a group of believers at an old people's home. With Rees Howells still in mind I chose prayer and intercession as my topic. I was fired up by this man of God's life of faith, sacrifice, and obedience, including the revival in East Africa and his many answers to prayer. These included praying for God to intervene in the battles of the Second World War and praying the State of Israel into being in 1948.

I was quite sure that many of the folk in the home had forgotten more about prayer than I would ever know. My concern for them was that although many had a dynamic faith, some, bowed under the weight of loss, pain and depression, were waiting to be 'called home' whilst watching daytime television!

Having delivered my stammering message an old lady thanked me and told me that "the Lord would use [me] to lead thousands to Christ". I thought that she was either being polite, confused or had mistaken me for someone else! At that time I knew very little of the gift of prophecy and to be honest did not realise that this woman was prophesying over me; for a start she had not given me a clue by saying, "Thus says the Lord." Her words were completely off my map, and so I forgot them. Almost thirty years later, however, when I had prayed for hundreds of people, they were brought back to my remembrance, and I began to offer them back to God in prayer. If these words were to be fulfilled, something needed to change both in my life and in my nation. I am powerless to fulfil any word of God. Our calling is not meant to be worked out in independence from God but in submission to and in relationship with Him. I now believe these words but feel that they have an application for many not just for me in the coming revival.

Signs of the times

We live in momentous days when the pace of world events can overwhelm us. Daily we are confronted by news of wars and both man-made and natural disasters. Such occurrences are increasing in their frequency and severity. The world economy is collapsing, and there has been rioting in the streets of Western nations.

In describing the signs of the end of the age Jesus told his disciples not to be frightened when they hear of "wars and revolutions" (Luke 21:9). However, later he said:

Luke 21:25-26
...On the earth, nations will be in anguish and perplexity at the roaring and tossing of the sea. Men will faint from terror, apprehensive of what is coming on the world.

Believers should not be afraid of the earlier signs, but the whole world will be petrified at the time of the latter signs. We live at this time. Following the Boxing Day Tsunami of 2004 and the Japanese Tsunami of February 2011 nations have been overwhelmed by "the tossing of the sea". We should take note: other waves are coming.

Signs, of course, have no inherent value in themselves. Their significance comes from pointing us towards an event or destination that is beyond them. A traveller journeying to Southampton would be disappointed if they stopped on the M3 before a sign and mistook it for the city it was pointing to fifty miles away! The purpose of a road sign is to reassure us that we are on the right road and encourage us to press on to our goal. More than signs we need a road map which will help us understand the happenings that are unfolding. Our road map is the Bible.

To move in the power of God it is important to understand the signs and seasons of God. We are told that the men of Issachar "understood the times and knew what Israel should do" (1 Chronicles 12:32). They were commended in scripture because they gave their allegiance to David whom God had raised up as King in their day. The Pharisees and Sadducees were condemned by Jesus, the greater David, for although they were able to understand the appearance of the sky they failed to "interpret the signs of the times" (Matthew 16:3). In asking for a sign these men failed to recognise the sign provided by God - His Son. It is important that we do not become preoccupied with asking for signs and fail to understand the signs of the times around us.

Against the backdrop of world events we can feel that we are puny and of no significance. Yet to believe this would be to embrace a lie, for our lives are pregnant with potential. Paul tells us:

Ephesians 2:10
We are God's workmanship, created in Christ Jesus to do good works, which God prepared in advance for us to do.

The word translated workmanship in this passage is the Greek word *poiēma*. In the same way that Jesus was the word who became flesh, our whole lives also are supposed to be a poem spoken by God. We should embrace the encouragement spoken to Esther that she had come into her "royal position for such a time as this" (Esther 4:14). Previous generations have gone before us and their time has passed, but a baton has been passed on; this is our time and we must determine to fulfil our purpose.

We should therefore live like it matters because it really does. In the oldest Psalm in the Bible Moses prayed that God might "teach us to number our days aright that we may gain a heart of wisdom" (Psalm 90:12). This thought was expanded by Paul when he said:

Ephesians 5:15-17

Be very careful, then, how you live - not as unwise but as wise, making the most of every opportunity, because the days are evil. Therefore do not be foolish, but understand what the Lord's will is.

Why is this? Paul again provides the answer:

1 Corinthians 5:10

We must all appear before the judgment seat of Christ, that each one may receive what is due him for the things done while in the body, whether good or bad.

If we live to please ourselves we will fail both to please the Lord and to fulfil our purpose.

Restoration

After the healing of the man crippled from birth at Gate Beautiful in Jerusalem, Peter said the following to the crowd of onlookers:

Acts 3:19-21

Repent, then, and turn to God, so that your sins may be wiped out, that times of refreshing may come from the Lord, and that he may send the Christ, who has been appointed for you—even Jesus. He must remain in heaven until the time comes for God to restore everything, as he promised long ago through his holy prophets.

There waits then a time for God "to restore everything". The word translated 'restore' in this passage is the Greek word *apokatastasis*. It carries the dynamic meaning of reconstitution, a putting back together, as well as restitution, recompense and a return. Before the return of Christ a divine revolution must come in which our upside-down world will be made upright. This process will only be completed by the return of Christ but must begin in our hearts.

The New Testament gives little information about how the early church functioned on a daily basis. One glimpse we are supplied with is shortly after the day of Pentecost; we are told that the believers...

Acts 2:42-43

...devoted themselves to the apostles' teaching and to the fellowship, to the breaking of bread and to prayer. Everyone was filled with awe, and many wonders and miraculous signs were done by the apostles.

The 21st Century church would do well to adopt this simple 1st Century programme of devotion to apostolic teaching, fellowship, breaking bread and prayer. The impact and the effect recorded in Acts speak for themselves. The church age should end as it began - in the power of the Holy Spirit. The church has to be restored.

For this to take place we need to co-operate with God's plan to restore our hearts and "restore our soul" (Psalm 23:3). As we do we will learn practical ways in which every one of us can be used by the Father.

In the last very dramatic words of the Old Testament we read:

Malachi 4:5-6

See, I will send you the prophet Elijah before that great and dreadful day of the LORD comes. He will turn the hearts of the fathers to their children, and the hearts of the children to their fathers; or else I will come and strike the land with a curse.

In the last line, the 2010 New International Version uses the words "strike the land with total destruction".

The phrase "turn the hearts" found in the New International Version quoted above is translated "restore the hearts" by the New American Standard Version. The title and theme of this book comes from here.

In answer to the question "What is to be restored?" we are told, "All things." How can everything be restored? Jesus tells us, "Elijah comes and will restore all things" (Matthew 17:11). Some familiar with the context of these words will say that the Elijah has already come and that he was John the Baptist. I believe that this is only partially true. There are 'Elijah people' who are to come. An essential part of the Elijah task is that "He will turn the hearts". I notice that the father's hearts will be turned to "their children", and likewise the hearts of the children will be turned to "their fathers". We understand that the children need to acquire the same hearts as the true fathers possessed or that the fathers' hearts might be inside the children. We do not need other fathers or other children but for our hearts to be turned back to the ones we have.

Ideas for this book began to come together when I attended the All Nations Convocation at the Ramat Rachel Kibbutz Hotel in Jerusalem in 2007; these Malachi verses were the theme of ten days of intensive prayer and intercession. Over a thousand Christians from 180 nations gathered to pray for both the peace of Jerusalem and revival among the nations. The event was born of the vision of Tom Hess, an American pastor who made his home on the Mount of Olives in 1987, when he established a 24/7 prayer house to prepare the region for the return of Christ. So the ministry of what has become the Jerusalem House of Prayer for All Nations (JHOPFAN) was born. I have been gripped and inspired by his vision ever since.

In our society we see a failure of both care and relationships. Fathers are estranged from their children and children are in rebellion against their fathers and mothers. In the United Kingdom some 2.7 million children live without either a biological or step-father. In this context how can the church make a difference? There is a growing gulf of alienation between the generations with each regarding the other with suspicion and distrust. There is an acceleration of the disintegration of society. Western culture is dying of a sick heart.

The Elijah Revolution

So what does Malachi mean and how does it apply to our world? Why does the world need another Elijah, if that is what is being said?

The Archbishop of York, Dr John Sentamu, quoted in the popular press in Spring 2009, has called on the silent majority of Christian Britons to stand up for their heritage in a climate of mounting, if petty, persecution [2]. In doing so I believe that there is a need to cherish and return to the Christian ideals, values and principles that have been handed down to us by a previous generation. I see that there needs to be a restoration of the hearts of this generation to the fathers of the past. Incidentally there are a diminishing number of countries, at last count only thirty, where overt persecution does not take place.

At a small worship conference in 1995, the Belfast singer and songwriter Robin Mark released on his unsuspecting audience of just fifty people a song that was to change his life: 'Days of Elijah'. Overnight he went from being unknown to being well-known in Christian circles. It opens with these words:

These are the days of Elijah
Declaring the Word of the Lord
And these are the days of Your servant Moses
Righteousness being restored
And though these are days of great trials
Of famine and darkness and sword
Still we are the voice in the desert crying
Prepare ye the way of the Lord [3]

It speaks in visionary terms of the Lord's return. The song has touched a chord in his audience and has gone around the world. Over the years there been a growing understanding of what living in "the days of Elijah" should mean for the believer.

The Atlanta Pastor Johnny Enlow has written a book entitled 'The Seven Mountain Prophecy'. In it he describes what he saw as the coming Elijah Revolution that will affect the entire world and will prepare the way of the Lord before His return. This revolution will complete the great commission given by Christ to make disciples of all nations, as God's end-time ambassadors in effect confront seven nations "greater and mightier than we" that currently occupy our Promised Land. These are the Hittites, Girgashites, Amorities, Canaanites, Perizzities, Hivites, and Jebusites, and they correspond to seven 'mountains' of global society - Media, Government, Education, Economy, Religion, Celebration/Arts & Entertainment and Family [4].

The prophetic teacher Lance Wallanu has explained that Christ's commission recorded at the end of Matthew, "Go and make disciples of all nations" (Matthew 28:19), has often been interpreted as converting individuals. However, the command is much greater and encourages us to lift our eyes beyond the individual to the nations that they fill. To do this we do not need large numbers of converts but rather for Christians to take up strategic points of influence as the gatekeepers at the top of the seven mountains of influence. The days of the ministry church being the province of one man have ended. All of us need to heed the encouragement written by Paul to Archippus and "see to it that you complete the work you have received in the Lord" (Colossians 4:17). We are enrolled in the priesthood of all believers.

In the book of Revelation the angels and the multitudes of the redeemed joined in singing:

Revelation 5:12

Worthy is the Lamb, who was slain, to receive power and wealth and wisdom and strength and honour and glory and praise!

Each of the seven attributes to be returned to Christ (who gave them in the first place) – "power and wealth and wisdom and strength and honour and glory and praise" - can be seen to correspond to one of the seven mountains of influence. Everything has proceeded from the Father via his Christ and must be restored to him.

What will the reader discover from this book and its relevance to their lives and this moment in history? I have tried to write the type of book that I would want to read. Being aware of the power of testimony when joined with God's word I have divided each chapter up into stories, teaching, suggested action and prayer points. Prayer is a running theme through this book. For me a book has not really worked unless it has stirred me to seek God. Books cannot give us all the answers. However, sometimes we can read something that brings us to a God who not only understands the unspoken questions of our hearts but has all of the answers. Ultimately it is only God who can restore our hearts.

'Restoring our hearts' is written largely about the last of the seven mountains: the Family. In writing, I draw upon my experience as a son, brother, husband and father of four children as well as twenty-two years' experience of social work with children and families in English inner cities. In writing I try to be both honest and encouraging. I share stories from my life and my family including my testimony of my ongoing healing from the impact of child sexual abuse. I am very aware of both the pain and privilege of family life. It is my conviction that families work best with the passionate engagement of a father. However, when a human father fails or is absent, God the Father will not fail and remains especially present.

Action!

In the days that we are living in I suggest that it would be good to be familiar with the three chapters from the synoptic gospels that deal with the signs of the end of the age: Matthew 24, Mark 13 and Luke 21. Think about what signs have occurred and what remain unfulfilled. By way of a background to this book you might find it helpful to read through the story of Elijah recorded in 1 Kings 17 to 2 Kings 2 and 2 Chronicles 21:12-15.

You might also consider the extent to which Elijah was succeeded Elisha and John the Baptist. What, if anything to you feel remains of the Elijah task spoken of by Malachi?

Prayer Points

- Pray that the church would have clear prophetic understanding of the times that she is living in.
- Pray that all of us would discover, walk in and fulfil our destiny.
- Pray that the Church would become more and more relevant and welcoming to the many worried and wounded people of the world.

REFERENCES

1. Grubb, Norman P, *Rees Howells: Intercessor;* published by Lutterworth Press (May 2003); ISBN: 9780718830274.
2. Daily Mail: 13th February 2009. Read more: http://www.dailymail.co.uk/news/article-1144203/Archbishop-York-John-Sentamu-tells-Christians-wake-defend-beliefs.html#ixzz11Qe11mrc
3. Mark, Robin, *Days of Elijah* (1995) and *Revival in Belfast* (1999)
4. Enlow, Johnny, *The Seven Mountain Prophecy: Unveiling the Coming Elijah Revolution;* published by Creation House (2008); ISBN 9781592797673.

Who are the Fathers?

Malachi 4:5

...the hearts of the fathers.

The Legacy

When I attended the annual All Nations Prayer Convocation in Jerusalem in the autumn of 2008, I was greatly impacted by the scope and vision of the Hong Kong church and business leader Hugo Chan. Hugo is a remarkable man whom the Lord has gifted with a strategic wisdom that is now shaping his own and other nations. I was struck, among other things, by his impeccable English accent. Talking to him briefly after one of his presentations, I was astounded to learn that he had become a Christian in my own city of Southampton and had graduated from the Faculty of Law from the city's university in 1978. That, along with the fact that Hong Kong was an English colony, explained his accent! I had travelled all this way and met a man from another quarter of the globe whose spiritual roots could be traced back to my adopted city.

Hugo testified that he and his wife owed much to the mentoring that they had received from a man regarded as one of the fathers of the charismatic and new church movement, Arthur Wallis. I recognised Hugo as a father in the church, but before he had become a father he had first been a son. Arthur's advice and visits had been a safeguard when, on returning to Hong Kong, Hugo and his wife had commenced church leadership. It is also true that Arthur was himself greatly impacted by what he saw of the revival that had begun in the Chinese world following the eviction of Western missionaries from China [1].

Many Christians around the world remain indebted to both the life and works of Arthur Wallis. This is particularly felt by the church that I have been part of in Southampton for the last twenty four years. Bryn Jones, who had led Covenant Ministries, described the first time he met Arthur:

I knew in my spirit that in some way this man, who was then twice my age, was an Elijah and I a young Elisha ... I must follow. [2]

Born the son of 'Captain' Reginald and Mary Wallis in Dublin in 1922, Arthur attended Monkton Combe School, near Bath, before going on to first Sandhurst and then wartime service in the Royal Tank Regiment. With his older brother Peter he had come to know the Lord before he left Dublin. He was wounded at the Anzio Bridgehead in Italy, an event that led him to question the compatibility of his army service with his sense of calling to the Christian ministry. This calling grew when his own father, himself a preacher and a writer, died suddenly while Arthur was a young man of seventeen. At that time he felt his father's mantle being passed to him.

After the war, Arthur had married Eileen Hemingway on 11th July, 1946, and the couple had one son, Jonathan. From a Brethren background, Arthur came into the experience of the baptism of the Holy Spirit in 1951, within a few weeks of his lifelong friend, the former Southampton City Missioner, Oscar Penhearow. Following in his father's footsteps, Arthur embarked on an itinerant preaching and teaching ministry, with a particular emphasis on revival, prayer, the work of the Holy Spirit, and the 'restoration' of the church. His uncompromising quest caused estrangement from his old friends but led him to forge many new ones. He had been deeply impacted by accounts of the revival that began on the Isle of Lewis in 1949. Arthur visited the revival during its later stages. His book 'In the Day of Thy Power' [3] was the fruit of this visit and his subsequent studies. Duncan Campbell, the man of God who was at the heart of the Lewis revival, wrote the foreword to this book.

From 1983, I became increasingly aware of both Arthur's reputation and influence and had the privilege of listening to him many times. He was of the same generation as my own father and shared both his forename and army background. I esteemed him, as did many others, as a father figure.

One of the things that struck me when I joined the Community Church in Southampton in 1987 was that Arthur made efforts to remember my name with occasional success! I remember that after hearing me pray on one occasion he kindly took me to one side and told me that I did not need to say "Lord" more than once when addressing the Almighty as He would not forget that I was talking to Him! Taking this advice to heart has, I trust, made my prayers easier on the ears of human listeners over the years. Few leaders take such practical fatherly care and interest in young believers. There is a need for many such fathers and mentors in the church.

Many of Arthur's words still ring in my ears as clearly as if I had heard them yesterday. A few months before he died in 1988, I heard him speak on the subject of the widow's jar of oil taken from 2 Kings 4:1-7. In his preamble he said that as he grew older as a preacher he found himself saying more and more about less and less, going deeper into small sections of the Bible. This proved illustrative of the point that he was making concerning the abundant nature of God's miraculous supply. Speaking prophetically he said that the church, like the widow in the story, should realise her bankruptcy, shut the door to the world and turn to a jar of oil, a picture of the Holy Spirit. He emphasised that we should all be "shut up to a jar of oil". The widow's capacity to receive was the only limit on God's supply. These words were amongst the last that I heard Arthur speak. I have often thought about them since.

Arthur wrote and taught on the Christian life and travelled widely (in particular to the USA, Australia and New Zealand). His books reflect his uncompromising commitment to the Bible allied to his continual seeking of the power of the Holy Spirit. For much of his life Arthur lived in the tiny village of Talaton in Devon, moving in the last decade of his life, first to Yorkshire to join Bryn Jones' Covenant Ministries and later in 1981 to Southampton to be part of the leadership of the Community Church. I remember how he shared that the Lord had confirmed his move to Southampton by drawing his attention to Psalm 107:7: "He led them by a straight way to a city where they could settle." The journey from Bradford to Southampton is virtually straight down from North to South. That God could speak so specifically through scripture was a revelation to me.

Shortly before his death Arthur spoke to Eileen of wanting no other memorial than "fruit in people's lives". His greatest passion was for the revival that he never experienced in his own land but did much to prepare the church for. He had a vision for much more than he experienced. Those who had the privilege of knowing him testify to the lasting impact that Arthur made upon them. Arthur's vision for revival is as fresh and as relevant now as it ever was. His book 'God's Chosen Fast' [4] is an acknowledged classic on the topic of fasting, whilst 'The Radical Christian' [5], which he said was his most difficult to write, continues to call Christians to live for Jesus in an uncompromising way.

Amongst many other things, Arthur and Eileen Wallis were intercessors. They knew what it was to pray and prevail before God. This was the testimony of those who prayed with them and those who had been prayed for by them. Although he is best remembered for his books and public ministry, this secret service was perhaps his most productive. He died suddenly in September 1988 at a prayer retreat with other church leaders at Whirlow Grange in Sheffield. He had just won a game of croquet when he turned to help his partner do the same. He had seen the large wooden cross on the lawn, stepped towards it (some guessing that he glimpsed the glory of God) and died of a massive heart attack. At his memorial service Bryn Jones said that the last words he heard on earth would have been the first words that he heard in heaven: "Well done, Arthur; you've won!"

Speaking at the same memorial service Oscar Penhearow said that his friend had been like "a burning and shining lamp", adding that "you were willing for a time to rejoice in his light" (John 5:35, New King James Version).

These words had been first applied by Jesus to his cousin John the Baptist. When Arthur went to be with the Lord, the comparatively young leadership of the church keenly felt the absence of his prayer covering over their lives. I am not sure that it was replaced. We all need fathers [6].

In the New Living Translation of Malachi 4 it is written:

Malachi 4:5-6
Look, I am sending you the prophet Elijah before the great and dreadful day of the LORD arrives. His preaching will turn the hearts of fathers to their children, and the hearts of children to their fathers. Otherwise I will come and strike the land with a curse.

When a church father like Arthur dies, we can feel abandoned. However, as Jesus said, "I will not leave you as orphans" (John 14:18).

Who are our Fathers?

We must ask, "So who are our fathers?"

The importance of this question has been underlined for me by my encounter with Leif Heitland, a Norwegian-born evangelist now based in the United States. Leif has a fruitful ministry preaching the gospel in the Islamic world where he has seen large numbers make a commitment to Christ. In a number of messages that he preached in Southampton in 2009 he emphasised that in these days the church is moving from being an institution to a family. In so doing, sons needed to come into alignment with their fathers. In the way that Elijah fathered Elisha, so there is an obligation upon existing church leaders not to just train or mentor the next generation of leaders but to father them. This is the only remedy for the many that have come into the church nursing an 'orphan spirit'. Bill Johnson, the inspirational leader of Bethel Church in Redding, California has reiterated this, making the point that God was raising up fathers in the Church around whom people would gather rather than institutions that would contain them.

I now want to consider those that scripture tells us that we should call fathers. This is a vital topic if in these days we are to know which way our hearts should turn. I believe that a right understanding of fatherhood will have a revolutionary impact upon us as individuals and the church. Ultimately, for us to know God as our Father we must know the God of our fathers. I believe that the fathers are:

1. Biological fathers.
2. The Patriarchs.
3. The Jewish people.
4. The Church fathers.
5. God the Father.

Biological Fathers

The first and most obvious answer to this question "Who are our fathers?" is our earthly, biological fathers. Of these Jesus, quoting Moses, said, "Honour your father and your mother," and "Anyone who curses his father or mother must be put to death."

However, the Pharisees, to whom Jesus was speaking, were once again guilty of missing the big picture. He reproved them saying:

Mark 7:10-12

But you say that if a man says to his father or mother: 'Whatever help you might otherwise have received from me is Corban' (that is, a gift devoted to God), then you no longer let him do anything for his father or mother.

Jesus was, of course, quoting the fifth commandment in Mark's gospel (Exodus 20:12). It is one of only two of the Ten Commandments that promotes rather than prohibits an action. As Paul tells us in his letter to the Ephesians, this is the first commandment with a promise attached:

Ephesians 6:2-3

...that it may go well with you and that you may enjoy long life on the earth.

The keeping of this command is therefore enlightened self-interest. Without the honouring of our father and mother, it will not go well with us, and potentially we will not enjoy a long life! The family unit is very much a building block for society. When families fall apart, society itself disintegrates. The Pharisees thought that they were honouring God when they were dishonouring their parents. The truth is that we honour God only when we honour our parents and we dishonour Him when we fail to do so.

Within the Church there needs to be a recognition and honour given to all the fathers. A recent concern has been that in the Western Church men have felt out of place. In part, this is as a result of doing a good job in catering for women. This is confirmed by the fact that fewer men attend than women. We must welcome and honour the men for fathers to be raised up and released. Bill Johnson speaks of creating what he calls "a culture of honour" amongst God's people. Our hearts must be restored to all of our fathers if our own lives are to be blessed.

This principle of honouring our fathers is not necessarily dependent upon them having been honourable or deserving honour. They might have been quite the opposite. For some, the term father has been debased by an abusive parent who makes the use of the word offensive. For others it is meaningless because of an unfilled void; there was, sadly, no father figure who was there for them. If that is the case, it will be necessary for our broken hearts to be healed before they can be restored to any father. However, in the same way that we still use money even though forged bank notes are circulating, the presence in the world of poor fathers does not obscure the need for good fathers. The presence of the counterfeit only serves to emphasise the need for the real. Both the church and the world need fathers. We need to seek to understand and be rightly related to all of our fathers. In a later chapter I will tell of my relationship with my own father.

The Patriarchs

This is the term used in the Bible to describe the wider group of the founding fathers of the Jewish nation. These included Abraham, Isaac, Jacob and the twelve tribal leaders who were the sons of Jacob. Joseph's two sons, Ephraim and Manasseh, are also included in this group of tribal leaders as Joseph inherited the double portion anointing of the first born son forfeited by his elder brother Reuben. These are primarily the individuals that headed the nation and whose lives instruct us still.

We begin to understand the importance of the Patriarchs from the incident when Jesus reproved the Sadducees. This group did not believe in the resurrection. In answering their heresy Jesus made the point that Moses, when he encountered God at the burning bush, had met the God of Abraham, the God of Isaac and the God of Jacob. Jesus then stated that He is not the God of the dead but the God of the living (Mark 11:27-28). The Patriarchs, then, through their faith continue to live and speak to us if we have ears to hear them.

The English word 'Patriarch' is derived from the Greek *patriarchēs*. This in turn is derived from two Greek compounds: *patria* which means 'paternal' and refers to a group of families or a whole race and *archō* which is a primary verb meaning to be first in either rank or power. So we understand that the Patriarchs or the Fathers were the first originators of a people group [7].

Speaking of Abraham, Paul said:

Romans 4:11

So then, he is the father of all who believe but have not been circumcised, in order that righteousness might be credited to them.

He became the father of many nations. Abraham through Isaac became the father of the Jewish nation and through Ishmael the father of the Arab peoples. However, in the passage just quoted we see that through faith he is the father of all who believe. Isaiah instructed us:

Isaiah 51:1-2

Look to the rock from which you were cut and to the quarry from which you were hewn; look to Abraham, your father.

So Abraham is both our foundation stone and our father through faith. Unless we know where we have come from we will not know where we are going.

Abraham's name is itself very significant. He was originally called Abram which means 'exalted father' but he was renamed Abraham by God which means 'father of nations'. He received this name when he was childless. The destiny indicated by his name was severely contested. It should be no surprise to us as children of Abraham that our God-given destinies will also be contested. Like Abraham, we must appropriate our promises by faith.

Back in Genesis, the Lord had said to Abraham (then called Abram):

Genesis 12:1-3

Leave your country, your people and your father's household and go to the land I will show you. "I will make you into a great nation and I will bless you; I will make your name great, and you will be a blessing. I will bless those who bless you, and whoever curses you I will curse; and all peoples on earth will be blessed through you.

The land he was promised was the land of Canaan and is now known as the land of Israel, although a much larger area was promised than that currently occupied by his physical descendants. Abraham became our father through believing God's promises. We become his true children when we do the same.

If we think that we have escaped the influence of the Patriarchs in the New Testament era, we are mistaken. They remain our foundation. We have to consider what Jesus said to His twelve apostles:

Matthew 19:28

I tell you the truth, at the renewal of all things, when the Son of Man sits on his glorious throne, you who have followed me will also sit on twelve thrones, judging the twelve tribes of Israel.

At the time of the "renewal of all things" there remains an important role both for the twelve apostles and the twelve tribes.

We are given more detail of this in the book of Revelation. The gates of New Jerusalem bear the names of the twelve tribes of Israel and its foundations the names of the twelve apostles. The only way into this city is through the twelve tribal gates, whilst the city walls are built upon the Patriarchs of the church, the twelve apostles (Revelation 21:9-14). It is not fanciful to see that the twenty-four elders on their twenty-four thrones around the throne of the lamb represent the twelve apostles and the twelve Patriarchs (Revelation 4-5). To inherit the blessings given to the fathers we must honour them.

The Jews

This leads us to the next group that might be described as fathers. One thing that the twelve Patriarchs and the twelve apostles have in common was that they all originated from the same ethnic group: the Jews. When Jesus met the Samaritan woman at the well he told her that "salvation is from the Jews" (John 4:22).

It is clear that the church owes a debt to Israel. The Jews are the fathers and the Christians are the children. This has been neglected for far too long by much of the church, but in these days God wants to restore the hearts of the Christian children to the Jewish fathers.

Salvation of course comes from the Jews because Jesus Christ is the promised Jewish Messiah. Hundreds of years before Jesus' birth, the prophet Isaiah had said:

Isaiah 11:10

In that day the Root of Jesse will stand as a banner for the peoples; the nations will rally to him, and his place of rest will be glorious.

According to the genealogical records that are outlined both in Matthew and Luke, Jesus' human ancestry could be traced back to King David whose father was Jesse.

Jesus was described as the "consolation of Israel" (Luke 2:28). Simeon prophesied concerning the infant Jesus when he met him in the Temple that He would be "a light for revelation to the Gentiles and for glory to your people Israel" (Luke 2:32). Nathaniel declared to Jesus, "You are the King of Israel" (John 1:49). In the book of Revelation, He is described as "the Lion of the tribe of Judah, the Root of David" (Revelation 5:5). Jesus was "sent only to the lost sheep of Israel" (Matthew 15:24).

The Saviour of the World is recorded as speaking to only four Gentile followers during his earthly ministry: the Syro-Phoenician woman, the Centurion living in Capernaum, the Samaritan woman at the well and a Samaritan leper. When the Greeks asked Philip if they could see Jesus (John 12) Jesus knew that the time for his departure had come. God chose one nation, Israel, to reach the world. It was only when Peter was commanded to go to Cornelius' house (recorded in Acts 10), perhaps some ten years after Jesus' ascension, that the gospel began to be made freely available to the Gentiles [8].

Paul, from the tribe of Benjamin and a Pharisee wrote:

Romans 9:3-5

For I could wish that I myself were cursed and cut off from Christ for the sake of my brothers, those of my own race, the people of Israel. Theirs is the adoption as sons; theirs the divine glory, the covenants, the receiving of

the law, the temple worship and the promises. Theirs are the patriarchs,
and from them is traced the human ancestry of Christ, who is God over
all, forever praised!

Although he clearly understood himself to be the apostle to the
Gentiles, he was broken-hearted for his people. Everywhere that Paul
preached, he honoured his Jewish brothers by telling them first the good
news about Jesus, only going to the Gentiles after they had rejected his
message. If we are not actively praying for the salvation of the Jewish
people, yes and all men, then we are missing the heart of our God who is
unwilling that any should perish. If we do not honour fathers we will not
be honoured by the presence of God.

Concerning God's ongoing plans and purposes for Israel, Jesus'
disciples asked:

Acts 1:6

Lord, are you at this time going to restore the kingdom to Israel?

More than once I have heard it preached that this question was a
further example of the disciples missing the point of Jesus' teaching.
However, this interpretation ignores the fact that they had just finished
forty days of teaching with their resurrected Messiah at the beginning of
which we are told he had "opened their minds to understand the
scriptures" (Luke 24:45).

It is more logical in this context to consider their question to arise
from their weeks of teaching rather than to be the result of confusion. So,
the disciples were aware of God's plan to restore Israel but not of His
timescales. In his answer Jesus did not say that the kingdom would not be
restored to Israel, as he could have done. Rather he said to them:

Acts 1:6

It is not for you to know the times or dates the Father has set by his own
authority.

Times and dates have been set by the Father's authority. The clock is
ticking. Paul tells us:

Romans 11:25
Israel has experienced a hardening in part until the full number of the Gentiles has come in.

Jesus said:

Luke 21:24
Jerusalem will be trampled on by the Gentiles until the times of the Gentiles are fulfilled.

The fulfilment of these scriptures began with the establishing of the modern state of Israel on the 14th May 1948 and the subsequent restoration of Jerusalem to Jewish control on the 7th June 1967 almost two thousand years after it was last in Jewish hands. Both these events have occurred at times of great blessing in the Church. The full number of Gentiles is being brought in, and the times of the Gentiles are fast being fulfilled. This paves the way for the removing of Israel's partial hardening and the spiritual revival in which Paul tells us:

Romans 11:26
All Israel will be saved.

Gentile Christians are warned three times in Romans that we should not be arrogant towards the Jewish people as we seek to love and follow the Jewish man Jesus. Paul makes it plain that the Gentiles are of the wild olive stock and have been grafted in to the cultivated olive root - that we do not support the root but that the root supports us (Romans 11:17-24). If as Christians we say, "Theirs was the Old Covenant; ours is the New," even in this we are mistaken, for in the words of Jeremiah we read:

Jeremiah 31:31, quoted in Hebrews 8:8
The time is coming, declares the Lord, when I will make a new covenant with the house of Israel and with the house of Judah.

There are a total of 69 references to Israel and 13 to Israelites in the New Testament. All but two of these clearly refer to the Jewish people or the land they were promised. In dealing with the two that do not, in the first Paul says:

Romans 9:6

For not all who are descended from Israel are Israel.

Here he is simply saying that to be part of ethnic Israel did not necessarily mean you were 'saved'. This has always been the case. No more does Church membership guarantee that your name is written in the Lamb's book of life.

In the second passage, he closes the letter to the Galatians by saying:

Galatians 6:16

Peace and mercy to all who follow this rule, even to the Israel of God.

From this text I have heard it taught that the Church is the new Israel and has entirely replaced the Jews in the plans and purposes of God. A better interpretation of this verse is in line with the other passage - that not all of the physical descendants of Israel are grafted into the true olive tree. The New Covenant is with the house of Israel, and Gentiles can only share in it by faith and through the grafting process.

Jeremiah tells us:

Jeremiah 33:24-26

Have you not noticed that these people are saying, 'The LORD has rejected the two kingdoms he chose'? So they despise my people and no longer regard them as a nation. This is what the LORD says: 'If I have not established my covenant with day and night and the fixed laws of heaven and earth, then I will reject the descendants of Jacob and David my servant and will not choose one of his sons to rule over the descendants of Abraham, Isaac and Jacob. For I will restore their fortunes and have compassion on them.'

Speaking of the context of God's future for the Jewish people, Paul said:

Romans 11:29

...for God's gifts and his call are irrevocable.

In my homeland, John and Charles Wesley, Lord Shaftsbury, William Wilberforce and Charles Spurgeon also prayed and worked towards the end that Britain might be a 'Cyrus Nation' and serve the re-establishment of a Jewish homeland. Cyrus had been the Persian ruler who had ordered the return of the Jewish people and the rebuilding of the Temple (prophesied in Isaiah 44:28-45:13) in the time of Ezra. Many Christians believe that the declaration made near the end of the war by the then British Home Secretary, Arthur James Balfour, on 2nd November 1917, that "His Majesty's government view with favour the establishment in Palestine of a national home for the Jewish people" marked the beginning of the end of "times of the Gentiles" (prophesied in Luke 21:24).

This view of these British church fathers was reinforced by their reading of the 700 scriptures that promise the land of Israel to the Jews and was the view that prevailed across the British church until the 1920s. Some 90 years later it is not; 'replacement theology' which asserts that the church has entirely replaced the Jewish people in the plans and purposes of God is now predominant. It is, I believe, a heresy choking the church. Derek Prince and David Pawson amongst others have observed how quickly the British Empire collapsed following the end of its mandate in Palestine when it had opposed the establishment of a Jewish state.

The first century church moved in unprecedented power and authority whilst acknowledging its Jewish roots. We will not be able to do the same until the Christian children's hearts have turned around to acknowledge and honour their Jewish fathers.

The Church Fathers

Paul wrote:

1 Corinthians 4:15

Even though you have ten thousand guardians in Christ, you do not have many fathers, for in Christ Jesus I became your father through the gospel.

Paul's relationship with Timothy was that of a father. This was evident when he wrote to the Corinthians:

1 Corinthians 4:17

I am sending to you Timothy, my son whom I love, who is faithful in the Lord.

Later he referred to Timothy as "my true son in the faith" (1 Timothy 1:2).

By contrast Jesus commanded:

Matthew 23:9

Do not call anyone on earth 'father,' for you have one Father, and he is in heaven.

We should not give to men honour that should be directed to God. However, there is honour due to men of God that should be bestowed. We are told that the elders who direct the affairs of the church well are worthy of double honour, especially those whose work is preaching and teaching (1 Timothy 5:17).

Unless we give this honour, we will forfeit a double portion of our father's anointing. Like Elisha we must press close to our Elijah. The essence of being a father in the church is to lay down your life for the flock. Some years ago, my wife, Carol Ann, told me that I should mentor a young man; more than that, she kept saying it to me until I did something about it! I felt that I lacked spare time in the evening, but I have never minded getting up in the morning to pray. At church, when I met a university student called Alex Bailey who had a heart to pray, it seemed logical to meet together to pray once a week in term time. Almost five years later, the answers that we have seen to our prayers have transformed both of our lives.

Paul tells us that there are many teachers in the church but few fathers. Indeed there is a famine of fatherhood. It is easier and less costly to share words than it is to share your life. As the Bible teacher Eric Delve has said, "to become a father always entails pain."

John defines a father when he writes to the "fathers, because you have known him who is from the beginning." (1 John 2:13) You cannot, by implication, be a father unless you know the Father or, indeed, function as a father unless you have been effectively fathered.

Those who become regarded as fathers in the church are trailblazers and forerunners who move in the spirit and power of Elijah. The book of Ephesians outlines the foundational fathers upon whose lives and ministry the church is built. In it we are told:

Ephesians 4:11
God gave some to be apostles, some to be prophets, some to be evangelists, and some to be pastors and teachers.

The church cannot and will not be built by committees or maintained by bureaucracy. In saying this I do not decry the need for good communication or administration. However, the fathers of the church are those that open up a way that others may follow. These are often those who re-define through their lives and faith what is possible for the Christian. They have helped to restore to the church some lost purpose or truth. As such they have often suffered serious persecution and had to pay a price for what others after them come to accept as 'normal' Christianity.

I have no doubt that Arthur Wallis was a father to many in the modern charismatic Church. However, over the centuries there have been many other fathers. I think of the reformers Martin Luther and John Calvin and the revivalists John Wesley, George Whitefield, Jonathan Edwards, Charles Spurgeon, Charles Finney and more recently Duncan Campbell. These men were fathers to the Church of their day. They also stand as prototypes who have made the impossible possible. Many, though not all, of these former saints, although separated by their different perspectives and the centuries, were united by their love for the Jewish people whom they came to honour as their fathers.

For example John Wesley in his notes on the book of Romans wrote:

So many prophecies refer to this grand event [of the restoration of Israel] that it is surprising that any Christian can have doubt of it. And these are greatly confirmed by the wonderful preservation of the Jews as a distinct people to this day. When it is accomplished, it will be so strong a demonstration, both of the Old and New Testament revelation, as will doubtless convince many thousand Deists, in countries nominally Christian. [9]

In the Pentecostal era, men like Smith Wigglesworth and John G Lake and women like Kathryn Kuhlman and Maria Woodworth Etter have redefined 'normal' Christianity. We squander our Christian inheritance if we ignore the biographies of these and other saints [10]. These are days when our hearts need to be turned back to the faith of our spiritual fathers. For the latter glory of God's house to surpass the former glory as is promised in the last days (Haggai 2:9), we need to consider the former glory and pray for its recovery. As Arthur Wallis often said, "The best is yet to come."

God the Father

David said:

Psalm 27:10
Though my father and mother forsake me, the LORD will receive me.

He was speaking from painful experience for when the prophet Samuel had visited his house for a feast, no one had thought to invite him! Ultimately all sources of human support will fail us in some way and at some point, but if we rely upon Him, God will not. Samuel would not sit down to eat until David had been brought in from the field to the banquet. God remembers us too.

Jesus made a similar point much more starkly:

Luke 14:26
If anyone comes to me and does not hate his father and mother, his wife and children, his brothers and sisters - yes, even his own life - he cannot be my disciple.

Does this mean that we should literally hate our family? If we were to reach this conclusion then we would be at odds with the rest of scripture. No; rather the answer lies in what Jesus described as the first and greatest commandment:

Deuteronomy 6:4-5 (first instance)

Hear, O Israel: The LORD our God, the LORD is one. Love the LORD your God with all your heart and with all your soul and with all your strength.

Beside our love for God, all other affections should look like hatred. In the three synoptic gospels Jesus expanded this command by adding that we should love God with our entire mind. This was not an option that was available to the Old Testament saints in the same way that it is to us possessing the revelation of the Father through Jesus.

Jesus' purpose was to restore everything to the Father. The first Adam led humanity away from the Father whilst the last Adam, Jesus, has made it possible for all to return. Paul said that...

1 Corinthians 15:24

...the end will come, when he hands over the kingdom to God the Father after he has destroyed all dominion, authority and power.

The revelation of the Father, although implied in the Old Testament, can only be fully revealed in the New. This is because, as has been said by Derek Prince, "It takes the Son to reveal the Father."

Jesus constantly addressed God as His Father. He taught His followers to do the same. This revelation was offensive to the religious and is more than the saint can comprehend. God, the Maker of the Universe, wants to be our Daddy. I believe that it is imperative that we learn to pray to God the Father in the name of Jesus in the power of the Holy Spirit. For many this will require a change of mind and of heart.

Everything has proceeded from God and ultimately must return to him. James said that...

James 1:17

...every good and perfect gift is from above, coming down from the Father of the heavenly lights who does not change like shifting shadows.

God is the first cause of everything.

Jesus said:

Matthew 11:25-27

I praise you, Father, Lord of heaven and earth, because you have hidden these things from the wise and learned, and revealed them to little children. Yes, Father, for this was your good pleasure. All things have been committed to me by my Father. No one knows the Son except the Father, and no one knows the Father except the Son and those to whom the Son chooses to reveal him.

Knowing God as our Father is not something that we can work out by our intellectual reasoning. It comes as a revelation through our older brother Jesus. It is through this revelation that we can begin to love God with our minds.

Jesus explained very clearly that He is the way, but our destination is the Father. Jesus answered a question from Thomas by saying:

John 14:6-7

I am the way and the truth and the life. No one comes to the Father except through me. If you really knew me, you would know my Father as well. From now on, you do know him and have seen him.

Through Christ we have the joy of becoming sons and coming into relationship with the Father. Paul wrote:

Romans 8:15

For you did not receive a spirit that makes you a slave again to fear, but you received the Spirit of sonship. And by him we cry, "Abba, Father."

Jesus taught His disciples to pray, "Our Father". He wants us to know His Father as our Father. We know that creation now "waits in eager expectation for the sons of God to be revealed" (Romans 8:19).

For the sons of God to be revealed to creation, it is imperative that we should begin to walk in a revelation of the Fatherhood of God for ourselves. We must realise that we are sons. If it is true for us that we "died, and [our] ... life is now hidden with Christ in God" (Colossians 3:3) then the words spoken over Jesus by his Father are true of us:

Matthew 3:17

This is my Son, whom I love; with him I am well pleased.

Most of us do not see ourselves as beloved sons and daughters. As I have, with friends, prayed this revelation down into my own and others' lives, God's power has been released. Now on more than one occasion comparative strangers have come and asked that I pray for their emotional healing, and as I have prayed this we have both dissolved in the father's love. We need to understand that we are "accepted in the beloved" (Ephesians 1:6, King James Version).

Action!

I believe that it is important to find practical ways to apply this teaching to our lives. Ask yourself how you might honour the fathers mentioned above. I have experienced angry feelings toward many of my father figures. I see that I have piled upon them a load of unrealistic expectations and then raged at their failures. These feelings get in the way of my being reconciled to them. There are two main reasons why it is difficult to honour our fathers. Firstly, unlike God the Father, every man standing as a father figure will have failed to perfectly fulfil his calling. Secondly, because of the failure of our human fathers, we struggle to believe that God is good and to trust Him. Whatever our perception, God really is good. You cannot honour or indeed know God the Father as a father unless you have been reconciled to those who have imperfectly represented Him.

Ask yourself what it means in practice to honour the Patriarchs. You could look again at the life of Abraham in Genesis and seek to learn from his example of faith. Perhaps you could find a biography of one of the church fathers that I have mentioned and read it. Concerning the Jews I am well aware that they are imperfect. However, they are chosen. I would encourage you to base your judgements of the situation in the Middle East primarily upon the scriptures, not upon information supplied by the news media. However, when you do hear news from this region I would suggest that you balance what you hear by occasionally visiting such websites as the Jerusalem Post or perhaps the International Christian Embassy in Jerusalem. This will help to correct the dominant bias against Israel.

We will need to work through our feelings of disappointment and hurt to find a way to authentically honour the fathers. Forgive and release any of the fathers whose failures, real or perceived, still haunt you. You might consider looking back over this chapter and examine where you have become angry. How do we honour a father with whom we have had a very difficult relationship? What if the father does not want to, or cannot, now communicate with you? Ask where your feelings about them come from and whether they are reasonable. You might try journaling these feelings and praying with a trusted older father or mother in the faith about them.

Prayer Points

- Let us pray that our hearts would begin to turn to connect more deeply with God the Father and that the Church would be released from every orphan spirit.
- Ask God to forgive us and free us from the consequence of having dishonoured any that scripture encourages us to call fathers. Particularly ask for a breaking of any stronghold of anti-Semitism over our lives and in the Church.
- Pray as well that we would learn to give proper honour to all of our forefathers that it may go well with us and that we may enjoy a long and fruitful life.

REFERENCES

1. One of the last of the eleven books that Arthur Wallis wrote is testimony to this: Wallis, Arthur, *China Miracle: A silent explosion*; published by Kingsway (1985).

2. Quoted in a special tribute published by Restoration Magazine in 1988.

3. Wallis, Arthur, *In the Day of Thy Power;* first published by Christian Literature Crusade (1956) and reprinted numerous times since.

4. Wallis, Arthur, *God's Chosen Fast;* published by Kingsway (1968).

5. Wallis, Arthur, *The Radical Christian;* published by Kingsway (1981).

6. Wallis, Jonathan, *Arthur Wallis: Radical Christian;* published by Kingsway (1991); ISBN 086065852X For those interested in reading more on this subject I would refer them to Jonathan's biography of his father.

7. Strong's Hebrew and Greek Dictionaries.

8. Luke, the only Gentile writer of the New Testament, was believed to have converted to Judaism before becoming a Christian.

9. Wesley, John, notes on Romans quoted in *A Nation Called by God: Britain's Leading Role in the Restoration of Israel;* published by Love Never Fails.

10. Liardon, Roberts, *God's Generals*; published by Whitaker House (1996); ISBN 0883689448. I recommend a book like this as providing a good introduction to the biographies of some of these people.

Things Fall Apart

Malachi 4:5

Before the great and dreadful day of the Lord.

Chris' Story

You may die of many things in social work but not of boredom. In 1997, I was working as a social worker in a Family Centre in the heart of what was Southampton's red light district. Sometimes in the lunch hour I went out to pray around the area and was propositioned by the prostitutes who worked locally. I knew enough of their lives for their offers to repel rather than attract me. I politely turned them down and prayed.

At this time I met Chris who was then 37 years old and, like many from his native Liverpool, he could charm the birds from the trees. I liked him immediately, but I was also wary of him because of his size and his self-confessed capacity for violence. Chris was the father of four beautiful children who lived in the area before they were removed from him and his then wife. When I met him his life and dream of a 'normal' happy family was falling apart.

The truth was Chris had never experienced anything approaching the happy family life he desperately wanted. He had suffered terrible cruelty and abuse as a child, spending ten of his childhood years in care. This was his normality. He became involved in crime and had spent thirteen of his adult years in a number of prisons. This included the notorious Strangeways prison. He had also become addicted to drugs. Given this was his reality, how could he hope to provide his children with what he had never experienced?

One story he told me which stuck vividly in my mind was of how when working in the prison kitchen he had become concerned that his wife at the time had been unfaithful. Here he cut off his finger in order to be transferred to the prison hospital. From there it would have been easier to escape in order to kill his wife. His plan came to nothing, but his missing finger was evidence of how serious he had been!

Chris was an intelligent and resourceful man, but when I met him he was running out of options. One time, he told me that he had injected just about every substance known to man and quite a few that it had occurred to no one else to inject. He came to the Family Centre to have the only contact that he was allowed with his children. Most of these visits went well, but sometimes there were problems. One day he shut himself in the toilet at the Centre and failed to come out. I had to knock on the door to find out what was wrong. After twenty minutes he came out stoned and swaying.

Around this time, I noticed that one of his eyes became bloodshot and swollen. I took him up to the Eye Casualty twice to get him treated, and he was admitted to hospital. I learned that his problem had developed from a fungus that he had got from a bottle of Jif lemon juice. Apparently, in order to help an addict process 'Crack' they inject it mixed with ascetic acid. When Chris had no ascetic acid he had injected lemon juice as a substitute. Thankfully, through the skill of the medical staff his sight was saved.

The time around Christmas was a very low point in Chris's life; his marriage had fallen apart, and his life almost came to an end. His behaviour became wilder as his despair increased. He was heading towards self-destruction. Some people did care and tried to help. I remember a call from his landlady begging me to do something for him. I phoned mental health colleagues to find out if he could be detained for his own safety. He could not. I found myself in tears pleading with God for his life. I have heard this described as 'liquid prayer'. I visited him in his flat with his drugs worker. He was in a wretched condition and had taken so many drugs as to be almost unconscious. When the drugs worker left the room for a moment, I prayed for God to save his life. I did not think that Chris would notice. The drugs worker arranged for him to go to a rehabilitation centre. Within a week or so, in January 1998, Chris chose to move into Yeldall Manor, a Christian Drug Rehabilitation and Treatment Service near Reading.

Some ten days after he had arrived, I received a letter from Chris. I was in tears before I had opened it. On the back of the envelope he had written:

2 Corinthians 5:17

Therefore, if anyone is in Christ, he is a new creation; the old has gone, the new has come!

In the letter he told how he had surrendered to God one night after another resident had shared what the Lord had done for him. To my surprise, he remembered my prayer for him. From that point on, Chris's life began to be utterly transformed. He became focused on maintaining a drug-free lifestyle and despite a few early setbacks went from strength to strength.

There was still pain to work through. Whilst still undertaking the rehabilitation, the care proceedings concerning his children were concluded. I understand that Chris was co-operative with all the professionals working with him during the care proceedings and was in agreement to the making of care orders with respect to all his children, with an adoption care plan for the youngest two. He stunned at least one of the social workers by hugging and thanking them for taking care of his children. No one in this line of work expects thanks, certainly not from a parent in Chris' circumstances. Chris met with the prospective adopters for his children, prayed with them, and consented to their adopting his children. I am not sure that I could have done this.

By then in a different job, I was present in the Court Building the day that Chris' daughters were adopted. Given that he was on the road to recovery, he recognised that he could not care for them and trusted them to God. It was planned that Chris would continue to see the children once a year. It was a bitter-sweet time, for although God was putting his life back together, his family had still fallen apart. Years later, after finishing his own treatment, Chris is employed as a trained therapeutic counsellor, helping those who are suffering addictions. If there is a hope and a future for our land, we must learn to help put people back together who the world has torn apart.

Things Fall Apart

I was nineteen years old when I was first gripped by the following perceptive poem which came from the pen of a secular writer:

The Second Coming

Turning and turning in the widening gyre
The falcon cannot hear the falconer;
Things fall apart; the centre cannot hold;
Mere anarchy is loosed upon the world,
The blood-dimmed tide is loosed, and everywhere
The ceremony of innocence is drowned;
The best lack all conviction, while the worst
Are full of passionate intensity.
Surely some revelation is at hand;
Surely the Second Coming is at hand...

'The Second Coming' was written by the Irish poet William Butler Yeats. [1] It borrows dramatic Christian imagery from the book of Revelation to help describe the atmosphere that existed in post-war Europe. It is full of foreboding. The coming spoken of appears to be of the antichrist rather than the Messiah. Phrases like "the best lack all conviction, while the worst are full of passionate intensity" anticipate the rise of the dictators, although it was written in 1919, twenty years before the Second World War. Yeats, although not a conventional believer, had a prophetic understanding of the 'signs of the times'; he recognised that the Second Coming is at hand. It still is. Logically, we are nearer now than when this poem was written (Romans 11:13).

The simple line from the poem "Things fall apart; the centre cannot hold" describes what Yeats saw as the collapse of Western civilization. The line was later borrowed by the Nigerian author Chinua Achebe for the title of his classic 1958 novel 'Things Fall Apart'. Writing in an African context, he described the destruction of a strong man, his family and his culture. Not just in Africa but across the world things really are falling apart. [2]

The psalmist asked the question:

Psalm 11:3

When the foundations are being destroyed, what can the righteous do?

In these days the foundations of society are being shaken and destroyed. Why is this the case, and how do we find ourselves in a situation where everything is crumbling around our ears?

Families Fall Apart

So what things are falling apart in society? Let us look behind the familiar symptoms such as drugs, alcoholism and violence to some of the underlying causes. For me, one of the most dramatic of these causes is the collapse of family life. The sociologist Carle C. Zimmerman, writing in 1947, made connections between the kind of family that dominate a culture and the health of its civilization. He concluded that the family is the most fundamental of all social institutions [3]. Most would agree.

After studying Greek and Roman civilizations, Zimmerman saw three basic types of family:

1. The trustee family - large but close-knit like a tribe or clan and usually headed by a strong chief who could be a woman or man.
2. The domestic family - centred on the smaller more immediate family group but maintaining close ties to the extended family.
3. The atomistic family - the claims of relationships outside the nuclear family combine to reduce the force and value of the family altogether.

He concluded that the first two strengthen society whilst the last leads to its downfall.

Zimmerman noticed that growing civilizations pass from one family type to another at various stages in their rising, and many have all three present at any given moment in their lifetime. In the West, even in 1947, what he perceived as the atomistic family had become the main family type. What he saw then is even more apparent over sixty years later. This is not good news. Greece and Rome both passed through all three stages before their final collapse. Western society is doing the same.

I see examples of this in my own family. My mother's parents, Norman and Janie Gray, were married on Christmas Day in 1912 when they were both 22 years old. They met when 'in service' to Lord and Lady

Morley who lived in the Georgian-built Saltram House near Plymouth in Devon. Norman had been a groom, working in the stables, and Janie had risen through the ranks of servants to assist the lady's maid. Norman and Janie's marriage lasted for over sixty years. They had ten children over a twenty year period: three boys and seven girls. Their family, which was certainly close knit, could be described as a trustee family. Whilst they were both honoured in the memory of their children, Janie was the Matriarch who held things together. They passed on values of sacrifice and selflessness and left a legacy of love. The Baptist Chapel, of which my grandmother was a part, helped nurture their 'tribe'.

Norman and Janie's children largely formed domestic families; their relationships with extended family remained important. In all, six of their children produced fifteen grandchildren for them. For many years, at the Whitsun weekend a coach would be hired and the entire family would go on outings together to different parts of Dartmoor. Theirs was a generation for whom divorce was unusual. Only one of my aunts divorced, but sadly almost half of their grandchildren, my cousins, have experienced this pain. We have dropped the baton. In the third and fourth generation from this couple the atomistic family has become the common family form. The Baptist Chapel has now closed. This pattern is recurring throughout society. Relationship breakdowns have occurred with increasing frequency. Families have fragmented. Things are falling apart.

In 1988, US research showed that children aged up to two were at about a hundred times greater risk of being killed by their stepfather than by their biological father. Psychologists call this the Cinderella effect. The research went on to look at British data, concluding that it indicated "considerable excess risk at the hands of stepfathers". Fathers who kill do so more out of sadness than in rage as stepfathers commonly do. The attachment relationship between biological children and their fathers is generally a protective factor [4].

Zimmerman listed eleven behaviours that he observed as indicators that a culture was entering its final phase and atomising. I will focus on only three of them [5]. Although he uses academic language, his observations have a prophetic importance and are truer now than when he wrote them.

INCREASED AND RAPID, EASY 'CAUSELESS' DIVORCE.

The 'no fault' divorce has been thought to be a great advance by society in reducing the blame that might be attributed to separating couples. Of course, there is some truth in this. This is not an argument for the perpetuation of bitter, joyless or violent relationships. However, it is right to ask if the marriage promises have reduced in value so that they are easily made and easily broken. Has the breaking of these promises led to the devaluation of all the promises upon which society is built? In the context of broken human promises, the unbreakable promises of God stand in dramatic contrast.

There are always consequences to a relationship breakdown. Sadly, when children are involved many of these are borne by them. In a study by Ben Wilson published in June 2010 it was reported that 3.8 million British children live with only one of their biological parents. There are 2.7 million who live with just their mother whilst 200,000 live with a lone father. Of the rest, 500,000 live with cohabiting step-families and 400,000 in married step-families. In summary, nearly one third of children are growing up separated from one of their parents [6].

DECREASED NUMBER OF CHILDREN, POPULATION DECAY AND INCREASED PUBLIC DISRESPECT FOR PARENTS AND PARENTHOOD.

Speaking of the days immediately preceding His return Jesus said plainly:

Matthew 24:12
Because of the increase of wickedness, the love of most will grow cold.

Whilst the economic factors and the availability of birth control contribute to parents' decisions to limit family size, there is an underlying cause. If, as might be accepted, children are the result of human affection then falling family size is an indication of the simple lessening of love.

Remember, Zimmerman was talking in 1947 about how Europe and the United States had by then already stopped having enough children to grow their civilizations. Since that time, family size has continued to decrease rather than increase. With the exception of the period referred to as the 'boom' generation into which I was born, Western Civilisation has only grown because of immigration. Although two children remains the most common family size in the UK, the average number of children per family has dropped - from 2.0 in 1971 to 1.8 in 2007. [7]

Families the size of my grandparents' with ten children, whilst never the norm, were not uncommon a few generations ago. Now such large families among white Europeans are virtually unheard of. Muslim, Sikh and Hindu households in Great Britain are larger than households headed by those of any other religion. In 2001, households headed by a Muslim were largest, being most likely to contain children and the highest number of children [8]. Based on current growth projections, Islam will take over the West simply by human reproduction and without aggression. I am aware that such statistics can be used by some to generate fear and promote hatred. That is not my agenda. Love is the answer. Without an honouring of what we have received from our forefathers, we can have no future. Restoring Christian love into the heart of the human family is the only answer.

ELIMINATION OF THE REAL MEANING OF THE MARRIAGE CEREMONY.

If the marriage ceremony has no meaning and has become merely a contract for services akin to buying cheese in a supermarket rather than a covenant born of love, then one of the essential building blocks for society has been demolished. If people do not know the God of love, how can they credibly make promises of love before Him? That is not to decry the promises made by those of no faith or who marry outside of church. However, the currency of true love is devalued by being equated with a warm but ephemeral feeling that rises like the morning mist and has vanished by noon. Love that endures is a love that is selfless and has learned to sacrifice. Ultimately this is the love of God revealed in Jesus. Of course, Christians do not have the monopoly on love; God does because "God is love" (1 John 4:8).

The writer G. K. Chesterton said:

When people stop believing in God, they don't believe in nothing - they believe in anything. [9]

Western Civilisation has turned its back upon its Judeo-Christian origins. In this context, all beliefs are acceptable apart from those that brought the freedoms that we now see dissipated. The West has turned apostate. So have parts of the church. However, Christianity was and is the cradle of true civilisation, and without it this fragile child is doomed to perish. The Church needs to both repent and call society back to repentance.

Winston Churchill once said:

A nation that forgets its past has no future. [10]

Likewise families, the building block of nations, have no future when they forget their past. The older family forms referred to are the trustee family of my grandparents and the nuclear family of my parents' generation rather than the increasingly dominant atomistic family of this generation. The truth is, the family is not a recent invention but the God-given model for building a good society. Unless we maintain what we have received we will have nothing to pass on. We forget where we have come from and do not know where we are going. If we fail to cherish our families as something worthwhile investing in then they will not endure.

In recognition that many individuals have been damaged by their own family experience it has become commonplace to attack the family itself. However, if it is demolished there is nothing to replace it with. Many commentators, in attacking what is termed the 'traditional family', characterise the unit as being oppressive and dysfunctional but fail to acknowledge that for all its faults it is also the most successful way of raising children. Likewise Christian marriage is the preferred context for raising the godly offspring that God is seeking. The family, although often subverted, has been durable across time and cultures. It is God-given. There is simply no realistic alternative.

Dr. Zimmerman felt his academic colleagues, who ignored the evidence he gathered, denied history because the facts led them to conclusions they could not accept. All of these conditions are present in our current society. Yet it seems controversial to make this observation. In these days of political correctness it seems unlikely that Zimmerman would be able to find a publisher. Children hurt by divorce need their wounded hearts healed before they can begin to relate to God as a Father. The good news is that God wants to restore our hearts.

Shaking the Nations

Centuries before the first coming of Christ, the Old Testament prophet Haggai had foretold the "shaking of all nations". He said:

Haggai 2:6-7
This is what the LORD Almighty says: 'In a little while I will once more shake the heavens and the earth, the sea and the dry land. I will shake all nations, and the desired of all nations will come, and I will fill this house with glory.'

Before the end of this chapter the prophet proclaimed:

Haggai 2:21-22
Tell Zerubbabel governor of Judah that I will shake the heavens and the earth. I will overturn royal thrones and shatter the power of the foreign kingdoms. I will overthrow chariots and their drivers; horses and their riders will fall, each by the sword of his brother.

The shaking envisaged here is universal; no sphere of creation or human affairs will be untouched.

Referring back to Haggai the writer of Hebrews tells us:

Hebrews 12:27-28
The words 'once more' indicate the removing of what can be shaken - that is, created things - so that what cannot be shaken may remain. Therefore, since we are receiving a kingdom that cannot be shaken, let us be thankful, and so worship God acceptably with reverence and awe.

The shaking of everything should not alarm the Christian or undermine our faith but rather confirm it; God is fulfilling his word. He told us that it must happen and it is. Only what God has established, His Kingdom, can withstand this shaking.

Remember your Creator

So why is society in the condition that it is? Why have the Judeo-Christian foundations of society been undermined and the 'Christian West' turned apostate?

To give my own answer to these questions let me begin with a story. When I was 21 I undertook a part time theology course called Foundations for Ministry. It was set up and run from Southampton Community Church by the Bible teachers Don Lamb and Roger Hutchins with a number of guest speakers, including Arthur Wallis. It was an excellent course and laid a foundation in my life.

Roger Hutchins once taught on the topic of Eschatology (the end times) and said that those who follow the antichrist, also called "the man of lawlessness", would...

2 Thessalonians 2:10-12

...perish because they refused to love the truth and so be saved. For this reason God sends them a powerful delusion so that they will believe the lie and so that all will be condemned who have not believed the truth but have delighted in wickedness.

Referring to the "powerful delusion" here he said that he thought this was the theory of evolution. No one offered a different viewpoint, and those who expressed a view agreed. I thought then and think now that what he said made sense. In this passage we are told that we become vulnerable to this deception when we refuse to love the truth, and it is striking that it is a delusion sent by God.

As a family we know how important knowing God as Creator has been to all of our faith. When our eldest daughter Abigail was six years old she had a series of dreams in which she 'saw' God creating the world. A foundation of faith was laid in her life. Jesus said:

Matthew 11:25

I praise you, Father, Lord of heaven and earth, because you have hidden these things from the wise and learned, and revealed them to little children.

This revelation confirmed her confidence in the Genesis account of creation and sustained her through the evolutionary teaching that has bombarded her throughout her Primary and Secondary schooling. She is now a passionate Christian and creationist. I am concerned that other young people with the same background but without this revelation have greater struggles with their faith.

More recently I came across the well-reasoned teaching of Ken Ham. He makes the point that evolutionary theory (which might be better termed a *hypothesis*) is in fact a religious belief. This belief, using the language of science, poses as pure science and allows our secular humanist society to ignore both where it has come from and where it is going [11].

For a hypothesis to graduate to becoming a theory it must be tested, repeatable and provable. What is evolutionary theory cannot be.

Sadly the church seems to have broadly come to accept this hypothesis, with serious consequences. It has undermined the foundation of faith.

Let me make it clear, as Ham would, that I do not have a problem with the process described as natural selection which is plainly observable and repeatable. However, this process shows a transition within species and not a development from one species into another.

Southampton University conferred on me a Master of Science Degree in 1991. If I were minded I guess I could call myself a scientist; most of the time I do not. The truth is I have a limited area of expertise in the vast subject of the social sciences. There are huge areas of science that I am ignorant of. However, what is true of me is true of all scientists. Scientists all tend to know a great deal about the small area of their expertise, and there is a huge amount that they know nothing about. The trouble is that many hearing a scientist who is an expert on, for example, rocket propulsion think that he speaks with equal authority on the origins of the world. The truth is scientists do not and cannot because they were not there. There was only One eyewitness of the origin of the world.

Many times we people think that we are so clever. Isaiah, speaking for God, helps to put us in perspective:

Isaiah 55:8-9

"For my thoughts are not your thoughts, neither are your ways my ways," declares the Lord. "As the heavens are higher than the earth, so are my ways higher than your ways and my thoughts than your thoughts."

Paul writing to the Greek city of Corinth said:

1 Corinthians 1:21

For since in the wisdom of God the world through its wisdom did not know him, God was pleased through the foolishness of what was preached to save those who believe.

So worldly wisdom does not bring anyone to the knowledge of God and is indeed scorned by Him. A few sentences later Paul wrote:

1 Corinthians 1:25

For the foolishness of God is wiser than human wisdom, and the weakness of God is stronger than human strength.

Our brightest talents do not get anywhere close to God. In fact, when we rely on them they usually take us away from Him. We are finite and rather foolish creatures who will have to stand before an infinite and wise Creator.

Ken Ham quoted the prophetic words of Peter:

2 Peter 3:3-7

First of all, you must understand that in the last days scoffers will come, scoffing and following their own evil desires. They will say, "Where is this 'coming' he promised? Ever since our fathers died, everything goes on as it has since the beginning of creation." But they deliberately forget that long ago by God's word the heavens existed and the earth was formed out of water and with water. By water also the world of that time was deluged and destroyed. By the same word the present heavens and earth are reserved for fire, being kept for the day of judgement and destruction of ungodly men.

In days when those around us have wilfully forgotten where they come from, we should remember. This passage clearly predicts the days in which we are living including the teaching of evolution as a collective amnesia. We are urged to "remember [our] Creator in the days of [our] youth" (Ecclesiastes 12:1). If we remember our Creator when we are young, we will not forget him when we are old.

It is not surprising that the prospect of facing a Creator God should be so uncomfortable for the ungodly that they should actively choose an organised way of burying Him. If they were to admit that they were made by God they would have to accept that one day they will meet with Him. It is a terrifying prospect to meet your Creator as Judge without knowing Him as your Saviour. The thing is, Christians should not join them in what is called a delusion by the Bible.

In John we are told that everything was made by, and through, Jesus:

John 1:2

Through him all things were made; without him nothing was made that has been made.

In Romans it is written that the Creator can be known by considering what he has made:

Romans 1:18-20

The wrath of God is being revealed from heaven against all the godlessness and wickedness of men who suppress the truth by their wickedness, since what may be known about God is plain to them, because God has made it plain to them. For since the creation of the world God's invisible qualities - his eternal power and divine nature - have been clearly seen, being understood from what has been made, so that men are without excuse.

The same thought is poetically expressed in Psalms:

Psalm 19:1
The heavens declare the glory of God; the skies proclaim the work of his hands.

Christians, in giving credence to evolutionary theory, diminish their confidence in the rest of scripture and thereby their faith. A quote from the vehemently anti-Christian writer Richard Dawkins helps to illustrate this point:

Darwin made it possible to be an intellectually fulfilled atheist. [12]

At a fundamental level a belief in evolution is incompatible with belief in the Bible. We are told:

Hebrews 11:3
By faith we understand that the universe was formed at God's command, so that what is seen was not made out of what was visible.

This truth is so obvious that it amazes me that so much of the church is missing this. It seems that for a Christian to trust solely in scientific opinion, which is subject to constant revision and change, rather than the changeless word of God is like sawing off a branch of the tree that he is sitting on. If we do not stand on God's word we will not be able to stand at all. We will have no foundation.

How can we do the works of God if we do not believe the word of God? I come from a part of the church where there has been a great deal of prayer for the miraculous power of God. Many people are desperate to meet *Jehovah Rophe*, the Covenant name for God revealed in Exodus:

Exodus 15:26
I am the LORD, who heals you.

God is able to meet us where we are, but we are at a disadvantage in searching for God our Healer if we do not already know God our Creator. The two revelations of God are linked. We are handicapped in seeking the one if we do not know the other. Indeed at times our circumstances are so desperate that we need a creative miracle and to be assured:

Colossians 1:16-17

For in him all things were created: things in heaven and on earth, visible and invisible, whether thrones or powers or rulers or authorities; all things have been created through him and for him. He is before all things, and in him all things hold together.

Paul tells us:

Romans 10:17

Faith comes from hearing the message, and the message is heard through the word about Christ.

If we question God's word about the origins of the world and of life then how can we rely on any of the other promises of God? The truth is that if we want to we will find it much more difficult.

Paul said:

2 Timothy 3:16-17

All Scripture is God-breathed and is useful for teaching, rebuking, correcting and training in righteousness, so that the servant of God may be thoroughly equipped for every good work.

With respect to creation, God's word does appear to be very plain. If we have a problem with the supernatural account of the origin of the world then where do we draw the line? Do we throw out the miracles and resurrection of Jesus? If not, why not? Jesus and the gospel writers do appear to accept and rely upon the veracity of the book of Genesis; why shouldn't we?

All of the fundamental doctrines of Christianity have their origin in the first eleven chapters of Genesis. If we have rejected this God-given account then we have no explanation for sin entering the world and thereby have undermined the basis for the atoning death of Christ. If we accept that the world we now see came into existence through an evolutionary process that involved millions of years of death and decay then how could God have looked at such a world and said that it was good? It does not seem that he honestly could have done. Indeed the marriage of one man to one woman as a God-given relationship on which society is built is also undermined by rejecting the book of Genesis. This is ultimately why I believe we see society crumbling.

I wrote the following poem when I was at college, and it still seems to sum these things quite well.

Accidents

Hiding in the shadows,
unconsulted when created,
and insulted by the gift of life
men ignore their Maker
and look to make an end.

In the beginning,
man said, there was an accident,
a random collision of atoms,
then me – a chemical reaction.
So man awoke into the world
from soup of slumber,
and evolved into an adult,
and lived by chance.

And man looked
and saw that it was plausible,
and so by experimenting with embryos and bigger bombs,
attempted to ensure
that entry and departure from the world
for future generations
were all governed by –
Accidents.

Orphans and Atheists

There is a proverb that says:

Proverbs 25:26
Like a muddied spring or a polluted well is a righteous man who gives way to the wicked.

I believe that many Christians are guilty of yielding to an atheist agenda when they have a rock beneath them. The spring has become polluted. I remember, when studying English, reading the great poet Percy Bysshe Shelley and being fascinated by the central paradox of his atheistic ideology: he spent all of his energies locked in an argument with a God that he said did not exist. The same dynamic is at work amongst the new atheists. If there really were no God they surely could be content to leave it at that. They cannot. They have an evangelistic agenda and are constantly seeking to persuade themselves and others that they are right.

Both Psalm 14 and 53 open with the same blunt assessment of atheism:

The fool says in his heart, "There is no God."

The writer and teacher Mark Stibbe has made the point that Nietche and many of the leading atheist thinkers have been profoundly wounded in their relationship with their earthly fathers. The passionate rage in their argument is born out of an orphan spirit. In the same way it is has been observed that the rage of Islam has the same origin. The inscription written above the dome of the rock in Jerusalem is that "God has no companion" or in some renderings "no son". No wonder that "creation waits in eager expectation for the sons of God to be revealed" (Romans 8:19).

James tells us:

James 1:27
Religion that God our Father accepts as pure and faultless is this: to look after orphans and widows in their distress and to keep oneself from being polluted by the world.

It is vital that we, as the Church, should remember our Father and Creator rather than live like the orphans around us. We are charged to care for these orphans by showing them their Father. It is only as we walk in the revelation of being sons that we will be truly able to reveal the Father.

Action!

In this section, let me again try to give practical examples of how you might apply this teaching. I am aware that my views on creation will be considered controversial in some quarters and at odds with those of many sincere professing Christians. If that is the case for you, let's not fall out! My desire in writing these things is to generate a re-examination of this important subject in the light of the scriptures. I would urge the reader to be reconciled to their Creator and His word. Those interested in the science around this debate might consider looking at the websites for Answers in Genesis (www.answersingenesis.org) or Creation Ministries International (creation.com/articles).

What can parents do to begin to transform an atomistic family into a healthier family model? Outside of Christ I believe that the situation is hopeless. Yet we do know that God desires to "set the lonely in families" (Psalm 68:6). Ultimately this needs to be as God's family works as He intended. The Church needs to operate as the larger trustee or tribal family spoken of by Zimmerman. For this to take place every Christian family needs to be inclusive and not exclusive, to look out and not in. Allow the revelation of God the Father to transform you into a father, mother or sister to those that he brings into your life. It will be remembered that in the book of Acts it was said that there were "no needy persons among them" (Acts 4:34). This is where we have to get back to. God is inviting us to become a part of this transformation.

Developing this thought further, how can spouses guard their marriage? How can parents protect their children from an atheistic education and society? I believe that the answer to both questions is by building up and repairing the family altar. The family that prays together stays together. Read the Bible from cover to cover with your children and talk to them about its contents. This will transform you both. Parents should not rely upon even a good school to teach children right from wrong. The scripture places the primary responsibility for the education of children upon the parents. Parents need to make time to talk to their children and be familiar with the challenges that their developing faith is facing.

Where fathers are believers I believe that they have a priestly role in initiating times of prayer and conversation with their children. They need to be humble, gentle and approachable. Remember that half of conversation is listening. In this way qualities of healthy fatherhood can be developed. To be a healthy father you will need to be a healed father. We will consider this more in the next chapter.

Prayer Points

- Pray that men and women would remember their Creator and return to Him.
- Pray that there would be a greater confidence in the Church in the veracity and authority of scripture.
- Pray for the healing and restoration of families.
- Pray for the Church to walk in and reveal the love of the Father.

REFERENCES

1. Yeats, William Butler, *The Second Coming;* written in 1919; first printed in The Dial (November 1920) and afterwards included in his 1921 collection of verses entitled Michael Robartes and the Dancer.

2. Achebe, Chinua, *Things Fall Apart; published by* William Heinemann Ltd. (1958); ISBN 9780385474542

3. Zimmerman, Carle C., *Family and Civilization;* published by Harper and Brothers (1947, New York). Zimmerman was a prominent Harvard sociologist who lived from 1897 until 1983.

4. www.communitycare.co.uk/Articles/2009/04/09/111233/lurking-in-the-shadows.htm

5. Zimmerman, Carle C. Ibid: For completeness those cited by Zimmerman but missed out here are:
    *   Popularity of pessimistic doctrines about the early heroes.
    *   Rise of theories that companionate marriage or a permissible looser family form would solve the problem.
    *   The refusal of many other people married under the older family form to maintain their traditions while other people escape these obligations.
    *   The spread of anti-familism of the urbane pseudo-intellectual classes to the very outer limits of the civilization.
    *   Breaking down of most inhibitions against adultery. Revolts of youth against parents so that parenthood became more and more difficult for those who did try to raise children.
    *   Rise and spread of juvenile delinquency.
    *   Common acceptance of all forms of sex perversion.

6. Wilson, Ben, the Office for National Statistics, Population Trends 140 June 2010. *Opinions survey on children with a non-resident parent, carried out in 2008/09.*

7. BBC Tuesday, 6 November 2007, http://news.bbc.co.uk/1/hi/7071611.stm.

8. The Office for National Statistics News Release: *One-in-seven in Great Britain have no religion,* Focus on Religion, 11 October 2004. Issued by National Statistics, 1 Drummond Gate, London SW1V 2QQ.

9. http://www.quotedb.com/authors/gk-chesterton

10. http://www.winston-churchill-leadership.com/churchill-quote-epigrams.html

11. Ham, Ken, *The Lie: Evolution (Genesis - The Key to Defending Your Faith);* first published by Master Books (July 1987); ISBN 0890511586. Ken is founder of 'Answers in Genesis' and one of the chief advocates for Creation Science.

12. Richard Dawkins, *The Blind Watchmaker,* page 6; published by W. W. Norton & Company (1986); ISBN 0393315703.

A Heart Restored

Malachi 4:5

...he will restore the hearts.

Deliverance

On Monday 12th February, 2001, I was driving back from Basingstoke to Southampton in heavy rain at the end of the day. I was feeling unwell because of a cold and had not slept brilliantly the previous night. I found myself struggling to stay awake at the wheel. My eyelids kept drooping, and several times I felt that I was about to go to sleep. I was afraid but thought that this was an entirely natural phenomenon; I was tired, and when you are you want to go to sleep.

Since there was nowhere to stop the car on that stretch of motorway I tried different strategies to keep myself awake and alive. I opened the car window to let the rain splash my face. Instead of waking up I felt worse. Several times my head started to go forward, and I jolted awake. I was fighting for my life. I prayed loudly in tongues and then heard myself saying with great authority, "Spirit of death, be gone!" I could not recall thinking these words and concluded that they must have been an interpretation of my prayer language. Instantly the feeling of drowsiness peeled off me and I was wide awake, free to finish my journey in safety. I felt slightly stunned and thought, "Oh, was that what it was - a spirit of death?"

This dramatic episode raised a number of questions for me and was in itself a little confusing. I became a Christian when I was thirteen years of age and had walked with God, so I thought, in a fairly consistent way from the age of nineteen. When this deliverance occurred I was thirty-seven years old. What was this 'spirit of death', and how had it gained access to my life? How could it have remained dormant and untroubled through my many years of Christian observance? Although I had not been in a church meeting and no one had been praying for me, I had just been delivered from a demon.

Where did that come from? In many respects I had enjoyed an idyllic childhood in the beautiful county of Devon. Yet there had been something wrong. It is easier to see with hindsight that there had been a shadow over my childhood. I had strange fears and nightmares and an intermittent stutter. I just did not know what was wrong.

Beginnings

I was very much a child of the 1960s, born a few days before the assassination of John F Kennedy, the third of four children. My sister and brother are thirteen and eleven years older than me, respectively. Two and a half years after my birth my younger brother arrived. My parents at some point told me that I had been "an accident". They happily qualified this by saying that I was the nicest accident that they had ever had - but I was an accident nevertheless! Apparently, before my mum had even realised that she was pregnant, she had been visiting her mother, a woman who prayed and knew God. She took one look at mum who had just started back at work and informed her, "You are carrying God's child."

I was sent along to Sunday school at the East Street Baptist Chapel in Newton Abbot. I became familiar with Bible stories which I learned to love. Many years later an elderly lady called Alice Bowden, who had been my mother's Sunday school teacher, told me that my aunt Marie had often wept as she had prayed for me.

When I started secondary school I also went along to the Boys' Brigade. One evening in January 1977, when I was thirteen years old, I attended a Boys' Brigade Church Parade. That evening it was as though I was the only person in the room, and every word preached was addressed to me. Even then I was burdened by a weight of guilt and fear. I responded to the appeal and after praying for forgiveness asked Jesus into my heart. I remember walking home with my bemused younger brother, literally jumping for joy. I felt that day had been the happiest day of my life. My heart had begun to be restored.

When I got home I explained to Dad what had happened to me earlier that evening. I sat on his lap as I had done as a much younger child with him hugging me and weeping. I think it seemed to him like he had lost a son. In some ways he had.

Having made this commitment I don't think that I really knew what to do next. I read through my Gideon's New Testament. I went along to the Christian club at my secondary school and told my surprised friends what had happened in my life. I remember getting some stick when I tried to read my Bible during the library period at school. This was difficult for me because I also wanted to be popular and to fit in. In time I outgrew Boys' Brigade and my appearances at church became less frequent. Without really looking for them, other things started to fill my life.

I began to be filled with morbid thoughts about death and was certain that the end of the world was at hand. In reaction to this I went to lots of parties and drank too much. This was awkward for my conscience as earlier in my life I had sat temperance exams at Sunday school. I had certificates to prove how much I knew of the evils of drink. After a beach party one evening I was arrested for being drunk and incapable. In the three week walking holiday I went on after this I prayed that God would take me to where I could be what He wanted me to be.

A full year later, having come to the end of sixth form, I really did not know what to do with myself. My mother was not impressed with my vague plans of travelling. So three days before term was due to start I found myself travelling to college in Winchester to be interviewed. To my surprise I was given a place immediately.

On the train journey back, as I gazed out of the window at the green patchwork of fields, there was a vivid rainbow in the sky. I watched through a mist of tears and remembered the promise recorded in Genesis that God had made to Noah following the flood. I felt that God was answering the prayer that I had uttered over a year before.

Around this time I went for a walk ending up at the graveside of my Nan and Granddad. She had died some eight years before, a year to the day after she had last seen her husband, in January 1974. My mother had described to me how, as her coffin had been lowered into the ground, simultaneously the sun had come out and a strong wind had blown across the cemetery. Indeed the wind had been so strong that a stone vase had blown over with a crash at a nearby grave.

Whilst looking at the grave all those years later and feeling morose I 'heard' a voice asking, "Why do you look for the living among the dead?" These incredible words were not audible but were clear, and I did not believe that they had come from my own thoughts. I remember looking around, expecting to see someone, but no one was there. I recalled that the words had been spoken by the angels at Jesus' grave to the woman who came to search for his body (Luke 24:5). I had heard them at Easter services. I walked away from the grave feeling much lighter.

College

Starting college I gave little thought to God. I threw myself into the round of drinking and parties associated with student life. I managed to find a girlfriend. Early in my second term at college it seemed to me like God was everywhere. I bumped into Him on the radio, on the television and then one day even in the living room of the hostel where I was staying. It was very inconvenient!

After an evening in a pub I walked into a conversation being held between two Christian students, Stewart Keiller and Steve Flavin, and another who was an atheist. Others were watching, so I sat down for the entertainment. I was not allowed to be a passive spectator. At one point in the debate, and for no apparent reason, the atheist turned on me and demanded to know where I stood on the issues being discussed. Embarrassed, I admitted that I believed as the Christians did. He called me a coward for not standing up for what I believed, and I had to agree with him. My cover was blown! Later in the evening I went to Steve's room and prayed, rededicating my life to God. When I thanked the atheist later he was bemused; it had certainly not been his intention to push me back to God but this was what had happened. He was very apologetic; I was genuinely grateful!

A few days after returning my life to God I wrote the following poem expressing my gratitude to Him:

Saved

I've thought too much of pain and pleasure,
And in seeking or avoiding,
Receiving or inflicting,
Did not stop to feel and see,
The sun rise through the rain.

But the past is cut,
It cannot chain or blame me.
Saved from myself,
I am alive,
And living – love,
And loving - give,
Myself to God,
Whose greater gift,
Of greater love,
Though I repent,
I can't repay,
But only I hope there will be a day,
To heap my meagre thanks,
Upon His altar.

Whether in the past I had been looking up to heaven or down to the earth, it was all over. The important thing was that Christ now lived in me. The following Easter I was baptised at East Street Baptist Church in my home town. At around the same time I was filled with the Holy Spirit. From this time on I believed that I made quite steady spiritual progress. Surely I was 'sorted'.

After I left college I worked in a bookshop where I parcelled books and sent them off to different libraries around Hampshire. To my shock I discovered that a colleague was a heroin addict. This was in 'nice' middle class Winchester, which in 1986 was the richest provincial town in England, and he seemed a 'nice' middle class person. Over the years I have come to see that things are rarely as they seem. Beneath the surface many nice middle class people in our nice middle class society are falling apart.

When I was with this young man one evening he started to get sick and his muscles began cramping. He was experiencing withdrawal and needed a fix. I had read of Jackie Pullinger's work with drug addicts in Hong Kong's walled city, and so I offered to pray for him and he accepted [1]. His cramping pains went away immediately. Unfortunately his craving for drugs did not. Although I explained to him that Jesus could help him, he ended up in the local casualty demanding drugs from the medical staff on duty. I concluded something needed to change in both him and me for him to receive the freedom he evidently needed and for me to administer it.

The Call

I 'got the sack' from the bookshop, which was humbling for a graduate who felt he had so much to offer the world. Following some six months of unemployment, one of the leaders of my Church prophesied that I should get the first job that came along even if it was a 'dustbin' job in order to get out among the people that I was evidently so desperate to help. I knew exactly where I could get a 'dustbin' job and got a job as a hospital porter.

As a hospital porter it seemed as though God took me on a guided tour of the hospital. My mind was free whilst my body was occupied. I walked miles during the day, and if patients did not want to talk to me I was free to chat to God. There were long periods of sitting around in between jobs, and so I read books. I was impacted by Thomas à Kempis' five hundred year old classic 'The Imitation of Christ' and the slightly newer 'Practicing the Presence of God' by Brother Lawrence. At times the presence of God seemed more real than the hospital.

At this time I would have loved to work for the church, perhaps talking to people about God. I really wanted to serve the Lord and thought that this was the best way of doing so. However, the Lord had something else for me.

Carol Ann and I were married in Winchester in August 1987 and moved to Southampton so that I could train as a social worker. From that time I worked exclusively with children and families, many of whom had suffered abuse and were living with its consequences. It was only after a period of prayer and fasting that I had trained for this work. I came into the work with high aspirations of changing the world and setting the prisoners free. I often used to say that I needed a strong sense of the call of God into this work and needed this constantly reaffirmed to remain in it. Social work is like that. I would counsel anyone considering it as a career not to do it unless you have to! I would add that I had to.

The Curse

For the early part of my career I believed that the abused were other people. Child sexual abuse was an abstract concept, and its victims deserved my sympathy and professional help. The possibility that I might have been sexually abused as a child did not even enter my head. Then overnight everything changed.

It was Easter 1991. I had been qualified as a social worker for two years and was twenty-seven years old. Three weeks before, I had returned from a Christian Social Work conference in Sheffield on the issue of ritual abuse. Someone at the conference shared that from her experience those who had suffered abuse often made the most sensitive carers. At around that time I remember that I had been burdened to pray for abused children to be set free. To say that I was surprised by how that prayer was answered is an understatement. I never suspected that I was, in effect, praying for myself.

On Good Friday, 29th March 1991, I woke up at about 3.00am from a dream with a cry coming from my mouth. It was a cry of fear, pain and desolation. In the dream I was confronting some long forgotten dread. The details that I remembered were of my Uncle and Aunt's two boxer dogs, Bengo and Patch, and the pub where they had lived. Lying awake after the dream I had a clear conviction that something had happened to me when I was three years old. I recalled that a semi-vagrant alcoholic called Leonard, who had lived in the grounds of the pub, had assaulted me. As I explained this to Carol Ann I began to weep, and she prayed for me, thanking God that being healed from this experience would be part of my full salvation. Her prayer was prophetic. I began to understand for the first time the origins of the crippling guilt that had for so long ruled my life.

Piece by piece I began to recover the lost memories of the stranger rape that I had suffered. This slowly began to change my attitude towards those that I was trying to help. As a child I had read and been gripped by the story of the Catholic priest who gave his life in caring for leprosy patients on Hawaii's leper settlement on Molokai Island. In 1873 the young Belgian named Father Damien begged his bishop to send him to the colony. For years as he cared for the lepers it seemed to everyone that he was immune to the disease. Then one Sunday in 1885 he opened his sermon not with the customary "Brethren" but simply "We lepers" [2]. I might say, "We abused." I could not look down in a patronising way upon the abused any more. I was one of them.

Years later I would be able to say of my history as Joseph had said to the brothers who had sold him as a slave:

Genesis 50:20
You intended to harm me, but God intended it for good.

In the meantime I was puzzled at how I could have lived in ignorance of this foundational pain on which my personality appeared to have been built. I have come to see that the burying of this crippling memory ensured that I was protected until it could be properly processed. As Betsie Ten Boon told her sister Corrie whilst staying in the notorious Ravensbruck Concentration Camp before she died, "There is no pit so deep that God's love is not deeper still." [3]

I asked myself how I could have walked into a profession where I would be forced to face, again and again, people who had suffered the same pain. It seemed a strange and uncomfortable providence. Although I realise now I could not have coped with this revelation any sooner, at the time I felt both ambushed and betrayed. These feelings were of course associated with the original violation. Jesus said:

John 8:32
You will know the truth, and the truth will set you free.

For our hearts to be restored we need to be freed from self-delusion. I had no idea how painful the truth might be. I had no idea of the prevalence of this problem and how many of those who became caregivers had suffered in this way.

Although I did not vocalise it, my thought was, "How can I trust the God who allowed this to happen?" I also came to see that I felt an infantile rage against my own father although I had never told him as a child of this experience. At heart I felt I should have been protected. At some point, without recognizing it, I became depressed. I have come to see that depression is a form of buried anger, and so perhaps the depression began at that point. More likely I had carried this sadness from the time that I was three. At various points in my pilgrimage I thought that I had broken free of the pain of the past and had closed this chapter of my history. However, it kept coming back to haunt me in various ways.

What were the effects upon me? They seem to have been countless. I came to see that I suffered from an occasional stutter as a result of the abuse. This was because the perpetrator had effectively put a curse upon my tongue by saying that I was to say nothing of the assault. I saw that even my choice of career had been influenced by the inner vow that I had made as a child that what I had suffered should never happen to anyone else. I desperately wanted to rescue people. I came to understand that I carried anger against men that affected my perception of myself and relationships with other men. I was not really comfortable in my own skin. It also blighted my perception of God as a loving Heavenly Father.

At times I wished that there might be some prayer that I could pray, book I could read or meeting that I could attend and I would be 'fixed'. These were the routes that had served me before but did not seem to help me then. In Christian counselling I found a measure of help and healing. If I were to summarise this help I would say that it assisted me in living with the pain rather than freeing me from it. I also felt less lonely for a time. Underneath the pain that God was healing there always seemed to be another pain that He wanted to heal. The root cause was not fully addressed. I gained a better understanding of my problem but only partial release. I sought to anaesthetise this pain by retreating into the fantasy of television and drinking more wine than my conscience was content with. All this time I sought to pray for and help others. It helped me to make sense of everything and in some way redeemed my pain.

The Cure

On the 14th April 2000 I invited my friend and mentor Mark Iles to attend one of my counselling sessions and to pray with my counsellor for my healing. The time proved very significant. Mark had a very vivid word for me that spoke of how God wanted to reclaim my experience. He had a picture of the boy Arthur and the sword in the stone. A crowd was around the stone. This represented the crowd of problems that had the abuse as a rallying point. I was able to remove the sword, the stone disappeared into the undergrowth and the crowd dispersed. The problems would cease to be an issue. My only souvenir from the experience was to be "a dirty great big sword". The sword he saw was bigger than I was, and I would need to learn to wield it. The sense was that I needed to grow up into the sword. I also needed to pray that God would provide me with the armour that he had prepared to accompany it. Of particular importance, Mark stressed, was the armour covering my shoulders designed to protect me as blows rained down on my arms.

This prophecy pointed me towards ultimate victory but did not accomplish it. I had a further distance to travel. As I prayed and sought God for wisdom, answers came. Four months after I had been delivered from a spirit of death, on 18th June 2001, I awoke from a dream about my being buried alive. In the dream I had seen a child's skeleton that had been found inside a coffin with scratch marks on the lid providing evidence of having tried to claw its way out. Praying about this for the first time I understood that the abuse I had suffered had been as violent as a murder. In part this was how the spirit of death had entered my life as my will had been usurped. I had been praying that God would bring down the barriers that I had erected to protect me from people. This dream and the experience that had preceded it appeared to help do this.

In the autumn of 2003, in the month or so before my fortieth birthday, I set my face to seek God through a forty day period of prayer and fasting. This was something that had been on my heart for many years. I can remember Derek Prince challenging the readers of his book 'Blessing or Curse: You can choose!' that if they were serious about getting free then they should seek God through such a fast. Forty is a tremendously significant number in the Bible. It seems to symbolise a complete period of time or testing. Noah's flood came after forty days and nights of rain. Forty years is the length of a biblical generation. The Israelites wandered forty years in the desert and of course Moses, Elijah and Jesus all undertook forty day periods of prayer and fasting. It was also the age when life was supposed to begin! That was what I was looking for.

Desperate times require desperate measures. At the time of this fast I was concerned that the Lord should intervene in my family. Carol Ann and I were both depressed. This was starting to impact upon the wellbeing of our children. In addition we were concerned that their academic progress was impeded by problems such as dyslexia. Jeremiah said:

Jeremiah 29:13
You will seek me and find me when you seek me with all your heart.

This was to become my experience. I met God in a wonderful way through the fast.

A highlight during the fast was a healing that I received. A few months prior to fasting I had started wearing glasses. I tried to reconcile myself with the fact that I was getting older and this was to be expected. However, it rankled. Then during the fast I lost my glasses. I hunted high and low and could not locate them anywhere. After a few days of fruitless searching I prayed and felt the Lord say to me, "I am giving you new vision." At this very point I felt my eyes change, and my vision came back into focus. When I eventually found my glasses I had no need of them. The Lord was plainly referring to more than my physical eyesight when He said that He was giving me "new vision". My whole outlook on life was about to change.

On 14th February 2004 I travelled to the Church of the Synagogue of All Nations in Lagos, Nigeria with my two eldest daughters, then aged eleven and nine, and some other friends. It was our first visit to Africa. Britain had been for many years the colonial power governing Nigeria. This ended in the 1960s. Britain has been a father through its governmental influence and by bringing the gospel to many nations. For many years missionaries had left my homeland, indeed through my home city of Southampton, to live and work in Africa and other lands. We had exported Christianity to lands where it had taken root and flourished, growing far beyond the expression of church in our own land. I am grateful that there has been turning of the hearts of the fathers to the children and the hearts of the children back to the fathers. Having been a mission force, Britain and indeed the whole of Western Europe is now regarded as a mission field. Many Christians from African and other lands have heeded the Macedonian call to "Come over ... and help us" (Acts 16:9).

In March 2009 I heard Charles Abrahams, who is Nigerian born but British by adoption and a prophetic intercessor, explain the history of the Nigerian revival. He said that in the 1970s Christianity in his homeland was rather cold, ritualistic and formulaic. Church attendance tended to be regarded as a duty rather than a joy. Church membership seemed a mark of social standing rather than a consuming passion. Then the prophets started to prophesy a move of God and an explosion of growth in the Nigerian church. Generally speaking no one believed them. However, some must have prayed. Through 1980s and 1990s God has more than fulfilled these visions. Now Charles explained that a new church is planted in Nigeria every minute. As might be expected this has not been without persecution.

Lagos is the second largest city in Africa with a population of twenty million people, smaller only than the Egyptian capital Cairo. Until 1991 it was the capital city of Nigeria when it was replaced by Abuja. Nigerian roads and Nigerian driving are both an adventure. On our very exciting journey from the airport to the church, which included an armed police escort and detours onto the wrong side of the road to get past traffic, I saw a huge number and variety of churches and Christian businesses.

I had heard many reports from friends of the ministry of the prophet TB Joshua and went with a hungry heart. Aside from the many wonderful miracles that I saw in the lives of others, I was very grateful for what was accomplished in my own. On 18th February 2004 he prayed for me in the prayer line. I fell down on the floor and laughed. He then told me that I had been depressed. I had got used to my low emotional state and did not always recognise that I was depressed until after I was healed. He said that there was "something very bad" that had happened to me in the past a very long time ago. He went on, "You just need to forget it; it's over." He explained that in dwelling upon it I was allowing it to spoil my present and to endanger my future. "Forget it!" he repeated. He said that there was a brother (meaning the abuser) in the past; I just needed to forgive and forget. When I got up from the floor I felt like I was a different man.

I can honestly say that a burden was rolled away that night. Truly it is the anointing that breaks the yoke. The word of authority from the prophet brought me the freedom that all other words had failed to give. In Isaiah it is written:

Isaiah 32:4

...the stammering tongue will be fluent and clear.

Since this ministry, this has been my experience. When the Son sets you free, you will be free indeed! In another message, Prophet TB Joshua quoted another part of Isaiah:

Isaiah 43:18-19

Forget the former things; do not dwell on the past. See, I am doing a new thing! Now it springs up do you not perceive?

The grace of God began enabling me to leave my history and to enter into my destiny.

I am reminded of the title of a popular television show 'They think it's all over - it is now!' The show takes its title from words spoken by the commentator during the closing seconds of the 1966 World Cup (which England won). For a long time I had wanted to achieve what counsellors call 'closure' on my past but had failed to do so. There had been a number of false dawns when I had thought it was all over. Truly I believe it is now! That does not mean that I have not had problems since; far from it - only that this one has lost its power over me.

On the last day of my visit to Nigeria I had a very brief interview with the prophet, a kindness he extended to all his visitors. He prayed a blessing upon my children and me and handed me a piece of paper on which he wrote, "Acts 19:11".

It was not until I left the room that I was able to look the verse up. It said quite simply, "God did extraordinary miracles through Paul". I was stunned. I was sure that I had never seen that verse in my Bible before and would certainly have never had the audacity to apply it to myself. Now my confidence in the gospel to meet every need had been substantially enhanced. I had seen that it was simpler, more dynamic and more effective than I had seen it administered in my own land. This man of God, whom

I had witnessed bring to birth incredible miracles, had given me words that contained both extraordinary promise and responsibility.

Heart Trouble

It is often said that the heart of the human problem is the problem of the human heart. Jeremiah told us:

Jeremiah 17:9

The heart is deceitful above all things and beyond cure. Who can understand it?

We might be broken hearted, but our hearts can also be hard, divided and deceived. I heard Derek Prince explain that the word translated 'deceitful' in this verse in Jeremiah is the same as the Hebrew name 'Jacob'. Jacob means 'the deceiver' or literally 'he who grabs the heel'. We cannot rely upon our hearts to tell us the truth. In order to bind up and restore our broken hearts God first needs to deliver us from our self-deceit.

This is how the Message puts the verses from Malachi:

Malachi 4:5-6

But also look ahead: I'm sending Elijah the prophet to clear the way for the Big Day of God—the decisive Judgment Day! He will convince parents to look after their children and children to look up to their parents. If they refuse, I'll come and put the land under a curse.

These words are fresh and dynamic. For the children's hearts to be restored God must access the hearts of the fathers. For the father's hearts to be restored God has to be given access to the wounded heart of the child that they carry within.

How then do we begin to see hearts restored? I had been pondering this question for some seven months when a friend Marco Wilbrink put John Loren Sandford's book 'Elijah Among Us' into my hand. Although I had heard of John and Paula Sandford's ministry in inner healing and the prophetic I had not read anything by them before. I was gripped.

John and Paula Sandford run what they call 'The Elijah House' where people come for training and ministry. I gasped when I read John Sandford's account of a revelation that God had given him:

The Lord had recently come to me to say, 'You did not understand Malachi 4:5-6.' He said, 'You thought that it meant natural fathers and mothers, and of course it does. But, John, it means far more. The Jewish people are the fathers of the Christian faith; Christians are the children. The hearts of the fathers and the children need to be turned to each other. Pray for the peace of Jerusalem, knowing that this means far more than you think it does. For Protestants, Catholics are the fathers, Protestants are the children. Pray for reconciliation and unity in My Church. In any land colonists are the children, natives are the fathers. You are called to pray for reconciliation and healing between Native Americans and their fellow countrymen, as well as for the natives of other countries and their countrymen.' [4]

He had written out the secrets of my heart.

Some of the scriptures that I want to share with you have been keys to my own healing. When at college, one of my friends, possibly Stewart, said that if I read through two chapters of the Old Testament and one chapter of the New Testament a day I could read through the whole Bible in a year. I have found this to be invaluable and have tried to do so ever since.

In the Psalms it is written:

Psalm 119:9

How can a young man keep his way pure? By living according to your word.

This is good advice whatever our age. The Bible is given not merely to inform but to transform us. God's word has more practical benefit to us if we store it in our hearts than on a shelf. Again the psalmist said:

Psalm 119:11

I have hidden your word in my heart that I might not sin against you.

There is a divine design in our days that can only be discovered in our relationship with God and through his word. However we arrived in this world, I believe that no one is an accident as far as God is concerned. King David conveyed this thought beautifully when he said:

Psalm 139:13-16

For you created my inmost being; you knit me together in my mother's womb. I praise you because I am fearfully and wonderfully made; your works are wonderful, I know that full well. My frame was not hidden from you when I was made in the secret place. When I was woven together in the depths of the earth, your eyes saw my unformed body. All the days ordained for me were written in your book before one of them came to be.

It is also written in the book of Ephesians that "he chose us in him before the creation of the world to be holy and blameless in his sight" (Ephesians 1:4). We may not have fully connected with our purpose, but all of our lives have meaning. If we ask God to disclose His plans and purpose for our lives I believe that He will do just that.

Do you feel that you have failed God as I did? The sovereignty of God has anticipated and made provision for the redemption of our sins and failures. God remembers us although we might forget him. Paul said:

2 Timothy 2:13

If we are faithless, he will remain faithful, for he cannot disown himself.

God will not fail.

When struggling with sin we are told to "count yourselves dead to sin but alive to God in Christ Jesus" (Romans 6:11). Sin has no continuing jurisdiction over the dead. Our battle with sin is over, having been fought and won on the cross. We do have a responsibility to apply Christ's victory to our lives. We overcome "by the blood of the Lamb and by the word of our testimony" (Revelation 12:11).

Moses warned the Israelites:

Deuteronomy 29:18

Make sure there is no man or woman, clan or tribe among you today whose heart turns away from the LORD our God to go and worship the gods of those nations; make sure there is no root among you that produces such bitter poison.

He showed how a root of bitterness could produce the poison of idolatry and turn our hearts away from the Lord. Perhaps you have been wounded by abuse or betrayal. The grace of God is available for us to avoid cultivating this bitter root in our lives that would cause trouble and defilement (Hebrews 12:15). Forgiveness will free us from bitterness and keep us close to the heart of God. Unforgiveness will keep us in torment. Even if the person who caused our injury deserves punishment we are the ones who suffer if we withhold forgiveness. Self-pity will perpetuate our pain. Life is really too short for us remain consumed by bitterness. Make the decision to forgive as you have been forgiven. You will release yourself as you do so.

As a young man working as a hospital porter I was forced to look death in the face.

Ecclesiastes 7:2
It is better to go to a house of mourning than to go to a house of feasting, for death is the destiny of every man; the living should take this to heart.

I learned first-hand of the brevity of life; death is no respecter of persons. I prayed over many of the corpses I collected from the wards to take to the mortuary. Jesus said:

John 14:12
I tell you the truth, anyone who has faith in me will do what I have been doing. He will do even greater things than these, because I am going to the Father.

Although I did not see any results, no one complained! However, I have come to see that I myself have been raised from death to life. God has begun schooling me in compassion. I have been freed from the sickness of sin and from the spirit of death. Christ died the death that we deserved in order to give us His life. He is the resurrection and the life, but he intends that we should live our lives in the power of his resurrection.

Jubilee

Isaiah 61:1-2

The Spirit of the Sovereign LORD is on me, because the LORD has anointed me to preach good news to the poor. He has sent me to bind up the broken hearted, to proclaim freedom for the captives and release from darkness for the prisoners to proclaim the year of the LORD's favour.

Isaiah's words yield their richest meaning when considered in their Jewish context. In Leviticus 25, Moses laid down the regulations surrounding what was called the Year of Jubilee. This Jubilee was defined in Leviticus 25:9 as the Yoval, a sabbatical year coming after seven cycles of seven years (forty nine years in total). Jubilee means 'the sound of the trumpet blast'. On the Day of Atonement (Yom Kippur) in the fiftieth year, the trumpet was to be sounded throughout the land of Israel. This announced a time of the release of slaves, rest for the land and the restoration of ancestral property for the people. It was to be a festival of joy and celebration, a time to party. It was, in other words, a "year of the LORD's favour" as prophesied by Isaiah. At least that was the idea.

There is no record in scripture of the Jubilee being celebrated. King Zedekiah and his officials at first released and then, changing their minds, recaptured their slaves (Jeremiah 34). This is the only reference to any effort having been made to keep the Jubilee. This lack is confirmed when we are told that by the time of the exile...

2 Chronicles 36:21

...the land enjoyed its Sabbath rests; all the time of its desolation it rested, until the seventy years were completed in fulfilment of the word of the LORD spoken by Jeremiah.

God said the land was supposed to be rested once every seven years in addition to the Jubilee in the fiftieth year. For a seventy year rest to be necessary it must have been that the land had never been rested from the time of Joshua to the Babylonian exile. It is easy to put things off; obedience to God is never convenient! Delayed obedience is disobedience.

God is never thwarted by human disobedience, for every word of His must come to pass. In His providence He makes provision for it. There was a greater Jubilee to come - the one prophesied by Isaiah. Jesus, in his inaugural sermon taken from Isaiah 61 at his home synagogue in Nazareth, announced to His astonished audience:

Luke 4:21
Today this scripture is fulfilled in your hearing.

The words of Isaiah were about Him. The prophet's words became Jesus' manifesto as He set about practising what He preached. Again and again Jesus restored both broken bodies and broken hearts. Peter said:

Acts 10:38
God anointed Jesus of Nazareth with the Holy Spirit and power and how he went around doing good and healing all who were under the power of the devil, because God was with him.

Now the mantle that rested upon Jesus has been placed upon His body the church.

Action!

Let me try to give some practical advice as to how to apply this teaching. For example, what practical steps should someone take if while reading this they know that they need healing? Firstly we need to understand that there is providence in our pain. God allows in his grace what he could easily prevent by his power. God is good. If we understand that God is our healer, and He is, then if we are wounded He will not leave us that way. Jesus was a man of sorrows and familiar with suffering. God does not leave us alone in our pain. However, whether we have been a victim or a victimiser our sin is the connection point to our pain. If we choose to remain in our sin then we remain in our sickness. If we are disconnected from our sin then our sickness cannot long remain.

I have seen this principle very clearly outlined in my visits to the church in Lagos. When Jesus said to the paralytic who was lowered through the roof, "Friend, your sins are forgiven," (Luke 5:20) the man was as good as healed. In some way sin is at the root of all sickness. In the gospels no one is recorded as coming to Christ to have their sins forgiven. However, whether we perceive it or not this is the primary need of everyone. People come to Christ because of a wound or a need. He is delighted to accept us however we come to him, but to help us he has to go to the root of our problems. In order to demonstrate His authority to forgive sins Jesus said to the paralysed man:

Luke 5:23
I tell you, get up, take your mat and go home.

As Paul says:

1 Corinthians 15:56
The sting of death is sin, and the power of sin is the law.

I have been deliberately detailed in describing both my wound and my healing. The blessings of God always carry a responsibility. They are never entirely about our comfort and happiness, wonderful though these things might be. Jesus said to his disciples:

Matthew 10:8

Heal the sick, raise the dead, cleanse those who have leprosy, drive out demons. Freely you have received, freely give.

By implication he was sending them to do for others what he had first done for them. He had saved, healed and delivered them. They had to go and do likewise. We are saved to save others. We are healed to heal others. We are blessed to bless others. As the Bible teacher Bill Johnson has said, "We can only truly keep what we are prepared to give away." We are to go and do likewise. Begin to ask God how He would have you respond.

If someone has a father-shaped wound in their lives because of a negative presence or an absence in their childhood, this will blight their relationship with God the Father and other father figures as I described that it did for me. Self-pity will be of no help but will perpetuate the pain. Forgiveness makes the future possible. If you do not have a spiritual father, perhaps you should consider asking for one? Ask God to help you locate or identify those who could serve as a spiritual father to you.

Prayer Points

- If you don't know Jesus Christ as your Lord and Saviour, you have now read enough to surrender to his claims upon your life. Bring to him all the wrong that you have done and all the wrong that has been done to you. Ask his forgiveness for your sins and forgive those who have hurt you and let you down. Now give him your whole life. Ask him to come in and take charge giving you a heart of flesh and taking away your heart of stone.
- Thank God for your history and pray for God to reveal and help you embrace your destiny. Spend some time praying over your childhood and ask if there is any pain or wound there that the Lord would heal.
- Rejoice that God has good plans for you to give you a hope and a future. Pray that you will discover and walk in more of these plans and the purpose of God.

- Pray for your own healing and ask God to use you to comfort others with the comfort that you yourself have received.
- Pray for a binding up of the broken-hearted around you.

REFERENCES

1. Pullinger, Jackie, *Chasing the Dragon;* published by Hodder & Stoughton Religious (1980). ISBN 9780340257609.
2. Time Magazine, *"We Lepers"*, Monday, 1st May 1933
3. Ten Boon, Corrie, *The Hiding Place,* with John & Elizabeth Sherrill (1971); ISBN 0912376015.
4. Sandford, John, *Elijah Among Us,* p133-134; published by Chosen Books (2002); ISBN-13 9780800793036.

Lessons from Elijah

Malachi 4:5

...the prophet Elijah...

Opposition

In the autumn of 1989, within three weeks of starting my first job as a social worker, a profession I knew God call me into, I had been threatened with a knife and beaten up by a disgruntled teenager that I had been trying to help. I remember during the prolonged incident telling him what Jesus had done for him and that I would not punch back as his fists flew at me. I was then working in an area where one of the social workers had been murdered some years before. I forgave the young man who assaulted me and despite the misgivings of others continued to work with him for another two years. I concluded this work by taking him out for a meal on his eighteenth birthday. I have often summarised social work as attempting the impossible for the ungrateful.

In the autumn of 1991, two years later, I was attacked again in two separate incidents a matter of weeks apart by two different alcoholic parents whose children I had been assigned to help. In the first of these two assaults I sustained a whip lash injury to my neck. Later that day I was taking up a responsibility for leading a house group within the church for the first time. Fear was sown into my heart until the prayers of friends uprooted it. In the ordinary course of work I was sworn at and spat upon and threatened more times than I could count or remember. At that time I noticed the following proverb:

Proverbs 20:30

Blows and wounds cleanse away evil, and beatings purge the inmost being.

Jesus said:

Matthew 5:11-12

Blessed are you when people insult you, persecute you and falsely say all kinds of evil against you because of me. Rejoice and be glad, because great is your reward in heaven, for in the same way they persecuted the prophets who were before you.

Paul tells us:

2 Timothy 3:12

Everyone who wants to live a godly life in Christ Jesus will be persecuted.

Although we are engaged in spiritual warfare and our battle is not against flesh and blood (Ephesians 6:12) the enemy often works through human agents against God's servants. With Elijah it was Jezebel.

In July 1996, I had a dream of a man whose family I served shutting a door to me. Before the end of that year he, his partner and their children moved into one of the council-owned houses opposite ours and we had to move home.

For some time Carol Ann had been of the conviction that we should move. We had two small daughters and were then expecting our third child. She lived a long way from friends and the school that our eldest daughter was due to start, and we then had only one car. Overnight I came to agree with her! I was aided in reaching this conclusion by having rubbish regularly dumped on our lawn, having our car tyre let down and having our brick outhouse broken into and garden tools stolen from it among other things. Particularly persuasive were the threats that this drunken man made to do me harm in front of my wife and small children on 1st January 1997. Although the police were fairly certain that his reference to having "friends with shooters" was a bluff, it was not something that I liked to leave to chance.

The presence of God is very real at the most difficult of times. On the 14th April 1997 I woke dreaming of a brown envelope out of which fell a key and I heard the word 'go'. The week after, we identified the house that we were to move to. We were greatly encouraged when on the

25th April 1997 our then four-year-old daughter Abigail reported to us that she had had a dream of a house strapped on the back of a lorry. She said that Jesus was driving the lorry. Everyone who saw this sight was laughing. At that time some very generous friends of Carol Ann's parents made us a large loan that enabled us to make an offer on the house that we wanted and begin the process of moving.

God is able to bring victory out of defeat. In Hosea it is written:

Hosea 2:15

There I will give her back her vineyards, and will make the Valley of Achor a door of hope.

God did the same for Elijah. God met him, on Mount Horeb, in the place of fear and apparent defeat and gave him new direction and a strategy for ultimate victory. The same can be true for us.

In October, 2006, in a time of prayer in Israel, I heard the word 'Smyrna'. Intrigued I looked up the mention that was made of this now Turkish town mentioned in the book of Revelation. As I read, these words jumped out at me:

Revelation 2:10

Do not be afraid of what you are about to suffer.

I knew that God was speaking a warning to me and that He was serious, but given my previous experiences I confess that I was very afraid. As I prayed, God began to deliver me from my fears. It says in Psalms:

Psalm 34:4

I sought the LORD, and he answered me; he delivered me from all my fears.

The only way that we can overcome our fears is to face them. Like Elijah, it is right that we should only be governed by the fear of God and free from the fear of man.

The morning after we landed back in England from our trip to Israel my kindly social work manager died suddenly of a heart attack and was replaced by someone far less sympathetic. I did not understand it at first, but this change signalled that I was entering a much harder and colder season. Thinking of Jezebel I was reminded of what Ephesians teaches of how a Christian's spiritual struggle is not waged against any human opponent but against the spiritual evil that fills the world (Ephesians 6:12).

Around Christmas 2006, I was struck down by a strange flu-like virus. I was used to praying for and receiving healing, but this condition which was later diagnosed as hepatitis stubbornly refused to budge. I remember suffering an incredible pain in my neck and being dosed up on painkillers just to help me function and sleep a lot. As I was self-employed, I tried to work through this time. One night, towards the end of January, I saw Jesus in a dream. His appearance was glorious. He was on a path up above me, and I was required to lift up my head to look at Him. Even in my dream I was conscious of how uncomfortable this was because of my neck. He then started to move away from me. I did not want Him to go and felt Him say, "Follow Me."

Throughout Jesus' ministry the words "Follow Me" were spoken: to Levi, Peter, Phillip and Nathanial, the rich young ruler and many others. They came without explanation and had to be obeyed without negotiation. Some followed; others did not. We need to hear and obey them for ourselves. My healing and comfort were not an issue as important as my following Him. After some weeks of continuing discomfort I was completely healed, but this was why - that I might 'follow'. Elijah did and so must we. The important thing is that we should move from being believers in Jesus to being followers of Him.

Persecution

When I was healed of hepatitis in 2007 I thought that my season of suffering indicated by the Smyrna time had ended when in actual fact it was only just beginning. This healing marked the beginning of an intense period of persecution that eclipsed my previous professional difficulties. It began when a number of what I deemed unreasonable complaints were made against me. This was not uncommon in social work but what was unusual was that it was decided that I was in the wrong without the basis of the complaints made having been investigated.

On 28th June 2007 I was two days into what was to be a twenty day season of prayer and fasting when the Holy Spirit came upon my then ten-year-old daughter Keziah. She came home from school reporting seeing angels. I will tell more of this in a later chapter. On the same evening, as I was reading the Bible to her, she reported seeing writing in golden oil on my bedroom wall. She carefully read to me the words that only she could see: "God does not sin, for it is sin itself that sins. We can sin, but only when we punch back."

The house was filled with the presence of God. For several weeks after this she continued to see angels around our home. Keziah had no idea, but God had used her to tell me how to handle the complaints and accusations that I was facing. I was used to fighting for others but now I was told that I must not "punch back".

Following the fast, I became convinced that I should give a gift to a poor mother whose children I had previously served as a social worker. As I prayed, I found the thought of giving this woman £500 would not let me go. I had been praying for and moved by her plight for over a year and had concluded working with her some seven months before. I wanted to help her in some practical way but felt powerless to do so. My other difficulty was that although I wanted to give her this gift, I had no money to do so. I had canvassed professionals still involved with her as to how I might make a discrete gift to her, but they offered no real help as to how. I then prayed for the money, and within a week of having done so, out of the blue, a generous friend sent me a cheque for £500. At the end of July, 2007, with a certain amount of fear and trepidation, I sent the woman the cheque and some Christian literature. In the letter that accompanied this I said that she "needed a miracle, probably several."

I did what I believed was the right thing, with hindsight doing some of it in the wrong way. Then it seemed that all hell was unleashed against me.

You certainly do not know what you have lost until it is gone. For ten years I had had the privilege of serving some of my country's most vulnerable children and their families in the Courts. I had been the court-appointed expert who advised what should happen in some of these most difficult family cases. People had looked up to me and relied upon me. With hindsight I see I had become proud. I could not have done this work without my Christian faith; now I could not do it at all. One day in February, 2008, I went to court as I had done hundreds of times before, and all but two of my cases were taken off me. Walking there that day, knowing what was before me, the apparent end of my professional life, I saw Jesus walking ahead of me. I saw him as a crucified king. It was an incredibly painful time, but to have been afforded just that glimpse of Jesus was breathtaking. There is nowhere we can go outside of God's presence.

All this culminated in my standing on trial for my professional life before the General Social Care Council from 14th-16th October 2009. The story was summarised reasonably well in an article published in the Southern Daily Echo where it hit the front page on 16th October 2009, under the banner headline of "Miracle Worker":

A SOCIAL worker gave cash to a vulnerable mother because God wanted her to visit a Nigerian prophet.

Paul Collett, 45, from Southampton, has admitted writing to the woman, after her five children were taken into care, telling her she "needed a miracle, probably several".

The father-of-four, who is appearing before the General Social Care Council in London on charges of misconduct, enclosed religious DVDs, a newspaper Faith Cometh and a personal cheque for £500 with the letter he sent in July 2007.

He told her she could use the money to visit Prophet TB Joshua, whose website advertises 'miracle' cures for Aids and cancer, and he could put her in touch with someone who could help her make travel arrangements.

He told the hearing, "It was my conviction that God had spoken through my conscience to give this money to her," adding, "It was a very Christian thing to do."

Collett, who had previously acted as a court guardian for the woman's children, said, "Perhaps the letter could have been better worded but there was no mischief intended. In my Christian circles it would not have been problematic.

"It was not my intention to upset the mother or impose my faith on her." Collett, who has 20 years' experience as a social worker, went on to say that he had directed the woman to the prophet after he had helped him through a bout of depression.

During my three day trial for 'misconduct' I was represented by the brilliant legal team at the Christian Legal Centre headed by Paul Diamond and Andrea Minichiello Williams. Again and again they have represented Christian professionals who have found themselves falling foul of their employers. Their stories have been making the press: a nurse and a BA stewardess wearing a cross; a nurse offering prayer for a patient; a counsellor, foster carers and registrars making a stand on their Christian principles.

Paul Diamond commented that he had been afforded more respect and given a much more sympathetic hearing when he had been representing a convicted murderer than he had in defending these 'wicked Christians' in such cases.

The outcome of my case was that I was admonished but remained free to work in social work. The process took over two years to resolve. This would have been fine (although still rather stressful), but for a year no one had wanted me to work for them despite a national shortage of social workers. I was unemployed.

It was a time to draw near to the Lord. Like Elijah being fed by ravens, my family and I learned much of the miraculous provision of God. Money and food were given to us. We learned to face and overcome our fears and grow in our faith. At this time I was also given money to go to Nigeria and Israel and prayed with fasting for direction. On Friday 20th June 2008 to my surprise I also found myself on a trip with a friend to Evan Roberts' home town of Loughor. We stayed in Island House where Evan had grown up, and my friend stayed in Evan's bedroom.

Evan received a vision of God writing him the cheque for 100,000 souls for Wales. The day before being launched into his revival ministry, when he was 24, Evan Roberts met Seth Joshua. Joshua had been praying for some years that God would raise up a young Elisha who did not have a formal ministry training to lead a revival. On this day of prayer and fasting, 22nd September 1904, Evan Roberts received an anointing of the Holy Spirit with great power in a meeting conducted by Joshua, and the Welsh Revival began.

The roots of the revival went back further. Young Evan Roberts had been praying for an outpouring of the Holy Spirit for eleven years. Following this encounter in response to a further vision, he returned to his home in Loughor from Newcastle Emlyn where he had been a student in a Bible College. During his first few meetings the heavens opened. God's presence filled the air. Many were prostrated with conviction, others cried for mercy and many were so filled with the Spirit that they pleaded with the Lord.

During our visit, my friend and I were given the opportunity to pray in the Moriah Chapel and the school room next door where the revival started. It seemed that God has not gone anywhere! The sense of God's presence was very strong as we interceded together. Amazingly we were joined by four intercessors from Indiania who had come on the same assignment: to reopen the wells of revival. One of the women, Janet McGee, was President of Heart of God Ministries in the US and a Director of Aglow international. She was taking her team to a number of strategic sites around the country to pray for revival.

In our time together, Janet McGee brought me a helpful prophetic word. She saw my hands tied and me being dragged by God into my destiny. She said that I did not look worried but was laughing. She saw me as a completely empty but colourful vessel that was being filled. She said she felt that in effect I just had to print my business card to validate myself and recognise the authority that God had placed within me. Following this, after further waiting on the Lord, I began writing this book (admittedly a little bigger than a business card) in response to this word.

In the end I was unemployed for the year between May 2008 and June 2009. All that time I was told I was free to work. When a third of social work posts were standing vacant, no one gave me anything. This was despite my previous twenty years' experience and exemplary record. Although a very challenging time, I learned to receive it as a gift from God. During those days I filled out numerous applications and attended many interviews but, after initial enthusiasm from employers, was rejected. I also prayed, studied, ran the family home, did a lot of gardening and wrote a great deal. God encouraged us as a family and spoke to us again and again, often through our children. He also miraculously provided for us in a variety of ways. Amazingly although things became very uncomfortable at times we did manage to keep paying our mortgage. This was because of the incredible generosity of our God expressed through His people. Then after a year of attending fruitless interviews, to my great surprise, a door swung open for me return to social work.

A few weeks after I started working there, when our finances were at their lowest ebb, a friend put £5000 in our bank pushing us into the black for the first time in a year! When someone tried to oust me from my new job within the month starting, I passed a car with a bumper sticker that read, "When Jesus says 'yes', no one can say 'no'." It seemed to sum things up well.

The Mantle

It is my conviction that the Church in these last days must learn to walk in the spirit and power of Elijah. Malachi prophesied, "I will send you the prophet Elijah." Why Elijah? What was so important about him? To answer this and understand the process of 'restoring our hearts' it is helpful to first look at this Old Testament prophet and how hearts were restored through his ministry.

Elijah arrived with no herald. In fact he *was* the herald. Little is known of his origins or background. In the only picture we have of his appearance we are told that he was a man with...

2 Kings 1:8

...a garment of hair and with a leather belt around his waist.

His name means 'Yahweh is God'; in short this was also his message. Although we are told that he was a Tishbite, a settler from Tishbe in Gilead, east of the Jordan river, there remains uncertainty about the location of his hometown, although it is associated with the archaeological remains at modern Listib. There is no other reference in Scripture to it (1 Kings 17:1).

Elijah is regarded by some Jewish scholars as the first of Israel's prophets. He was not Israel's first prophet chronologically but was perhaps first in eminence. He stands as a prophetic prototype. Elijah became a father of the prophets, setting up and running prophetic schools for the "sons of the prophets" which flourished under his protégé Elisha. He ministered during some of Israel's darkest days, when King Ahab was on the throne and the establishment was at its most corrupt. Elijah comes across as direct, plain-spoken and outrageously brave. He and the prophets who were his successors were not part of the governing party. In his day, God's messenger had moved from the mainstream out to the margins. In our society, like it or not, this is where the church now stands.

Before he had ever stood before men Elijah had stood before God. We are told in his opening words:

1 Kings 17:1 (NKJV)
As the LORD, the God of Israel lives, before whom I stand.

In Proverbs it says that "a gift opens the way for the giver and ushers him into the presence of the great" or, as other versions have it, "a man's gift makes room for him" (Proverbs 18:16). There can be no effective standing before men until we have stood before God.

Ahab was a king whose wickedness was only surpassed by that of his wife. Jezebel was introduced as a Phoenician princess, the daughter of King Ethbaal I of Sidon (1 Kings 16:31). She turned Ahab's heart away from the God of the Jews and toward worship of the Phoenician god, Baal, for whom she was a priestess. Baal was a nature deity supposedly responsible for rain, thunder, lightning and dew. Elijah fearlessly confronted the apostate nation of Israel, Ahab, Jezebel and Baal with God's word. Challenging Baal on his own ground Elijah said that there would be no dew or rain until he again permitted it. He then, as far as Ahab was concerned, disappeared.

Three and a half dry years later, Elijah returned, having been hidden first in the Kerith Ravine and later seventy five miles away in the Sidionian town of Zarephath. The name Kerith means 'cut off' and was a place of consecration, whilst the name Zarephath means 'refining'. In a spiritual sense we need to visit both places and allow ourselves to be separated to the Lord and then purified by Him. God cannot anoint what has not been consecrated. He can only trust Himself to what He sees of His likeness in us.

We know that during the drought Ahab made a fruitless search for his enemy. Whilst God's people suffered drought and famine in the Promised Land, Elijah had been miraculously sustained in exile. It is remarkable that for the last part of this time he was concealed in the land ruled by Jezebel's father where Baal worship had originated. He was literally living in enemy territory. Elijah was sent to a widow whose only prospect was death; she was about to cook her final meal. Although God chose Israel, His desire was always to reach out to all the nations through His people. In this story, Israel's disobedience resulted in this widow receiving mercy. Israel's later rejection of their Messiah would result in the Gentile people receiving mercy (Romans 11:31).

Much later Jesus infuriated the citizens of his home town of Nazareth when he drew attention to God's past favour to Gentile people, saying:

Luke 4:25-26

I assure you that there were many widows in Israel in Elijah's time, when the sky was shut for three and a half years and there was a severe famine throughout the land. Yet Elijah was not sent to any of them, but to a widow in Zarephath in the region of Sidon.

While the people of the true God had turned to idolatry, this former idol-worshipping mother and son embraced the God of Israel and His prophet. Not only were they miraculously fed through the famine but they experienced the first resurrection miracle recorded in scripture. According to Jewish tradition it was this woman's resurrected son who later became Elijah's cloud-watching servant.

Perhaps it is only by being taken out into the desert that a depth of trust we see in Elijah can be forged in our lives. In the wilderness we have to face God as we really are and not as we might prefer to think of ourselves. We are brought down to the bare essentials. P. G. Mathew said:

Elijah was not given even one day's food at a time, but received it little by little, one meal at a time. God wanted Elijah to seek him in prayer. If we are given in abundance, we as sinful people have a tendency to trust in our supply rather than in the Supplier. We begin to think that we don't need to pray or listen to God. We put our trust in our abundance, not in our God. This is one reason the church does not pray. We have so much that we don't even know what to do with all the things that God has given us. Elijah would receive his food one meal at a time. Then he would get down on his knees, pray, and watch expectantly for the ravens to come again. [1]

Graham Cooke has inspired many by his teaching on the wilderness. The following thoughts I heard first from him. Speaking through Hosea, the LORD says of Israel:

Hosea 2:14

Therefore I am now going to allure her; I will lead her into the desert and speak tenderly to her.

It is in the wilderness that we encounter the LORD as the lover of our souls. At one point Jesus said to His disciples:

Mark 6:31

Come with me by yourselves to a quiet place and get some rest.

The King James Version translates the phrase "quiet place" in this passage as a "desert place". In the Song of Solomon the attendant friends ask:

Song of Solomon 8:5

Who is this coming up from the desert leaning on her lover?

Only when our own strength has been broken can we learn to lean upon the LORD as our lover and our strength. This was what Elijah learnt, and we must do the same. I remember at one time expressing my frustration with the Lord, feeling that I had been overlooked. He told me in reply that my life had not been overlooked but hidden. If we want to ever stand in the spotlight before men we must allow our lives to have been searched by the light of God.

Unlike Elijah, in my times of persecution I had friends from a supportive church around me that were able to pray for my protection and against the destructive rule of fear and intimidation in my life.

Deuteronomy 32:39

See now that I myself am He! There is no god besides me. I put to death and I bring to life, I have wounded and I will heal, and no one can deliver out of my hand.

Resurrection

Through His relentless pursuit of God, we see that Elijah's movements were filled with divine purpose. Ours should be the same. God has a plan for us:

Acts 17:26

From one man he made every nation of men, that they should inhabit the whole earth; and he determined the times set for them and the exact places where they should live.

There is a divine design in our dwelling places. In 1990 when Carol Ann and I moved into our first home in the St Denys district of Southampton we became more aware of this.

One morning, very early, the telephone rang. We had inherited the phone number from the previous house occupant. On the other end of the line was a nurse at the General Hospital. She asked me to transport the elderly couple who lived opposite us to see their son who was dangerously ill. At that time I hardly knew them.

The hospital had our number in their notes from the former home owner. In common with some of their generation the couple had no telephone themselves. I hurried to get dressed and went across the road to wake my neighbours and take them into the hospital. On route they explained that their son, who had learning difficulties, had been assaulted three weeks prior by another resident of the institution where he lived.

Following the assault he had partly choked on his own vomit. This had resulted in his developing a chest infection.

Still bleary-eyed I sat with my neighbours as their son died. It seemed that we had only just arrived when the nurse, putting her head around the cubical curtain, asked how long he had been like this. We had not noticed that he had just stopped breathing. The nurse moved us to another part of the ward and supplied us with cups of tea. I talked to my neighbours about their son's life and death. The charges being faced by his assailant would be upgraded to manslaughter. Having only just moved into our home we were suddenly launched into a much closer relationship with this couple than we could have possibly imagined. It came with the house.

It is too big a task for us to love the whole world. God has already demonstrated that. Heidi Baker says that we must "just love the one in front of [us]".

In the life of Elijah we see God's concern for widows and orphans through his provision for the widow of Zarephath. The lonely prophet became an effective father in this widow's household. The Lord is always reaching out to those on the margins, and so should we [2]. In James we read:

James 1:27
Religion that God our Father accepts as pure and faultless is this: to look after orphans and widows in their distress and to keep oneself from being polluted by the world.

Elijah was able to release the resurrection life of God at a time and in a place where there was only death. We should ask to do the same. Reports of resurrections are reported as an almost commonplace event in parts of Africa and other lands. Smith Wigglesworth, who died in 1947 and started out as a Bradford plumber, saw over ten people raised from the dead through his prayer of faith. The children to whom our fathers brought the gospel have outstripped the faith of Western Christianity. The Lord wants to bring resurrection to and through the Western Church. In these days I have heard it repeated that these are days in which the rich man's request for his brothers is being answered:

Luke 16:30

If someone from the dead goes to them, they will repent.

Only three resurrections are recorded in the Old Testament. Prior to the days of Jesus, who we know to be the resurrection and the life, only Elijah and his spiritual son Elisha had called the dead back to life. These again are the days of Elijah.

Elijah on Carmel

Malachi 4:5

I will send you the prophet Elijah.

At the top of Mount Carmel, during his contest with the 450 prophets of Baal and the 400 prophets of Asherah, Elijah asked the people of Israel how long they would waver between two opinions. Interestingly the Hebrew word translated 'waver' is the same word that is translated 'danced' in verse 26. Elijah said:

1 Kings 18: 21

If the LORD is God, follow him; but if Baal is God, follow him.

Plainly the people were trying to do both and succeeding at neither as they danced between two opinions. He challenged them to make their minds up. Our God is a jealous God, and we cannot afford to sit on the fence any more. Indeed the day is coming when the fence will become electrified, and we will have to leap off on one side or another. This is what happened in Elijah's day. We cannot serve two masters.

Later in this account, just before the Lord sent fire on the offering that had been drenched with water, he had prayed:

1 Kings 18:37

Answer me, O LORD, answer me, so these people will know that you, O LORD, are God, and that you are turning their hearts back again.

This gives us a clear insight into what the Elijah prophesied by Malachi might do. Part of his task was to restore, or turn, the hearts of the people back to the God of their fathers and indeed back to God the Father.

In October, 2006, and again in September, 2007, I had the privilege of standing on the top of Mount Carmel on two of my trips to Israel. What is called Mount Carmel is actually a 24 mile long coastal mountain range in northern Israel stretching from the Mediterranean Sea towards the southeast. The summit offers spectacular views of the vast Jezreel valley which scripture indicates will be the location of the final battle of Armageddon. The headland at the north-western end of this range is often specifically referred to as Mount Carmel and may be the location of Elijah's famous contest. The name Carmel literally means 'God's vineyard'. As such it represented the land of Israel itself which was often described in scripture as a vineyard (see Isaiah 5).

We are told by Jesus' half-brother James that...

James 5:17
Elijah was a man just like us.

This is reassuring. Although a great man of God we see his frailty in being subject to a bout of depression, self-pity and fear. Following Jezebel's threat to kill him we read:

1 Kings 19:3
Elijah was afraid and ran for his life.

In the following verse he prayed that he might die saying, "I have had enough, LORD," and "Take my life." He felt isolated, repeating, "I am the only one left" (1 Kings 19:10,14). This was despite the fact that Obadiah, Ahab's godly servant, had earlier said that he had hidden one hundred true prophets in two different caves (1 Kings 18:13).

Elijah's desert years, whilst preserving him, reinforced his perception that he was alone. The Lord Himself also corrected him saying:

1 Kings 19:18
I reserve seven thousand in Israel - all whose knees have not bowed down to Baal and all whose mouths have not kissed him.

The apostasy of the land had been great but was not total. Although we might feel alone when we have surrendered to Christ, we never are. Many years later the Apostle Paul drew attention to Elijah's lesson concerning Israel when he said:

Romans 11:5

...so too, at the present time there is a remnant chosen by grace.

By revelation he reached the conclusion that there was a future for the remnant of the Jewish people. Along with Israel there is also a future for the faithful remnant in the church.

Like Elijah I have experienced times of depression when I have felt overwhelmed by the scale and ferocity of the opposition that I have faced. This has never been welcome or comfortable. Sir Winston Churchill, himself familiar with depression, frequently referred to it as the "black dog". It is the grit, however, that produces the pearl. In the bestselling book 'The Shack' by William P. Young there is a scene in which Jesus explains to the main character that a pearl is the only gemstone created by suffering and released by death. This is a picture of Jesus himself. The gates of heaven are made of pearl, emphasising the fact that Jesus is the only way in [3]. Jesus said:

John 12:24

I tell you the truth, unless a kernel of wheat falls to the ground and dies, it remains only a single seed. But if it dies, it produces many seeds.

Hebrews 11 with its gallery of the heroes of faith provides a portrait of Elijah's life at this time. He was amongst those that...

Hebrews 11:37-38

...went about in sheepskins and goatskins, destitute, persecuted and mistreated - the world was not worthy of them. They wandered in deserts and mountains, and in caves and holes in the ground.

The life of the true prophet had much danger and little glamour.

Revival Prayer

Elijah may have been a man just like us, but what made him distinct was his earnest prayer. If we want to see results like Elijah we need to learn to pray like him. This was the ultimate secret of his success.

James 5:17-18

He prayed earnestly that it would not rain, and it did not rain on the land for three and a half years. Again he prayed, and the heavens gave rain, and the earth produced its crops.

It is striking that one word from Elijah stopped the rain and one prayer brought the fire. To pray with this effect we must know both the mind and the will of God. We can be sure that Elijah was praying God's ideas, not his own. Indeed, in answer to a single prayer of the prophet, God's fire consumed five things: the sacrifice, the wood, the stones, the dust and even the water that drenched the sacrifice and filled the ditch around it (1 Kings 18:38). This was far more than he had asked for. The people's awed response that "The LORD - he is God! The LORD - he is God!" (1 Kings 18:39) echoed like a chanting of the prophet's name 'Yahweh is God'. Our God not only answers by fire but is Himself a consuming fire (Hebrews 12:29).

On Mother's day, 14th March 2010, I had been preparing breakfast for my wife and family. I left a tea towel on the cooker top when bringing the croissants out of the oven not realising that my mother-in-law had left the gas ring on. Shortly after I had sat down to eat I had to get up quickly when the fire alarm went off because of the fire in the kitchen. As my then ten-year-old son Daniel and I put out the fire, the song that was playing on the Christian Radio station was 'Lord, light the fire again'. I commented to Daniel that this was a prophetic sign. He was so excited that he shared the event at church later that morning and read out the story of the fire on Carmel. Another member of the congregation had been meditating upon this same passage and said how she had been struck by how the Lord added impossibility to impossibility when Elijah commanded the drenching of the altar and how he was doing the same in many of our circumstances. The Spirit of God then fell not only upon her but on many others. As on the day of Pentecost, the Lord wants to send fire on His church. He is still the God who answers by fire.

In considering the repair of the altar on Mount Carmel I heard a message delivered by Dr Niko Njotarahardjo of Indonesia while in Jerusalem in September 2007. He said that in order for the fire to fall, the body of Christ must repair its broken altar. The altar is firstly emblematic of our place of prayer and points towards our need to repair our relationship with the Lord. Secondly this altar speaks of spiritual warfare. A challenge had to be issued to the Baal worshippers to build their altar with a confidence that our God will answer with fire. Thirdly this altar is a place of colossal sacrifice. Never mind the bull that died; it seems extraordinary that at the end of three-and-a-half years of drought some twelve gallons of water should be hauled to the top of Carmel only to be poured over the altar. In the same way the Lord will ask for costly sacrifices from his people, be that in forgiveness or other ways. Finally, Dr Niko made the point that the construction of the altar from twelve stones, representing the twelve tribes of Israel, was a picture of how the unity of the church must be both repaired and improved for the fire of God to fall.

In this sudden moment of national revival many hearts were restored. We long for such a move in our day in our own land. The fire seemed to fall from a clear blue sky. However, we need to pray and make preparation for the sudden moving of God. Our focus is on the fire on the top of Carmel, but this showdown had been many years in the making. The drought was called, the challenge issued and then the contest arranged. Each step of obedience prepared the pathway for the coming of God. Every detail had to be attended to. Likewise the 'Elijah church' must prepare the way for the return of the Lord.

At the end of Elijah's earthly ministry we read that he and Elisha were walking along and talking together when "suddenly a chariot of fire and horses of fire appeared and separated the two of them, and Elijah went up to heaven in a whirlwind" (2 Kings 2:11).

Speaking of the ministry of the future Elijah and the coming of the Lord we read in Malachi:

Malachi 3:1

See, I will send my messenger, who will prepare the way before me. Then suddenly the Lord you are seeking will come to his temple; the messenger of the covenant, whom you desire, will come," says the LORD Almighty.

Following the resurrection it was recorded:

Matthew 28:9

Suddenly Jesus met them.

Concerning the Lord's return, we are told in Mark:

Mark 13:36

If he comes suddenly, do not let him find you sleeping.

Also on the day of Pentecost it was recorded that...

Acts 2:2

...suddenly a sound like the blowing of a violent wind came from heaven and filled the whole house where they were sitting.

We need to be ready, for God can and will come in a moment, suddenly.

On Thursday, 5th December 2010, the second day of the Jewish festival of Hanukkah, the feast of dedication (mentioned in John 10:22), a fire started on Carmel. (In the past I have prayed for the fire of the Holy Spirit both on top of Carmel and in Kehilat Ha Carmel - the Carmel Assembly - the congregation planted by David and Karen Davis. We need the fire of God.) Apparently this fire was caused by a small piece of charcoal tossed by a teenager after smoking a nargila (hooka) in a Druz village situated near Haifa. Only a week before the fire, Israel's chief rabbis were calling the nation to repent and cry out for rain. The fire soon began to rage, and for over three days became an out-of-control inferno. Just as God called to his people from a burning bush at the creation of the Jewish nation (Exodus 3), he was calling people back to himself. The fire consumed over five million trees on twelve thousand acres of land, left forty-three people dead, destroyed seventy homes and damaged another

250; over fifteen thousand people were evacuated from their homes. Israeli Prime minister Netanyahu called the fire a "disaster on an international scale"; it was by far the most devastating to befall Israel since its inception.

Although the fire fell quickly, it required seven of Elijah's prayers to release God's rain. Why was this? We know that seven is the perfect number in scripture for on the seventh day God had rested from His work of creating the world. Seven speaks to us of completeness. If Elijah had stopped praying before the seventh time there would have been no rain. We see that God's fire is given more easily than His rain, in the same way that judgement is deserved whilst grace and mercy are not. Even in a season of rain we must ask for it (Zechariah 10:1). Prayer that prevails requires passion and persistence. When you have received the fire, do not settle for the fire alone but ask for the rain. The fire will awe the people but the rain will revive the drought-stricken land.

Although he never married, Elijah was a father figure. We see him operating as a father in the home of the widow of Zarephath. He was also the father of the prophets, but at this time he had no successor to whom to bequeath his legacy. Fleeing from Jezebel, Elijah was at the end of himself. God tenderly cared for His servant's needs. Elijah fell asleep under a broom tree. Rest is the only real remedy for exhaustion. An angel then baked bread for him and brought him water not once but twice because the Lord was concerned that the journey ahead would be too much for him. After this the Lord met with Elijah on Mount Horeb, also known in scripture as Mount Sinai, where Moses had previously received the Law.

Fasting

This journey to Horeb is one of the many links in the Jewish mind between Elijah and Moses; not least because Elijah made the journey without further food or drink as Moses had done years previously and as Jesus was to do in the future. Together with Jesus, they are the only characters recorded in scripture as having undertaken a period of forty days of prayer and fasting. Others no doubt did so too but their exploits went unrecorded.

I vividly remember the very first time that I fasted. It was 1984, and I was still a student at college and new to the things of God. The great American evangelist Billy Graham was conducting a number of large meetings in football stadiums around the country as part of what was termed Mission England. A Winchester businessman had paid for coaches to go to the event in Bristol. I set my face to seek God for my friends at college that they might go to the meeting and that they might be saved. For the first time in my life I did so with fasting. I invited many, and three said that they would come. Billy Graham gave the clear and straightforward gospel presentation that he is famous for, and at the end when he called for a response, hundreds of people from all over the stadium began walking forward onto the pitch. To my utter astonishment the three friends that had come with me were amongst those who went to pray, committing their lives to Christ. One of them, Graham Applin, was later the best man at my wedding.

If we do not acquire a pattern of prayer and fasting then we will not accrue the spiritual resources that will fit us for these days. Neither will we be able to move in the spirit and power of Elijah. It should be noticed that the followers of both Islam and Hinduism practice fasting, and it is this discipline that is responsible for their dynamism. In his classic book on this topic 'God's Chosen Fast' Arthur Wallis made the point that when teaching his disciples on fasting Jesus said, *"When* you fast" (Matthew 6:16), not "if". [4] It is during this time of the bridegroom's absence that fasting has become imperative (Matthew 9:15).

In Jewish thought Elijah is linked to Moses in a number of other ways too. The Jews were expecting God to raise up another ministry like that of Moses. This was because Moses himself had promised:

Deuteronomy 18:15
The LORD your God will raise up for you a prophet like me from among your own brothers. You must listen to him.

In many ways Elijah fitted the bill. As Moses confronted the demonic idolatry of Egypt so Elijah took the same stand against the idolatry that had taken root within his own land. So must we. Like Moses, Elijah was miraculously sustained by heaven-sent bread in the desert region beyond the Jordan. This is the order of provision that God has reserved for these days. Both Moses and Elijah parted the water - Moses the Red sea and Elijah the Jordan. He will again make a way where there is no way.

Succession

Like Moses, Elijah had a successor; Elisha completed the calling and task of Elijah in the way that Joshua completed the call of Moses. Elijah and Moses were forerunners whilst their successors were finishers. Joshua's name means 'Saviour' and is thus linked with that of Elisha which means 'My God is salvation'. Both these names are linked with Jesus the Saviour. The Hebrew rendering of Jesus is Yeshua and is the name that has also been translated Joshua. In the New Testament we read that John the Baptist prepared the way for Jesus as one coming in the "Spirit and power of Elijah" (Luke 1:16). The ministry of Elijah is one that is vital in preparing the way for the Messiah.

Although Elijah had no biological children, Elisha became his true spiritual son. We see in this a picture of fathers turning their hearts to their sons and sons having their hearts restored to their fathers. Elisha came to wear his spiritual father's mantle and more importantly was invested with a double portion of Elijah's spirit. The double portion in scripture always speaks of inheritance. Whereas Elijah has a total of eight miracles that are assigned to him in scripture, Elisha has sixteen (including the resurrection that took place when a corpse touched his bones sometime after his death).

When Elijah ran away from Jezebel it seems that he should not have been on Horeb; on the mountain the Lord twice asked him:

1 Kings 19:9, 1 Kings 19:13
What are you doing here, Elijah?

Scripture records no specific instruction for him to travel to Horeb as he had had to go to the Kerith ravine or to Zarephath. Nevertheless, God was more than willing to meet with Elijah when he was in the wrong place. We need to shun the contamination and manipulation of Jezebel. It is reassuring that should we ever be in the wrong place, God will meet with us.

Although running away from Jezebel, in travelling to Horeb, Elijah was making a positive journey to the place where the covenant had been given to Moses. Indeed earlier in Moses' journey this was where he had been commissioned by God when he called to him through the burning bush. Although not told to go to Horeb, repeatedly referred to as "the mountain of God", Elijah's journey to this place reveals wisdom for us in going back to our roots and back to the promises of God when under pressure. If we are ever unclear about our guidance from God it is wise to recall the last thing that we understood. Malachi later urged the people of God to...

Malachi 4:4

...remember the law of my servant Moses, the decrees and laws I gave him at Horeb for all Israel.

Elijah's encounter with God at the summit of this mountain has close parallels with Moses' encounter with God in the same place. Moses, the lawgiver, represented the fathers of faith that the children's hearts are supposed to return to before the day of the Lord.

In recognition that the prophet's task could not be finished by him alone, the Lord instructed Elijah to anoint three individuals who would complete the judgement of God that he had commenced. So Elijah was told to anoint and commission Hazael as king over Aram, Jehu son of Nimshi as King over Israel, and Elisha son of Shaphat as his own son and successor in order to judge Israel, destroy Baal worship and the house of Ahab (1 Kings 19:15-17).

It is interesting that the only anointing that Elijah directly fulfilled was that of his successor Elisha. It was Elisha who completed the anointing of Hazael and commissioned the anointing of Jehu. Jehu was in fact anointed by one of Elisha's spiritual sons, the sons of the prophets. The three generations had to work together to get the job done: father, son and grandson. This is both a consolation and a warning; our God-given but unfinished tasks will be given to another. We must look for spiritual successors. It is not enough for us to walk with God ourselves; we must train others to do so.

So what were Elijah's methods and his recipe for success? Having prayed, he obeyed. He was a man of faith and of few recorded words who continually operated in the power and under the direction of the Holy Spirit. His word brought drought and released the rain. He confronted errant Kings, uprooted and established kingdoms, released miraculous provision, called down fire from heaven not once but three times, split the river Jordan enabling him to cross on foot, and raised the dead. When the Spirit of God came upon him he could outrun Ahab's chariot for a distance of thirteen miles! Let us be clear - none of these actions were the result of his good ideas. He was following the Lord.

To top all of these achievements, at the end of his spectacular career Elijah was caught up to heaven in a fiery chariot in a whirlwind without dying. When Elijah did so he left his mantle with his successor, Elisha, who was granted his request of inheriting a double portion of his Spirit. It is plain that Elijah's mantle was and is transferable. Elisha had not worn it out at the end of his ministry; the last of his miracles was accomplished after his own death (2 Kings 13:20-21). This emphasises that this colossal ministry was so important that it transcends any one man's lifetime. Sons must come into alignment with their fathers, and fathers must release the burden of their hearts to their sons.

Some later Jewish rabbis interpreted Malachi as saying that Elijah would himself physically return. Indeed Elijah is still invoked weekly at the Havdalah ritual that marks the end of Shabbat (Sabbath) and in other Jewish customs, among them the Passover Seder (meal). The fifth cup of wine at this meal is traditionally called the Cup of Elijah and is poured out for the prophet. In Jewish observance, this is an extra cup of wine displayed (sometimes at an empty place setting) to welcome the prophet of hope who would announce the Messiah's coming. Traditionally Elijah is said to visit each Jewish home on Seder night as a foreshadowing of his future arrival at the end of the days to announce the coming of the Messiah. While left empty or untouched in Jewish observance, in the Christian Seder it represents the Cup of Redemption, the Passover, "shed for you ... [for] the forgiveness of sins," and is used symbolically as the cup of the Eucharist or communion [5]. So for both Christians and Jews there is a common understanding that Elijah has unfinished business and that his ministry awaits completion.

In the book of Malachi, the Lord raised the question about His honour when he asked:

Malachi 1:6

A son honours his father, and a servant his master. If I am a father, where is the honour due me?

Later Malachi asked:

Malachi 2:10

Have we not all one Father? Did not one God create us? Why do we profane the covenant of our fathers by breaking faith with one another?

The fullest revelation of God the Father awaited the coming of Jesus the Messiah but is clearly implied in these verses. It does take the Son to reveal the Father. We begin to understand the sense in which the Elijah who is to come will restore the hearts of the children to the fathers by turning them back to God the Father.

Action!

As we consider the lifestyle and walk of Elijah there are likely to be adjustments that we need to make to our lives. In doing so you may wish to fast for the first time. I would suggest some preparatory reading around this subject. (I have mentioned Arthur Wallis' book 'God's Chosen Fast' but would also recommend Derek Prince's book 'Shaping History through Prayer and Fasting' as being good places to start.) There are different types of, and durations of, fast detailed in scripture. For example there is the Esther fast (described in Esther 4:16) which entailed abstaining from both food and drink for a period of three days. Then there is the Daniel fast (outlined in Daniel 10:3) which involved a three week abstinence from meat, wine and lotions.

Establishing the right motivation to start a fast is crucial. To this end have a look at Isaiah 58. If you are looking to "loose the chains of injustice" then fasting would be a good response (Isaiah 58:6). Faith is also imperative, without which it is impossible to please God. It is perhaps obvious, but fasting should be accompanied by prayer. Fasting should not be for a selfish end but for the glory of God. I would suggest that fasting should be built up gradually. In the same way a weekend jogger should not to be expecting to run the marathon without considerably training, perhaps you should not start out with a forty day fast. Fasting a single meal or for a day might be a good way to begin. It is important to take medical advice if you have a condition that makes it necessary to eat regularly. A 'Daniel fast' might be considered for those who must eat regularly. There are times and seasons when to fast from television or the computer would be of benefit in freeing time to pray.

Prayer Points

- Ask God for the courage and fortitude of Elijah. Pray that all the people of God would be governed by the fear of God rather than the fear of man.
- Pray for the release of the resurrection power of God. Pray, "I believe; help me overcome my unbelief."

- If Elijah was a man just like us, let us begin to ask God for a prayer life like Elijah.
- Pray that we as individuals and the church as a whole might walk free of depression and every mental affliction.
- Pray that we would make the transition from being believers to being followers.
- Pray that the church would no longer tolerate that woman Jezebel and that her contaminating influence would be removed from the lives of God's people.

REFERENCES

1. P. G. Mathew, M.A., M. Div., Th.M., sermon preached on 9th September 2001 entitled *Faith versus Fear.*

2. Davis, David, *The Elijah Legacy;* published by Kehilat HaCarmel (2003); ISBN 0497210000

3. Young, William P, *The Shack,* published by Hodder Windblown; first edition (17 July 2008); ISBN-10 0340979496

4. Wallis, Arthur, *God's Chosen Fast;* published by Kingsway (1968).

5. Bratcher, David, http://www.crivoice.org/seder.html

The Coming Elijah

Malachi 4:5

I will send you the prophet.

Both from my work as a social worker and through my own family experience I am aware of the heartache and sorrow caused by alcohol problems. As student social worker I read that 92% of violent crime took place following the consumption of alcohol [1].

I undertook my first social work placement with the Catholic Society of St Dismas. The society then ran a number of 'dry houses', a day centre and later a detoxification centre, all for vagrant alcoholics. At that time, in my ignorance, I was shocked to discover that not all of those who I found in the gutter (sometimes quite literally) had been born there. Some had the benefit of middle class upbringing and a degree but were still defeated by addiction.

As a young teenager I came to dislike alcohol in any form. I undertook Temperance Training through my Baptist Sunday School and believed that I had a thorough understanding of the evils of drink. I remember my Boys' Brigade Captain, a wonderful man of God, saying that believers who drank alcohol could be responsible for leading many astray. I took this very seriously. However, as an older teenager the temptation was too much for me, and I drank in excess. I only began to sober up when I was arrested for being drunk and incapable after a party one evening. Education, upbringing and religion are no defence against temptation or addiction. Sin is a spiritual force.

In subsequent years I wavered back and forth in my attitude towards (and relationship with) alcohol. I knew that drunkenness was wrong but was uncertain of where the line should be drawn short of this. Some seemed to like to push the boundary as far as was reasonable and then take it a bit further. Jesus, at the wedding feast in Cana in Galilee, turned the water into wine and not, as some evangelicals would have preferred, the other around. Paul said to Timothy:

1 Timothy 5:23

Stop drinking only water, and use a little wine because of your stomach and your frequent illnesses.

The church that I settled in had a more liberal attitude to wine than the Baptist Church that I had grown up in. This is fine until we seek to deliver those whose lives are ruled by an addiction. You will never deliver an alcoholic by taking him to the pub. You simply cannot rule over a spirit that controls you.

In another of his letters Paul said:

Ephesians 5:18

Do not get drunk on wine, which leads to debauchery. Instead, be filled with the Spirit.

Onlookers on the Day of Pentecost thought that the disciples had had too much wine; being filled with the Holy Spirit was and is intoxicating. In the end I felt that if I had to make a choice I would much rather be filled with the Holy Spirit than drunk with wine.

How much alcohol I should drink became an issue for me a few years ago. It came to a head when a group of men from the church were camping together for a couple of days. I knew that part of the budget had gone on alcohol, and I was talking to God about how much I should drink. I felt the Holy Spirit say to me to "feel free to drink" only what one particular friend was drinking. When, after setting up camp, I went over to him and offered to get him a beer I discovered that he was teetotal. He laughed when I told him of my conversation with the Lord and said, "It looks like you are going to have a dry weekend." This was not what I really wanted to hear, but it was what I needed. I did find that his taste in strong coffee reinforced my own liking for the drink.

John the Baptist

John the Baptist literally started where Elijah left off. From the centuries immediately after Jesus' time, the place thought to be where Elijah's ascension to heaven took place has been known as Elijah's Hill.

This small natural hill is about two kilometres east of the Jordan River and forms the core of the ancient settlement called "Bethany beyond the Jordan" in the New Testament (John 1:28). This was where John was thought to be living when he baptized Jesus [2].

The name of the prophet Elijah is mentioned some 29 times in the New Testament. Elijah also makes one special guest appearance on the Mount of Transfiguration. Occasionally his name was linked with that of Jesus who from time to time was mistaken for him. More frequently he was aligned with John the Baptist. This started even before John was born when the angel Gabriel visited his father Zechariah and said:

Luke 1:16-17

Many of the people of Israel will he bring back to the Lord their God. And he will go on before the Lord, in the spirit and power of Elijah, to turn the hearts of the fathers to their children and the disobedient to the wisdom of the righteous - to make ready a people prepared for the Lord.

John the Baptist ministered in the spirit and power of Elijah but was clear that he was not the returning prophet himself. Malachi had been God's final word to the people of Israel until the 430 year silence prophesied by Amos (Amos 8:11-12) was broken by John the Baptist. The famine of the word of the Lord that preceded John's coming had the dual effect of intensifying people's hunger for God's word and highlighting the importance of John's message. John, rather than Malachi, became the final messenger of the Old Covenant and the herald of the new age of the kingdom of God. Jesus said:

Matthew 11:11

I tell you the truth: Among those born of women there has not risen anyone greater than John the Baptist; yet he who is least in the kingdom of heaven is greater than he.

No wonder the crowds flocked to hear him.

Breaking the Silence

As the barrenness of both Sarah and Hannah were the preludes to significant births, so this long prophetic silence was the prelude to a significant voice. The silence of God that preceded the voice of John crying out in the wilderness had a sequel in the circumstances of the prophet's family before his birth. Before the son spoke, the father was silent. When Zechariah was told by Gabriel that his wife would bear a son he questioned, "How can I be sure of this?" (Luke 1:18)

He gave voice to his unbelief and became mute. Unbelief will always rob us of our voice. On the other hand we notice in Jesus' silence before Herod that God has nothing to say to unbelief. In the Psalms we read:

Psalm 25:14

The LORD confides in those who fear him; he makes his covenant known to them.

Also we know that...

Hebrews 11:6

...without faith it is impossible to please God.

Thinking more about the subject of silence, earlier in the history of Israel the Lord told Ezekiel:

Ezekiel 3:26

I will make your tongue stick to the roof of your mouth so that you will be silent and unable to rebuke them, though they are a rebellious house.

In this instance this prophetic sign was given because of the nation's (not the prophet's) unbelief. When the judgements that the prophet had long announced began to break upon the land "[his] mouth was opened and [he] was no longer silent" (Ezekiel 33:22). In Ecclesiastes we are told:

Ecclesiastes 3:7

There is a time to be silent and a time to speak.

Both speaking and silence have a season. When Moses questioned his calling he explained to the Lord:

Exodus 4:10

I have never been eloquent, neither in the past nor since you have spoken to your servant. I am slow of speech and tongue.

Then the LORD answered him:

Exodus 4:11

Who gave man his mouth? Who makes him deaf or mute?

God's voice created the world, sustains all things with his word and will finally wrap things up. He also determines who will really speak for Him and what they will say. He told Moses:

Exodus 4:12

Now go; I will help you speak and will teach you what to say.

Zechariah's tongue only became free when he wrote down the name that the angel Gabriel had told him his son should be called. When his words lined up with God's, his voice regained its power. When we do the same, so will ours. In Luke we read:

Luke 1:63-64

He asked for a writing tablet, and to everyone's astonishment he wrote, "His name is John." Immediately his mouth was opened and his tongue was loosed, and he began to speak, praising God.

In these days we desperately need to become a people who agree with what God is already saying. The name John is derived from the Hebrew name Johanan and means 'Yahweh favoured' or 'God is gracious'. Announcing God's grace and favour is also our privilege.

Zechariah's life and future were preserved through his being mute. If our hearts are wrong our words will be full of poison. Graham Cooke taught that we can destroy with our character what we seek to build with our gift. The silence imposed upon Zechariah allowed his faith to grow up to the call on his life. Having been, as he had, in the glory of God, Zechariah had the power to kill the promise he had just been given in the same way he had received it: through words. As teacher David Herzog said, "God had to take away his words by allowing him to be mute so that he would not undo or prophecy the wrong thing." [3]

In Isaiah we read:

Isaiah 32:4
The stammering tongue will be fluent and clear.

The ancient Rabbis believed that when He came the Messiah would perform three signs: he would heal a leper, give sight to a man born blind and give voice to the mute. Jesus performed all three of these signs and many more besides. Not only did he silence the demons (Mark 1:23-28), he opened the mouth of the dumb. The disciples brought Jesus "a demon-possessed man who was blind and mute, and Jesus healed him so that he could both talk and see" (Matthew 12:22).

Only Jesus can restore to us our vision and our voice.

There have been a number of significant preachers and orators who have been literally unable to speak until God enabled them to do so. Both Benny Hinn and the English preacher Ian Andrews were healed of painful stutters. For both preachers their healing and call came together as God touched and claimed ownership over their tongues in a moment. Winston Churchill grew up with a stutter. It is characteristic of his perseverance that despite his staggering handicap he became one of the greatest orators of the modern era. In the Oscar winning movie 'The King's Speech' the story of King George VI's battle to overcome his stutter is retold. It is remarkable that the two men used to lead the free world through the Second World War both suffered a speech impediment. Truly God chooses the weak to shame the strong; Hitler had no such difficulties with his magnetic oratory.

Although never mute I have known, at times, an acute and crippling hesitancy in my speech. This was made worse by my burning conviction that I should speak and, when I committed my life to Christ, that I should speak for Him. As an adult I came to understand that having been raped as a three-year-old boy my assailant had effectively put a curse upon my tongue by telling me never to speak of this event. It is a marvel to me that the Lord healed this symptom by addressing the underlying cause, and I found myself in the position to give a voice to voiceless children.

Throughout the gospels both Jesus and John the Baptist were repeatedly asked whether they were "the Prophet" (i.e. Moses) or "Elijah". The real Moses and Elijah appeared with Jesus on the Mount of Transfiguration (Matthew 17:1-13). They represent the Law and the prophets which both find their ultimate fulfilment in Jesus the Messiah.

Typically Peter, not knowing what he was saying, offered to build shelters for Moses, Elijah and Jesus. In this moment he saw Jesus as being on a par with these Jewish heroes of old. God the Father cleared up his confusion, emphasising the uniqueness of Jesus, saying:

Matthew 17:5
This is my Son, whom I love; with him I am well pleased. Listen to him!

The other two witnesses were then taken from his sight and he saw no one else, "only Jesus". How, like him, we need our horizon cleared of all competitors and to see no one except Jesus.

The Elijah to Come

When asked, "Are you Elijah?" John the Baptist answered plainly, "I am not" (John 1:21). Apparently contradicting this, Jesus said of John:

Matthew 11:14
And if you are willing to accept it, he is the Elijah who was to come.

Later in the same gospel, on the way down from the mountain, having met the original Elijah (and Moses), the puzzled disciples asked Jesus:

Matthew 17:10
Why then do the teachers of the law say that Elijah must come first?

Jesus replied:

Matthew 17:11-12

To be sure, Elijah comes and will restore all things. But I tell you, Elijah has already come, and they did not recognise him, but have done to him everything they wished.

The disciples understood that Jesus was speaking of John the Baptist.

How do we resolve such a paradox, that John both was and was not the Elijah prophesied by Malachi? Sometimes it is better to embrace rather than explain such paradoxes in scripture. It seems that both John and Jesus were right in the answers that they gave. John was not the Elijah in the sense that the proud Pharisees were asking, the literal Elijah, but Jesus could honestly point his disciples to him and say that if they were willing to accept it he was the Elijah to come. Jesus did not say that John was the actual Elijah.

Many of the prophetic scriptures of the Old Testament have a double fulfilment. The Jewish people at the time of Jesus expected their Messiah to come as a conquering King, not as a suffering servant. With the wisdom afforded by hindsight some Christians have scoffed at this misguided expectation. However Jesus is both Martyr and Messiah and will fulfil the scriptures about the conquest of his enemies at his second coming. At the time of his first coming he revealed himself as a suffering servant and friend of sinners. Speaking from eternity, God views both comings as accomplished facts. As Christians we need to be careful that we are not caught out by Jesus' return as the Jews of the first century were by his first appearance.

In the same way we can see that John the Baptist only partially fulfilled Malachi's prophesy about the return of Elijah. John prepared the way for the Messiah's first coming. At this time John pointed at Jesus and said, "Behold the Lamb of God" (John 1:36). There is a further fulfilment in which an Elijah people must prepare the way for the Messiah's return. This people will point not to a Lamb but to the "lion of the tribe of Judah" (Revelation 5:5). In Luke, the angel Gabriel, speaking of John the Baptist, said:

Luke 1:16

He will go on before the Lord, in the spirit and power of Elijah, to turn the hearts of the fathers to their children and the disobedient to the wisdom of the righteous.

John was mandated to turn the hearts of the fathers to their children but was not required to turn the hearts of the children back to the fathers. As such he fulfilled only the first part of Malachi 4:5-6, suggesting that the latter part of the verse, the "turning of the children to the fathers", was left for later fulfilment. The Jewish people in this instance are the fathers and the Gentiles are their children.

The first apostles were all Jewish, and their hearts were turned outward, be it ever so reluctantly, from their own people to the Gentiles. This required a miracle. It took Peter's vision to convince him that he should "not call anything impure that God has made clean" (Acts 11:9) and to visit Cornelius' house. The Jews believed that the Law forbade them to visit the homes of Gentiles. The Gospel spread out in concentric circles from Jerusalem to the ends of the earth, and before the close of this age the Bible foretells that it must return from the ends of the earth back to Jerusalem. For this to take place the Gentile children's hearts must turn back to the Jewish fathers. This will require another revelation and a miraculous change of heart. By and large, Gentile Christians are no more disposed to love the Jews than the first century Jewish Apostles were inclined to love the Gentiles.

Preparing the way

Jesus said:

Matthew 17:11

To be sure, Elijah comes and will restore all things.

We gain insight into who John the Baptist thought he was when, using the words of Isaiah the prophet, he said:

John 1:23

I am the voice of one calling in the desert, 'Make straight the way for the Lord.'

His ministry was literally to prepare and make a people ready for the first coming of the Messiah. He was the wedding attendant getting the bride ready for her groom. So before what Malachi describes as "the great and dreadful day of the LORD" we must again expect the ministry of Elijah to prepare the bride for his return.

Malachi's words that are linked to the returning Elijah "See, I will send my messenger, who will prepare the way before me" (Malachi 3:1) are twice quoted in the New Testament (Matthew 11:10 and Mark 1:2). In both these passages John the Baptist is the messenger.

So how was John like Elijah? In answering this question I considered the thoughts of the monk and church father known as the Venerable Bede of Jarrow, in Northumbria, who lived from c. 672 until 735. He wrote that he had spent all his life "in this monastery" applying himself "entirely to the study of Scriptures." [4] His extensive Bible commentaries reflect this richness. He observed that:

Both Elijah and John were celibate. Both wore rough dress. Both spent their lives in the wilderness. Both were heralds of the truth. Both underwent persecution for justice's sake at the hands of a king and queen - the former at the hands of Ahab and Jezebel, the latter at the hands of Herod and Herodias. The former, lest he be killed by the wicked, was carried up to heaven in a fiery chariot. The latter, lest he be overcome by the wicked, sought the heavenly kingdom by his martyrdom which was accomplished in spiritual combat. [5]

It might be added that both Elijah and John the Baptist were dependent upon God for their sustenance and had a strange supernatural diet: bread and meat brought by ravens, the multiplied bread of the widow of Zarephath, bread baked by angels, and locusts and wild honey. However, unlike Elijah, John's ministry was not attested to by miracles.

Thinking again of the fathers of the church, I turned to the writings of Matthew Henry who lived from 1662 until 1714. The great revivalist

George Whitefield acknowledged his debt to him throughout his life and was said to have read his works, as he did the scriptures, on his knees. Henry wrote in one of his classic Bible commentaries on Malachi 4:

> *Elijah was a man of great austerity and mortification, zealous for God, bold in reproving sin, and active to reduce an apostate people to God and their duty; John the Baptist was animated by the same spirit and power, and preached repentance and reformation, as Eli had done; and all held him for a prophet, as they did Elijah in his day, and that his baptism was from heaven, and not of men. Note, When God has such work to do as was formerly to be done he can raise up such men to do it as he formerly raised up, and can put into a John Baptist the spirit of an Eli.*
> [5]

It appears that both John the Baptist and Elijah were bound to a lifelong Nazarite vow (detailed in Numbers 6). The angel Gabriel instructed Zachariah that his son was...

Luke 1:15

...never to take wine or other fermented drink, and he will be filled with the Holy Spirit even from birth.

Unlike Samson, these men guarded their consecration to the Lord. By implication Jesus affirmed this when he said:

Matthew 11:18

For John came neither eating nor drinking, and they say, 'He has a demon.'

John certainly did not have a demon; but to the evil, light appears as darkness and darkness appears to be light.

We might ask, "Was this sort of consecration just for that day?" Somehow I don't think so. God does not change with the times in His dealings with men. God is calling His people in these days to lifelong consecration and devotion as he did John the Baptist and before him Elijah. Many believe that God is raising up a Nazarite generation. Some will be familiar with the promise that the Lord made: "I will repay you for the years the locusts have eaten." (Joel 2:25) As God releases the mantle of Elijah that John the Baptist walked under upon his consecrated church, I believe that, as with John, locusts that have devoured our years will become our food. God will rebuke the devourer and destroy the destroyer.

Elijah and John were both known by their attire. Elijah was recognised from the clothes he wore:

2 Kings 1:8

He was a man with a garment of hair and with a leather belt around his waist.

From this simple description of him the king could say, "That was Elijah the Tishbite." Likewise in Matthew we are told:

Matthew 3:4

John's clothes were made of camel's hair, and he had a leather belt around his waist. His food was locusts and wild honey.

They plainly had the same tailor!

Consecration is a vital prelude to conquest. In this modern age it can be so easily overlooked. To our modern eyes it might seem that characters like Elijah and John would have been rather odd in their appearance, diet and behaviour. No doubt they stood out even in their own day. These men plainly cared nothing for human fashion. In our hearts we know that neither should we. As the LORD said to the prophet Samuel:

1 Samuel 16:7

The LORD does not look at the things man looks at. Man looks at the outward appearance, but the LORD looks at the heart.

There was only One that Elijah and John dressed to impress.

Pleasing God rather than pleasing men was the primary consideration of both Elijah and John the Baptist. In Proverbs we read that the "fear of man will prove to be a snare" (Proverbs 29:25) whilst in the same book we are told that "the fear of the LORD is the beginning of knowledge" (Proverbs 1:7).

Plainly the fear of the LORD governed these men of God. They would no doubt have been relieved not to have been walking under the word that Isaiah the prophet carried when for three years he walked "stripped and barefoot" "as a sign and portent against Egypt and Cush" (Isaiah 20:3).

At least they got to wear clothes!!

Self-denial and obedience are an unattractive prospect to many. During a time of prayer on the 3rd June 1993 the Lord spoke to me very clearly, and I made a careful note of what I felt He said:

These are not days when you should seek great things for yourselves. Do not seek them. For you have heard it said, "Seek first the Kingdom of God and His righteousness and all these things will be added to you," but I say to you many have sought that which would be added to them and have forgotten to seek My kingdom and My righteousness.

I am a Jealous God who is jealous for your affection. For I call you to lay down the idols of your ambition so that I might fulfil My ambitions for you. I cannot give you what I want until you give Me what you have. I would have no competitors. You are seeing every earthly Kingdom shaken and all human glory debased and brought to shame. Therefore do not seek human greatness. If I grant you 'success' do not rely upon it and if you see 'failure' do not despair. For 'success' and 'failure' are human terms that I will not judge you by, but rather I am looking for a people who will obey Me from the heart. Let those who boast, boast in this that they know and understand their God. Be preoccupied with My kingdom and My righteousness, not with seeking to establish empires for your ambitions.

For as you see an end to all human greatness and ambition you will see your God who alone is exalted and without equal. My glory shall yet fill the earth as the waters cover the sea.

The words took my breath away. At first, being used to bringing words for other people and to the church, I thought that what I had received was for someone else. I prayed about the words, and not being released to bring them to anyone else I put them on the shelf. Some months later I returned to these words and was again struck by their power. I again asked who they were for. This time the answer came in the words that Nathan had once brought when confronting David: "You are the man!" (2 Samuel 12:7)

I was caught off guard and did not want it to be true. I liked the thought of bringing these words to someone else but not receiving them for myself. There was an important principle that I had to learn: if you cannot take it you should not give it!

When I consider the loneliness and ignominy of the end of John the Baptist's life, his calling has appeared harsh and unattractive. He ended his days being totally eclipsed by Jesus (something he welcomed) but also imprisoned and dying a martyr's death (which would have been less appealing). Many others have been called to walk the same road.

On 3rd April 1968 the American civil rights leader Dr Martin Luther King Junior addressed a rally at Mason Temple. His flight to Memphis had been delayed by a bomb threat against his plane. In closing this speech, he made reference to this threat, and said the following:

And then I got to Memphis. And some began to say the threats, or talk about the threats that were out. What would happen to me from some of our sick white brothers? Well, I don't know what will happen now. We've got some difficult days ahead. But it doesn't matter with me now. Because I've been to the mountaintop. And I don't mind. Like anybody, I would like to live a long life. Longevity has its place. But I'm not concerned about that now. I just want to do God's will. And He's allowed me to go up to the mountain. And I've looked over. And I've seen the Promised Land. I may not get there with you. But I want you to know tonight, that we, as a people, will get to the Promised Land. And I'm happy, tonight. I'm not worried about anything. I'm not fearing any man. Mine eyes have seen the glory of the coming of the Lord. [6]

King was assassinated on the following day.

Prior to the coming of Jesus no one had exercised such spiritual power and authority as Moses and Elijah. Jesus surpassed them, yet he promised to his followers that they would do "greater works" in his name. Jesus said that the "least in the kingdom of heaven is greater" than John the Baptist (Matthew 11:11). This then is the destiny of the people of God. At the end of the Bible, in Revelation 11, we are told of the two witnesses who by their exploits (including calling fire from heaven, stopping rain, and turning rivers to blood and sending plagues) are strongly identified with both Moses and Elijah.

Two is the biblical number of witness. Jesus sent his disciples out in twos. We are told that "a matter must be established by the testimony of two or three witnesses" (Deuteronomy 19:15). As such, these characters in Revelation offer the final fulfilment of Malachi's words to send Elijah before the coming of the great and terrible day of the Lord. We are told that these individuals are "the two olive trees and the two lampstands that stand before the Lord of the earth" (Revelation 11:4).

What does that mean? I believe that the Bible is the best interpreter of itself. Earlier in Revelation we are told that "the seven lampstands are the seven churches" (Revelation 1:20). So the lampstand represents the church, but what of the olive trees? Jeremiah described Israel as a "thriving olive tree" (Jeremiah 11:16). The passage in Revelation refers back to Zechariah when he saw that these two olive trees were "the two who are anointed to serve the Lord of all the earth" (Zechariah 4:14). In the New Testament Paul tells us that the Church has been "grafted into a cultivated olive tree" (Romans 11:24) which means Israel. The two olive trees and the two lampstands appear to merge to the point that they become indistinguishable. It seems then that these witnesses represent God's covenant people, Israel and the church. This is exactly what is written in Ephesians:

Ephesians 2:11-18

Remember that formerly you who are Gentiles by birth and called "uncircumcised" by those who call themselves "the circumcision" (that done in the body by the hands of men) - remember that at that time you were separate from Christ, excluded from citizenship in Israel and foreigners to the covenants of the promise, without hope and without God in the world. But now in Christ Jesus you who once were far away have been brought near through the blood of Christ. For he himself is our peace, who has made the two one and has destroyed the barrier, the dividing wall of hostility, by abolishing in his flesh the law with its commandments and regulations. His purpose was to create in himself one new man out of the two, thus making peace, and in this one body to reconcile both of them to God through the cross, by which he put to death their hostility. He came and preached peace to you who were far away and peace to those who were near. For through him we both have access to the Father by one Spirit

God's desire and intention is to create one new man comprised of both Jewish and Gentile believers. It is not "either the Church or Israel" but, in these last days, both being attested to and endorsed by the power of God. Both need to recognise that God has bound all men over to disobedience so that he may have mercy on them all (Romans 11:32).

Jim Elliot, an American Christian missionary to Ecuador, was seeking to reach the Waodani people. His journal entry for 28th October 1949 contains his now famous quotation, expressing his belief that missions work was more important than his life:

He is no fool who gives what he cannot keep to gain that which he cannot lose.

Jim, along his with four friends, was murdered on 8th January 1956 trying to reach out to the Waodani people. Ultimately if we love our lives we will lose them, but if we are prepared to lay them down then we will secure them eternally. This is what John the Baptist did.

Before the return of the Lord, God is determined to have a people who will move in the spirit and power of Elijah, an Elijah people. If we are to move in a measure of Elijah's spiritual power then we must be prepared to match the prophet in both his preparation and consecration.

Many want to share in the "power of the resurrection" spoken of by the Apostle Paul but are reluctant to embrace "the fellowship of sharing in his sufferings, becoming like him in his death" (Philippians 3:10) that he mentions in the same breath. It seems that the one is linked to the other, and we cannot have the former without the latter. Indeed the suffering and the power are both a direct result of knowing Christ. May we be found in the company of the overcomers described in Revelation:

Revelation 12:11

They overcame him by the blood of the Lamb and by the word of their testimony; they did not love their lives so much as to shrink from death.

Action!

Let us again consider practical examples of how to apply this teaching. Perhaps a Nazarite calling of the type described in Numbers 6 will not be for us. However, consecration and holiness are supposed to be a part of every Christian life. In the same way that we are used to upgrading our computer in the modern world, perhaps we might consider upgrading our consecration to the Lord. Take time to consider what this might look like in your life. For each of us there will be different answers. What needs to be uprooted? What needs to be sown? For certain we will reap what we sow.

How do we become a prophetic voice in practice? I am aware that no true prophet is self-appointed. Prophets are called and commissioned by God and then validated by their fruit. We all need to spend time to understand and hear God's call upon our lives. Calling comes from God. Comparison with others will lead us to despair or frustration whereas walking in our calling will lead to fulfilment. Everyone has a calling from God that is far more fulfilling than the wildest dreams and ambitions that we have had for ourselves. We perhaps will need to lay one down to take up the other. If there is any uncertainty about your calling spend time talking and praying with a trusted church leader about it.

What steps can we take towards fulfilling this calling and our destiny? I believe that the church as a whole needs be more vocal on issues of justice and righteousness. A quote ascribed to Edmund Burke summarises this:

> *The only thing necessary for the triumph of evil is for good men to do nothing.* [8]

We will fail to be truly prophetic if we do not understand God's central plan in choosing and using Israel in these last days. This is imperative if we are to "understand the times" in which we are living. Parts of the church that do not perceive this will be shut out of God's purposes, confused and deceived.

When I was younger I aspired to a ministry that would be recognised. More recently I have come to understand that God's "Well done!" is better than human recognition. Jesus said:

Matthew 7:22

Many will say to me on that day, 'Lord, Lord, did we not prophesy in your name, and in your name drive out demons and perform many miracles?'

Funnily enough prophesying does not impress God. If we do it well we are only repeating what we have heard and if we do it poorly we are in trouble! However, everyone prophesies only in part (1 Corinthians 13:9). Many years ago I heard it asked, "If you were put on trial for being a Christian would there be enough evidence to find you guilty?" It is not a bad question to ask as many are being called to stand up and be counted. I do not decry the need for individual prophetic voices to be raised up. Moses said:

Numbers 11:29

I wish that all the LORD's people were prophets and that the LORD would put his Spirit on them!

Prayer Points

- Pray that the prophetic voice of the church would be restored and that the people of God would boldly both live and cry out a message of repentance from the wilderness.
- Pray that God would raise up a Nazarite generation who would consecrate their whole lives to the Lord in unswerving obedience. Pray also that God would help you to remain faithful to him in the trouble that is coming upon the world.
- Pray that the church would increasingly be able to stand for righteousness and against wickedness and would be fearless of the cost or the consequences.

- Pray for those who are called to take a costly stand for their faith in this land and overseas, that they would know God's comfort, courage and provision.

REFERENCES

1. *Drink and Crime*; Community Care (2nd April 1987)

2. For example see http://baptismsite.com/content/view/7/3/lang,english/

3. Herzog, David, *Glory Invasion*; published by Destiny Image (April 1, 2007); ISBN-13: 9780768424348

4. Bede, *Ecclesiastical History of England (Historia ecclesiastica gentis Anglorum)*, 5. 24

5. Oden, Thomas C, *Ancient Christian Commentary on Scripture,* p9; published by InterVarsity Press (8th July 2005); ISBN-13 978-0830814183.

6. Henry, Matthew, *The comprehensive commentary on the Holy Bible: Volume 3.*

7. Quoted from Montefiore, Simon Sebag; *Speeches that Changed the World: The Stories and Transcripts of the Moments that Made History,* pp. 155; Quercus (2006). ISBN 1905204167.

8. Burke, Edmund, *Thoughts on the cause of the present discontents* (1770).

The Hearts of the Fathers

Malachi 4:5-6

He will turn the hearts of the fathers.

Journey to my Father

Often we do not understand what we have until it is gone. I had set aside 6th November 2005 to visit my Mum and Dad. Dad had been admitted to Torbay Hospital in Devon a few days before on the 1st November 2005 because of breathing difficulties. As I was just setting out, my elder brother telephoned me to say that Dad had taken a turn for the worse and that he was not expected to live much longer.

On my 125 mile journey from Southampton to South Devon I prayed that my father might live long enough for me to see him again. It had long been my prayer that I might be with him when he died. When I arrived at the hospital my brothers and sister together with their partners were already gathered. Dad had rallied from earlier that day and appeared to be bright but very breathless. Mum went home to rest and everyone left so that I was alone with Dad for a few precious hours.

Now in this hospital bed Dad wanted to review his previous life and pass something on. He needed to talk about his early life. My father, Arthur Roy Collett, was born in Bath, Somerset on the 17th July 1920, the eldest child and only son of Harry and Minnie Collett. He was only ever known as 'Roy' to his friends or of course 'Dad' to his children. William Wordsworth said perceptively that "the child is father of the man".

The Father of the Man

Before Roy had become a father he had been a son. Although in his eighties, Dad's childhood was a living memory. The type of father he became was, to an extent, defined by the type of father he had had. His father, my grandfather, Edwin Henry (or, as he preferred, 'Harry' Collett) had enlisted in the Somerset Light Infantry at Bath on 16th August 1913.

Harry was a regular soldier at the outset of the war and could be properly called an 'Old Contemptible'. To have this distinction you needed to be a holder of what was called the Mons Star for army service between 4th August and 22nd November 1914. The term itself came from a speech made by Kaiser Wilhelm II, King of Prussia and Emperor of Germany on the 1st October 1914, referring to the British army as "General French's contemptible little army". This insult became a badge of pride. However, Harry could hardly have been described as old, being only sixteen years of age when he signed up. In later life he reflected that he was probably the youngest Old Contemptible.

Harry served in France during World War I and was part of the first British Expeditionary Force. He and his sergeant were captured, escaped and were recaptured by the Germans after fighting at Mons and Charleroi. One night the sentry guarding them fell asleep enabling their escape through an unguarded window. Harry believed that they would have faced a firing squad in the morning if they had not freed themselves that night. They managed to reach Boulogne disguised as French peasants and pretending to be deaf and dumb.

The 1st Battalion fought on the Western Front for the duration of the War, and battle honours were awarded, including the retreat from Mons, Le Cateau, the two awful battles of the Somme in 1916 and 1918, and Ypres in 1915. Quite what atrocities Harry witnessed and survived can only be imagined. One thousand soldiers in the battalion left with him to go to France but only 226 men made it all the way through, many of whom were invalided out.

Harry was wounded at the first battle of the Somme. As a child I was shown the healed bullet wound in the top of his left shoulder. In fact, on his return to England in June 1916 he was in Hospital for 148 days recovering from this injury. This wound helped to preserve his life in keeping him out of much of the rest of the war.

My maternal grandfather, Norman Gray, a decade older than Harry Collett, was also a soldier. As a younger teenager he had served in the Boer War that ended in 1902. Having married in 1912 he joined the Light Infantry during the First World War and served as a machine gunner in India. Here he contracted malaria and recalled that he returned home a wreck. He had recurrent bouts of this disease throughout his life.

Child of the Empire

At the end of the war, Harry was twenty-one years old. He had married in the previous year in 1917 and, staying in Bath, worked as an army recruiting sergeant. At that time Britain still had an Empire. So in 1924, in service of that Empire, he sailed from Southampton to India on a troop ship called the 'Rawalpindi' with his wife, my then four-year-old father and his sister. Now, years later, living in the city that was his departure point to the nations, I feel a connection with both my father and his father.

It seems that Harry's Battalion, and therefore his family, was never in one place for very long; in Alexandria in Egypt, in 1929, they were based in Hong Kong before they moved back to India in 1930. Harry's medical records reveal his own fragile health during this period. He gave the impression of being the life and soul of the party, but his records indicated that he was prone to worry and anxiety and suffered recurrent stomach problems.

Harry was twice discharged from the army on the grounds of disability. This was something that he contested. The evidence of several tribunal hearing notes show that his requests for a more generous pension settlement for the injuries that he had suffered in the service of his country were declined.

In India Harry and his family were posted to Wellington, and the battalion was then split up: one company at Calicut, which was on the sea; the other of two platoons at Malappuram, which is the low-lying country inland from the coast. In India, Harry's battalion moved every six months between its two bases. My father loved India and spent more of his childhood there than anywhere else. As a child he learned to speak Hindi and developed a taste for Indian food. He worried his mother, coming in for his meals being too full to eat 'proper' food. As an adult he forgot Hindi but retained his love for curry. One of his sisters was born in Agra, in India, the home of the Taj Mahal.

So what was the impact of all of this upon my Dad? To say that the army lifestyle had an unsettling effect upon him would be an understatement. In later life it required a huge amount of persuasion on the part of my mother for him to travel anywhere! They never moved house. He had completely satisfied any wanderlust in his early years.

My father also felt that his formal education left a great deal to be desired. For much of his childhood he went to school for only six months a year for 45 minutes a day. The school that he attended only had one other boy and his three sisters as pupils. He recalled that he learned to write with a slate and learned his maths from a corporal who taught him to add up by playing darts with him.

Perhaps not surprisingly he fell behind with his reading and was sent away to a Catholic school in Wellington to catch up when he was twelve years old. He hated this school and felt that his father had wasted his money in sending him to it. Although in time he became a fluent reader, he was never really confident with writing and preferred to leave this to my mum.

The family returned to England when he was thirteen years old. He told me how the Catholic nuns in the Wellington school had been cruel to him, beating him because of his Protestant background. This damaged both his education and perception of Christianity. This said, he was confirmed into the Church of England by the Bishop of Guildford on the 22nd March 1934. Many did this as a rite of passage into adulthood. He received his first Holy Communion on the following Sunday, Easter Day, on 1st April 1934 at the Garrison Church, Deepcut, Aldershot. He was, however, a non-conformist at heart and for most of his life was not a regular church attendee.

The Fighter

On his hospital bed Dad recalled the last schoolboy fight that he had had when he was a fourteen-year-old living in Deepcut. He had been set upon by the school bully, and one of the masters at school, noticing the fight that had ensued, put a stop to it. He gave the boys boxing gloves and put them in a ring to 'resolve' their differences. Dad, who had previously won prizes for his boxing in India, was the easy victor. He said that the boy never troubled him again, and others who had been his victims thanked him for putting him in his place.

My father was a fighter and hated injustice. I am reminded of the words of Micah:

Micah 6:8

He has showed you, O man, what is good. And what does the LORD require of you? To act justly and to love mercy and to walk humbly with your God.

Dad once told me that he had been a communist like many of his generation. He wanted a fairer society. However, like many of his contemporaries he resigned from the Communist Party in 1956 when the Soviet Union invaded Hungary. At this point Joseph Stalin, who had appeared as the workers' champion (at least to those overseas), was exposed, and the nature of his regime began to be more widely understood. Dad conveyed to me something of his concern for social justice, and this in turn inclined me towards social work. He was unafraid to take a stand on things he believed in.

Another example of this was through his experience with Freemasonry. Like his father before him he was persuaded to join the Masons. It is reasonable to suppose that this might not have been at the same time that he was communist! His reasons for joining would have been principally social. However, he left promptly when his Lodge admitted a man who had been married to one of my mum's friends and had subjected her to domestic violence. He gave the Lodge the ultimatum that if they admitted this man then they would lose him. When they proceeded he stuck to his principles and resigned.

For a time after his discharge as Warrant Officer II in 1935, my grandfather, Harry Collett, ran the Working Men's Club at Deepcut before moving to Devon. After leaving the Service in 1936 until his retirement he was licensee of the Keyberry Hotel, Newton Abbot. Upon his retirement from the hotel Harry offered my parents the licence, but Dad declined. Having seen the impact of running a public house on other relatives he decided that it was not for him. Witnessing the effects of alcoholism he remained only a moderate drinker. He put his family's needs before possible financial advantage.

Roy started working for the Great Western Railway in 1936 when he was sixteen, where he cleaned the engines. He received a glowing reference for this work by the Reverend E. J. Dodge, Chaplain to the Forces on the 28th April 1936. Reverend Dodge had known him for three years and had taught him at the Day School at Blackdown and in the choir. He stated that he was "an honest, keen, intelligent youth" displaying "qualities of leadership" and added that he "could be trusted with anything".

My Dad moved on up from being a fireman to being an engine driver of various classes of steam engine. His father Harry re-joined the Colours in 1942 and following this was commissioned into the Royal Engineers attaining the rank of Captain. Much as Dad wanted to join the army at the outset of the Second World War, his mother really did not want another soldier in the family, and her view prevailed. Being in a reserved occupation, it was his service as a railwayman that counted as his war effort. He was a marksman and, in common with my paternal grandfather, Norman Gray, was in the home guard and worked during some of the bombing raids on Exeter railway station.

The Sins of the Fathers

Harry died aged 75 years on 29th December 1971 in Newton Abbot. He outlived his wife by two years. He had suffered from prostate cancer but I was told that he had been "given something" by the family doctor that had accelerated his death. The doctor himself committed suicide some years later. In the years following his death our family experienced a number of surprises that threw light on the man that we thought we knew.

The first surprise came one day when my father was in his seventies. He received a telephone call from a woman called Barbara. She had traced him through the telephone directory and having established that he was the son of Harry Collett explained that she was his half-sister. She said that her mother had lived in Bath during the early 1920s. She had had a liaison with Harry just before he had set sail for India, and Barbara had been born as a result. She had carried the shame of illegitimacy all those years as had her mother before her, who had never married. Although she had wanted to know her father, out of concern for the effect that this would have upon his legitimate family she had not made contact until she was sure that Harry had died. Although my father was convinced by Barbara's claim and was willing to have travelled to her, even inviting her to visit him, they never met; they exchanged letters and other telephone calls. It seemed to Dad that shame or inhibition held her back from entering into the relationships that her heart longed for.

This story has a resonance in today's world. Shakespeare said, "It is a wise father that knows his own child" (Merchant of Venice ii. ii. 69, 1596).

Following this disclosure Dad wondered how many other brothers or sisters he might have. He joked about it. His father had travelled very widely. He knew that he had run a brothel as a "service" to his soldiers whilst in India. Our family had suddenly changed shape and grown. We knew that all humanity is related, but now it seemed possible that we might have many more blood relatives than we had imagined!

A further surprise that caused my family to re-examine its legacy came around the same time that Barbara had made contact. I had always believed that my Dad's younger sister Beryl was childless, her husband having died some years before. It proved that this was not the case. In 1949, as a single woman, she had given birth to a little girl. The father had been an American serviceman. Harry had insisted that the baby should be adopted - that she could not marry unless the child was gone. Mum and Dad, on their honeymoon, had visited Beryl just after she had given birth. She was treated badly in the home where she had been sent. 'Arrangements' were made, and one day when Beryl returned to the room where she had been staying, her baby daughter was gone. She did not get to say goodbye. The girl was duly placed with a couple who adopted her. My parents were among the few members of the family to have met the baby.

When I reflect upon Beryl's life, she having died some years ago, it seems to have been shadowed by this secret sadness. She was funny and clever and by all accounts could have made a career of writing. However, she smoked and drank more than she should have and was shrunken with osteoporosis. Her older sister, Cynthia, knew everything, and without telling her sister, so as not to raise her hopes or fears, worked hard to trace her adult child. When she posted a newspaper advert in another part of the country, to her surprise she met with success.

The daughter, then a woman in her forties whose adoptive parents had both died, had not been told that she had been adopted. A surviving relative had confirmed to her shocked surprise that she had been adopted. As a married woman with four children of her own, the turmoil that this revelation would have caused can only be guessed at. However, after clearing the ground an awkward first meeting was arranged. Later during the weekend of that reunion I had the privilege of meeting her and her family. One legacy from her birth family seemed unarguable: Beryl, Cynthia, the woman and her four children all had red hair. This in turn they inherited from Harry Collett.

The reunion sadly did not result in a long-lasting relationship but did bring a measure of resolution. Beryl died only a matter of years later. Her daughter remained in contact with Cynthia. Reflecting on these episodes I have been struck forcibly by how the momentary pleasures of some have been paid for with a lifetime of suffering by others. There are always consequences from our actions. In these accounts the pleasure was largely the men's whilst the pain was largely born by the women. The sins of the father were indeed visited upon the children.

My father loved his father, honoured him, but did not live his life in the same way that he had done. He instilled an ethos of hard work in all of his children. He retired from British Rail in 1983 at the age of 63 having learned to drive the High Speed Train. Like many railwaymen, perhaps because of the shift work, he loved gardening. He was an allotment holder for over forty years, at one time maintaining two plots. He loved the fact that these provided him with both exercise and food for his family. He grew more than we needed and from his abundance gave away.

Towards Peace with God

From the time that my father retired I began to consistently seek God for his welfare. I was really concerned that he should know the Lord in the way that I had come to. Over the years friends stood with me as I prayed for him. At times I prayed with fasting. One of the first things that happens when we pray is that we change; my heart towards Dad changed.

I saw less of his faults and more of his fine qualities. I resumed greeting him with a hug and a kiss, something that I had stopped some years earlier. I could see my prayers were being answered.

A specific prayer that I saw answered was that others from his generation would be able to share Christ with him. I was aware that as his son my life had to speak more loudly than my words, and some things would come better from others. I was really excited when my parents went to stay in Australia for six months with Stan and Eileen King, my mum's sister and her husband. The couples shared a double wedding, and Stan had become a Christian a few years earlier. On their return Mum and Dad began going to church together, not every week but more than they had. The Baptist Church became much more open to the Holy Spirit, and when we went with them I often noticed Dad wiping tears from his eyes during services. For reasons that have never been completely clear to me, the good work of this church was spoiled when it fell apart.

Alongside Dad's love for gardening, he also loved Dartmoor which he knew intimately after many pleasant weekends exploring. However, none of his enthusiasms came anywhere close to his passion for his wife and family. Mum told me that when they had first met he had told her that he would marry her. This proved awkward as she was engaged to someone else at the time! True to his word he married Barbara Janie on the 12th March, 1949, and enjoyed 57 years of happy marriage. They had four children and nine grandchildren. He was not a conventional English gentleman. For one thing he was very free in demonstrating his emotions. He cried freely, hugged his children and left us in no doubt about his love.

Old age can be very hard. It is a time of both loss and adjustment. Dad did not enjoy growing old. In a time of prayer my friend, Mark Iles, had a picture of the hedge that had been around my parents, protecting them from being cut down. He did not know that a neatly manicured privet hedge had always surrounded their bungalow. When I next visited their home after Mark had shared this picture with me, I was shocked to discover that the hedge was gone because the work of maintaining it had become too great. It seemed that the Lord was speaking to them through this that they could no longer provide themselves with shelter and protection and needed to look to Him to do so.

Dad had a serious fall, in part because of the poor maintenance of his road, on 2nd December 2001, but also because of his balance. As a result of this fall he suffered a broken arm, a broken nose, damaged the nerves in his cheek and suffered cuts to his face that required ten stitches. His confidence was also severely dented, and he became depressed.

Seeing that his end was coming, which he reassured his children that he did not fear, he did make his peace with God notwithstanding the bruising that he had received from the church. Some years before his last stay in hospital, when my younger brother and his wife were expecting their first child and he was not sure that he would live to see this event, I felt God wanted to reassure him that he would hold the child. He did and there was a special bond between him and his grandson. In the hospital he allowed me to read comforting passages from the Bible to him and pray for him. We hugged and wept.

When I was a teenager I can remember having a number of blazing rows with my father. I cannot now remember what they were about although they had seemed so important at the time. My mother said that we argued so fiercely because we were so similar. There is a saying attributed to the American writer Mark Twain that when he was fourteen he thought his father the stupidest man alive but by the time he was twenty-one he thought that his father had made considerable progress! Likewise my assessment of my father changed over the years. The changes I observed speak as much about the transformation in my heart towards him as they do the change in him.

Returning from a weekend with my parents in December 1996, I had come away with many things left unsaid and had to write a letter to my father. I was very conscious that no one is promised tomorrow. In this letter, which I rediscovered in a box of my father's treasured papers, I made mention of Malachi 4:6, of the turning of "the hearts of the children to their fathers", and added:

> *My heart is turning towards you. When I was younger I would have been annoyed if people had said, "you are just like your father". Now I take it as a compliment. I have just as much difficulty in controlling my emotions as you and I am just as likely to cry. Thank you for giving me the*

example that big boys do cry. Jesus wept. There is nothing unmanly about tears.

Later in the letter I wrote:

Sometimes Dad, I get the feeling that you don't really know, deep down just how special you are, when all of the time its evident to all of your children. You are special. Dear Dad I love you very, very, very much. I am weeping as I write this as you probably are when you read it. What is more I know that God loves you very, very, very much. In fact, much more than I ever could.

On the night before he died he had a long and happy conversation with his sister Cynthia. Mum and I stayed in a room along the corridor from him. During the night a nurse woke us up and called us to his bedside. He had already departed before we arrived. Standing before his dead body with my dear desolate mother I felt the Holy Spirit say to me, "You have committed him into my care; into my care he has come."

My father, Arthur Roy Collett, died in hospital on 8th November 2005 at the age of 85. Like all of us he was not perfect, but he was a good Dad and I knew he loved me. It was both painful and a privilege to be with him and my family at the end. Much as his family all miss him I would not wish him back into a body where everything was breaking down. It was his time to go. Had he lived, doctors told us, he would have gone blind. His funeral celebrated his long life and also provided an opportunity for those who loved him to be together. I managed to remain composed enough to give a short address at his funeral and gave out broad bean seeds (which if planted would grow into my father's favourite vegetable). We always reap the same kind of seed that we sow. Dad sowed and reaped love. In Isaiah 53 Jesus was spoken of as a "man of sorrows" who was acquainted with grief. The Holy Spirit is known as the comforter. His comfort has been very real and precious to me and to my family.

Reconciliation

The Hebrew word translated in Malachi 4:5-6 above as 'fathers' might be equally translated 'grandfathers' or 'forefathers'. To fulfil the fifth commandment, as well as for our own health and blessing, we must find ways to honour all of our fathers. We have to become reconciled to our fathers by forgiving them their sins, celebrating their achievements or, more realistically, a combination of both. Whatever your father has been like, whether a rogue or a rock, your relationship with him is likely to define you.

We are all wandering prodigals at heart. Relationship repair is a central theme of the Bible; it says:

2 Samuel 14:14

God does not take away life; instead, he devises ways so that a banished person may not remain estranged from him.

Of the ministry of reconciliation we are told:

2 Corinthians 5:18-19

All this is from God, who reconciled us to himself through Christ and gave us the ministry of reconciliation: that God was reconciling the world to himself in Christ, not counting men's sins against them. And he has committed to us the message of reconciliation.

I appreciate that this may be easy to say but hard to apply. Let me try to summarise some of the teaching points that I have gathered from reflection upon the lives of my forefathers and in the light of scripture. All of us need to be able to pray about our history in order to embrace and fulfil our destiny.

As a child I had imagined my parents to be both invincible and immortal. It was a shock to discover they were neither. In the beginning of the 1990s, in his early seventies, my Dad suffered a heart attack. Praying for him at that time I had been directed to the scripture "Don't be afraid; just believe" (Mark 5:36). We firstly need to pray for our fathers. When I shared this with him it brought a great deal of peace and reassurance to both of us. He recovered well but had to live at a slower pace. If your father is still alive (and however your relationship is with him) you should seek to bless and honour him by praying for his soul; it will do you good. Forgive your parents for being fallible and weak. If you succeed in forgiving them you will find it easier to forgive yourself. After all, you are made of the same stuff as them and subject to the same temptations and pressures that they have been.

The American writer Henry David Thoreau wrote:

The mass of men lead lives of quiet desperation. [1]

This saying seems as true today as when he wrote it. In 1990 women made 143 million visits to the GP. Men made only 75 million visits. The overt message "big boys don't cry" may no longer be given but it is still generally understood [2]. Yet we are told that "Jesus wept" (John 11:35). He represents a different sort of masculinity than that which we often model or encounter. Classically men have grown up emotionally illiterate and inarticulate. To be able to express the gamut of emotions expressed by Christ in the gospels of tenderness, indignation, love and anger, and to do so without sin, is to be fully a man. We must learn to speak in the language of feeling. This is something we can aspire to for ourselves and promote in others.

From my career I am aware that fathers who have 'failed' in their relationships with their biological children don't just 'go away'. They invariably become stepfathers. Men in this position will carry a weight of unresolved and perhaps unacknowledged grief for children that they have lost as they struggle with a lack of attachment to children in their current household. This is where the word of forgiveness must be spoken and received. The intense bond forged between parent and child in the early weeks following the child's birth provides a safeguard that is supposed to protect an infant throughout their childhood. It is in the potential of a father to rescue or ruin their family. Child protection research shows that stepfathers, lacking this bond, pose a much higher risk to children in their household than biological fathers. Where there is no natural love it can be both grown and learned. However, it must be patiently nurtured. Before it can be given out by men it must be learned from God. Pray for stepfathers to have the revelation of the love of God the father.

Men have an instinct to bear burdens, make sacrifices and provide. When I consider the colossal sacrifice of my grandfathers' generation I am reminded of the words of Jesus:

John 15:13
Greater love has no one than this, that he lay down his life for his friends.

We rightly honour them. The freedoms that Western nations have enjoyed came at a high price. Men in previous generations were willing to pay for them, and it appears that sacrifices will be necessary to ensure their continuity. Some are already paying the price today. Freedom is fragile and is again under threat. At the very least we must pray the continuance of the gospel freedom that we currently enjoy and see if God wants to 'put legs on our prayers'.

God's prophetic clock is ticking. When I think of the legacy of the British Empire the words of Psalm 2 ring in my ears:

Psalm 2:8
Ask of me, and I will make the nations your inheritance, the ends of the earth your possession.

Many Bible teachers have agreed that Britain was permitted an empire for the furtherance of the gospel. The gospel is the ground of all of our freedoms. The King James Bible, first published in 1611, dignified the English language with the vocabulary of the grace of God. Indeed the United Kingdom sent many missionaries overseas. Whilst the faith and altruism of these Christians should rightly be celebrated we need to pray for the uprooting of any imperial legacy that has been sown with the good seed of the Kingdom that they carried. Just the year after my father sailed for India, the Methodists opened Central Hall (now the home of the Community Church of which I am a part) to the public on 18th February 1925. In the early days a banner hung from the entrance to the building saying "For Southampton and the World". The fire in the hearts of missionary fathers such as the former England Cricket Captain CT Studd, who as one of the Cambridge Seven left fame and fortune to follow Christ, needs to burn again in the children of today.

The term 'feckless fathers' has been coined in the press to describe fathers who have failed to fulfil their financial responsibility to their children. In the UK, the Child Support Agency was designed to hold fathers to their ongoing financial responsibilities. It has been criticised for failing to balance the needs of first, second and stepfamilies. A generation of fatherless children is growing up for whom the word 'dad' has been cheapened by a succession of short-term father figures. It is estimated that 5% of the population may have a different father to the one they think they are related to [3]. Fathers need to 'own' their biological children both emotionally and financially. The hearts of the fathers really do need to be turned towards the hearts of the children.

We read that King David sinned by first lusting after Bathsheba, the wife of Uriah the Hittite, whilst watching her bathe, then committing adultery with her and murdering her husband to cover up her subsequent pregnancy. Although David repented of his sin and was forgiven, there were consequences: a spirit of lust was released destructively in his family. The prophet Nathan foretold that he would reap what he had sown and that a sword would divide his own family. We see that David's son Amnon raped his half-sister Tamar (2 Samuel 13). David's subsequent failure to address this incestuous crime resulted in another son, Absalom, Tamar's full brother, taking the law into his own hands by murdering Amnon and then rebelling against his father. Absalom slept with David's concubines in broad daylight. With David's successor Solomon we read that he married many foreign wives against the command of God and they led him astray by worshipping other gods. Unchecked lust tore David's family and his kingdom apart. It still has the same consequences. We see it in our own land. This is a pain that must be healed for people to come into the relationship with God that he desires and intends.

As with David's sin I could see that there were consequences for my family from my forefathers' sin. Over the years I have become aware of its malevolent hold on society and as a secret sin in the church. I acknowledge a different and more helpful inheritance from Norman Gray, my mother's father. He was married for 61 years and fathered 10 children. My mother recalled him to be a loving and interested dad. God honours the faithful, but the unfaithful dishonour themselves. Pray for the strengthening of the integrity of fathers and for the forgiveness and restoration of those that have failed and fallen.

We need to see the church established as a redemptive community. As such it is a demonstration of the family of God. My parents were hurt and confused by being caught in a church split, and not surprisingly it put them off going to church. Jesus said:

John 13:34-35

A new command I give you: Love one another. As I have loved you, so you must love one another. By this all men will know that you are my disciples, if you love one another.

I wonder how many more people would be in heaven if the church obeyed this commandment. This is the responsibility of every Christian. Begin to ask God for a revelation of his love for your immediate neighbours both in the church and outside.

Leaving and Cleaving

It is important to ask how we might balance the principle of 'leaving and cleaving' with that of 'honouring our parents'. At first glance there would appear to be a conflict between the two and it appears difficult to obey the one without violating the other [4]. We first encounter the concept all the way back in Genesis.

Genesis 2:24

Therefore a man shall leave his father and mother and be joined [cleaved] to his wife, and they shall become one flesh.

The statement appears to have three aspects: leaving, cleaving and then becoming one flesh. All are important. Firstly, we see that the parent-child relationship is temporary and its natural conclusion should be "leaving". The husband-wife relationship is portrayed as permanent:

Matthew 19:6

...what God has joined together, let man not separate.

Secondly, the Hebrew word translated "cleave" refers to 'chasing hard after someone else and then being glued to that person'. So a man is to pursue his wife after the marriage (not just before) and then be 'stuck to her.' This cleaving indicates such closeness that there should be no closer relationship than that between the two spouses, not with any former friend or with a parent.

Thirdly, becoming "one flesh" refers to the forging of a new single entity from two separate individuals. There is to be such sharing and oneness in every aspect (physical, emotional, intellectual, financial, and social) that the resulting unity can be best described as "one flesh". Again, when there is more sharing or emotional support derived from the parent-child relationship than from that between the husband and wife, the oneness within the marriage is undermined. Distance is imperative for union to be effective. We cannot truly cleave unless we leave.

Of course there is more to leaving and cleaving than at first appears. Speaking of bridal love the psalmist says:

Psalm 45:10-11
Listen, O daughter, consider and give ear: Forget your people and your father's house. The king is enthralled by your beauty; honour him, for he is your lord.

The relationship between husband and wife, although profound in itself, is supposed to be a picture of Christ's love for his bride the church. That we can love at all is because we have first been loved. It is the higher love that has the greatest claim upon our hearts. The love of God eclipses all other loves.

Action!

In this section, I have suggested practical examples of how to apply this teaching. What does the Bible say about how fathers' hearts are to be turned to their children? Whilst expecting or demanding honour from their children, in the past fathers failed to obey the injunction not to exasperate them. Our model of biblical fatherhood needs to come from understanding that God is our Father. Simply ask, as the disciple Thomas did of Christ, to be shown the Father, knowing that if you have seen Christ you have seen the Father.

From the example of David we have seen that the Bible has much to say about the lasting impact of fathers on the lives of their children. A simple action when considering our inheritance from our forefathers is to forgive their sins. How we respond to this will depend on the extent and nature of the sins that they have committed against us. However, as we do so we will find it easier to forgive ourselves. In turn we will begin to find God's heart for our fathers. These are the first steps in relationship repair.

I would not have been able to write this chapter if my dad had not told me his story. This will not be possible for everyone, but I would say that listening to our fathers is the first way that we might consider honouring them. If we are unable to achieve this by asking them directly, then finding out about them will have to suffice. Even children separated from their fathers are surprised by the traits they have inherited from them. We carry their DNA. Practically we cannot learn from their lives if we are unfamiliar with their tragedies, triumphs and choices. As I have tried to convey, their story is our inheritance.

Problems occur in family life when the intended roles between a husband and wife are reversed and the parent and child relationship is treated as the primary relationship. It is not and should not be allowed to become so. Whilst parental guidance, when sought, can be liberating to the adult offspring, unwanted parental interference can choke the growth into maturity. When an adult child has married and this parent-child relationship remains primary, the newly formed union is threatened. Should you be a child conscious of this intrusion you should decisively seek to cut yourself from your parental apron strings and with humility assert the sanctity of your marriage. Should you be a parent convicted that you are allowing your reasonable concern to carry you to unreasonable lengths of interference, seek to step back and release your child to the care of the Father.

Prayer Points

- Pray over your legacy from your forefathers. Thank God for the good and forgive them for the evil that you inherited from them. If they are still alive, and as far as it is within your ability, pray for their salvation.
- Seek the Lord for deliverance from any besetting family sins that you can see blighting the lives of your relatives.

REFERENCES

1. Thoreau, Henry David, from *Walden,* published in 1854.
2. McMahon, Linnet, Ward, Adrian (editors), *Helping Families in Family Centres:* Chapter 7; Collett, Paul, Working with men in Family Centres; published by Jessica Kingsley (2001); ISBN 1853028355, 9781853028359.
3. Burn, Professor John, of the Institute of Human Genetics (Newcastle, 2003).
4. http://www.gotquestions.org/leave-cleave-honor.html/

The Hearts of the Children.

Malachi 4:5

...and the hearts of the children to their fathers."

Isaiah 11:6
The wolf will live with the lamb, the leopard will lie down with the goat, the calf and the lion and the yearling together; and a little child will lead them.

A Samuel Anointing

In 1997 I began to spend some time with Graham Cooke, a writer and conference speaker with a strong prophetic gifting, now based in California, who had then not long joined our church. I remember him speaking one evening at Central Hall, where our church met in Southampton, about a vision that God had recently shown him.

Graham shared how he had recently been ministering at a church in Switzerland. During the worship he had been visited by some angels and they had brought him back, in the Spirit, to Central Hall and through the roof into Room 4, which was then used as a Sunday school room. In this room they then showed him groups of children ministering to each other. Some were prophesying, others were teaching, others were praying for the sick. The strong impression was that the Holy Spirit was moving upon these children in a very powerful way. The children were then led by the leaders of the church into the main hall and continued ministering in the anointing to the adults. Graham heard the words "a Samuel anointing is coming upon the children". God was releasing a supernatural grace upon the children for them to know Him; they did not need to walk through rebellion and could have the ability to walk with God throughout their lives.

Still reeling from this vision, Graham was brought back to the church in Switzerland. He wisely asked God to confirm all that He had shown him. Barely had he finished asking for a confirmation than in another part of the room a German woman, who Graham knew did not speak any English, began to speak in tongues. She said in English, "A Samuel anointing is coming upon the children; a Samuel anointing is coming upon the children." She then shook violently and fell to the floor.

I received the account of this vision as a word from God, and I began to pray this into our young children. It was already our practice to pray over our children morning and evening. Following our reading of Francis and Judith MacNutt's helpful book 'Praying for your Unborn Child' Carol Ann and I had begun to pray for each of our four children from conception [1]. This couple believed that praying for unborn children would help them to be more disposed to love God as well as being happier and more secure. In addition, following a specific encouragement to do so, I also made sure that I prayed in tongues over the children before I went to bed each night. Within a month of hearing of Graham's vision, God had broken into our family in a most remarkable way.

Our eldest daughter Abigail, then aged four, had two recurrent questions she wanted answers to. The first was "Why did Jesus die on the cross?" and the second, having watched a number of baptisms, was "How old should I be when I am baptised?" At the time the thought of putting her head under the water worried her. These questions appeared very much God-given and would not let her go. We did our very best to give good, age-appropriate answers to our little girl, but nothing satisfied her. She just did not get it. Then suddenly all that changed.

Significantly, Carol Ann had encouraged Abigail to seek God for herself, and at this tender age she had begun to do so. God has no grandchildren - only sons and daughters. We have to make room for Him to forge a direct relationship with our children.

One morning Abigail told her mum that Jesus had come to visit her in the night. She had been having a terrible dream when she heard a noise and Jesus came. Later, when she drew His appearance she had Him clothed in a white robe with a blue sash on and a golden crown on His head. She said that her bedroom became very, very bright. Jesus then explained why he had died on the cross. She simply recalled Him telling her that he had died for her sin so that she did not need to die. She said that she had held up her hands and said, "I'm sorry; forgive me," and "Praise the Lord!"

He also told her about her baptism. He spoke of her being baptised when she was still a child. Ten was mentioned as the age at which she could be baptised (or maybe younger).

As the years slipped by, Abigail forgot much of her encounter with the Lord, although even now as a young adult she is able to recall seeing Jesus. As her parents it was our duty to remember the details. A lasting legacy of this visitation has been her love for and knowledge of the Lord.

Although Abigail had forgotten what the Lord had said to her, when she was nine she started asking about being baptised, so when she was ten she had been able to satisfy both her parents and our Church that the time was right. She was baptised in front of her friends and family and gave moving testimony to her love for the Lord. Even if we do forget, the Lord remembers.

Reflecting upon this I have been struck by the part that Hannah, Samuel's mother, had played in her son's life. She was a barren woman who pleaded to God for children; then when he answered her prayer she returned her son to God. She had made a vow to God and kept it, even though it cost her dearly. She loved her child but loved God more. She took her child to the tabernacle at Shiloh and presented him to Eli the priest for him to be raised in his care. It is absolutely no coincidence that only a few years following on from Hannah's prayers Samuel was called to be a prophet. Her obedience and sacrifice in giving the child whom God had given her back to God transformed her nation. The measure with which we give ourselves and our children to God is the measure with which God can take us both up.

All parents hold their children as stewards. You cannot keep them. Indeed they were never yours. They are a precious gift from God but will inevitably grow and go away from you. Parents who try to fight this, hurt themselves and their children. Better by far that we give them away to God than see them stolen by the world or the devil. If we want a 'Samuel anointing' to come upon our children and the children of this generation then we as parents need to have the attitude and show the courage of Hannah and give them away to God.

As a social worker I have shared the privilege and the pain of seeing many children separated from their birth parents and given to new adoptive parents. One wise judge said that since the abolition of the death penalty in the United Kingdom, society has had no greater sanction against the individual than the removal of their children permanently through adoption. There is no greater act of love than for a parent, knowing that they are unable to care for their child, to place them in the arms of another who can. It is far worse for those who cannot care for their children but refuse to release them. Losing our children is in one sense inevitable. For one thing, they will not stay children. We have a choice whether we do this well or badly. Better to place them into God's hands than to have them wrenched away by the devil.

One of the most remarkable accounts of a parent giving up a child to follow the call of God is given in Norman Grubb's book 'Rees Howells, Intercessor'. Following his marriage Rees Howells and his wife received a call to be missionaries. This meant leaving their newborn son, Samuel, at home in Wales with a foster family to obey this call. After this long and hard 'death experience' they both left for Africa. In response to this extreme step of obedience the Lord brought 100,000 Africans to faith in Christ through their ministry. Revival followed them to every mission station that they visited. Years later, the Lord returned his son Samuel to Rees first as a co-worker and then a successor as he led the Bible College of Wales. Jesus said:

Mark 10:29-31

I tell you the truth ... no one who has left home or brothers or sisters or mother or father or children or fields for me and the gospel will fail to receive a hundred times as much in this present age (homes, brothers, sisters, mothers, children and fields - and with them, persecutions) and in the age to come, eternal life.

The purpose of the anointing upon Samuel was to prepare the way for the coming King. Samuel was a good and godly leader, but his most important task came at the end of his life. Having once given the people the king (Saul) which they demanded (1 Samuel 8:7), he poured a flask of oil on David, the ruddy-faced shepherd boy who was the seventh son of Jesse. Samuel was called and anointed by God in order to anoint the King who was to come. So in our day this is the purpose of the Samuel anointing that God wants to release upon our children. God is raising up a generation that will welcome the soon-coming Messiah, the greater Son of David.

I Will Pour Out My Spirit

At West Point Bible camp near Exeter in August 2000 our girls (then aged 7, 5 and 3) had been prayed for to be filled with the Holy Spirit. Nothing outwardly had happened at the time. One evening a few days after our return, after Daniel (then a baby) was asleep, Carol Ann had gone shopping at a supermarket, and I was settling the three girls. As the evening went on they began to get sleepy until one of the girls complained of feeling afraid as she had suffered a bad dream. With thoughts of the Bible camp in mind I prayed for them to be filled with the Holy Spirit. Suddenly, first one and then all three of them received the Holy Spirit and spoke in tongues. Well that did it! All prospects of sleep vanished as they were bouncing up and down on their beds praying in tongues excitedly.

When Carol Ann returned she was somewhat bemused by my complete failure to 'settle' the children although she was delighted to see what the Lord had been doing in our daughters' lives. Eventually they did all go to sleep although in the morning we heard that one of them had continued praying in tongues on and off through the night periodically, waking her sisters up! There is no 'junior' Holy Spirit. Whatever God does and for whoever He does it, it is hugely significant.

This was not the children's only experience of being filled with the Holy Spirit nor should we expect to live off a single encounter with God any more than a car should be driven indefinitely after only one filling with petrol. Paul encouraged those in Ephesus to...

Ephesians 5:18

...not get drunk on wine, which leads to debauchery. Instead, be filled with the Spirit.

The Greek phrase translated here "be filled with the Spirit" could equally be rendered "be being filled" or "be continually filled with the Spirit". There have been other times over the years when we have prayed together as a family and have all been so overwhelmed with the power of the Holy Spirit that we have been unable to stand.

When our second daughter, Jemimah, was still a baby in 1995, many parts of the Church were experiencing what became known as the Toronto (or the Father's) Blessing; people were falling down under the power of the Holy Spirit, laughing, weeping and experiencing various sorts of healing. Jemimah had just learned to sit up and become steady in doing so from the age of about eight months. Carol Ann and I noticed that when we prayed for her whilst she sat on our bed she would gently fall backward - just as was happening at the adult meetings. I emphasise that we did not touch or push her, but this happened again and again when we prayed for her. For her part Jemimah did not appear unhappy about this; quite the opposite! Our other children did not have this experience when they were babies.

In February, 2004, I had been given the video entitled 'Prophet TB Joshua and the children' by some friends of ours. The video documents the wonderful healing of a nine-year-old boy from South Africa called Stefan who had been born deaf. Afterwards it shows the man of God praying with Stefan and his friends and teaching them how to pray for each other with power in the name of Jesus. Each child, under the prophet's supervision, took turns in praying for their friends and witnessed them falling down under the power of God. Although this was serious and holy, the children were evidently having a great deal of fun; laughter and joy accompanied the prayer.

As soon as I watched this video with my children they wanted to "have a go". At that time Abigail was eleven and Daniel was four years old. As the children took turns in praying for one another they each fell down under the power of Holy Spirit. The same happened when they prayed for me. I don't think Daniel had fully understood what was going on because when he had fallen down, thinking that his sisters had pushed him, he had punched Abigail! Even with the presence of the Holy Spirit in our children's lives they still require parental training and sanctification.

Such experiences have not been limited to my own family. In June, 2008, I had the privilege of attending a morning of waiting upon God with Years 5 and 6 at the King's School, which my younger children attend, near Southampton. We began with a time of worship led by Jane Wiseman, the children's class teacher. I shared from Romans that...

Romans 8:14-17

Those led by the Spirit of God are called sons of God. For you did not receive a spirit that makes you a slave again to fear, but you received the Spirit of sonship. And by him we cry, "Abba, Father." The Spirit himself testifies with our spirit that we are God's children. Now if we are children, then we are heirs - heirs of God and co-heirs with Christ.

I then spoke briefly about the spirit of adoption and sonship and mentioned biblical characters who had been adopted - namely Moses, Samuel and Esther. Other encouragements came from the children and the other adults. The Holy Spirit fell on the whole group of over twenty children. The first indication of this was when in the worship two of the Year 5 girls began to laugh. Across the other side of the room a Year 6 boy also began to laugh. This was not out of embarrassment but because of the presence of God. Then it seemed that the whole group began to sob, many without anyone knowing why.

Though it was difficult to measure what was going on in different children's lives, it did appear that some deep hurts were being healed and the Holy Spirit was revealing God as Father. Some children experienced deliverance; one child testified that they experienced a weight being lifted off from their chest. Burdens were rolled away from the children. In the United Kingdom I had up to that point never seen God move in such power as he did amongst these children.

In the autumn of 2003, towards the end of an extended period of prayer and fasting, I awoke from a vivid dream at 2.00am. In this dream I had gone downstairs to pray in our dining room in the pitch darkness. In prayer I had the following conversation with the Lord. I pleaded, "Show me Your glory," to which He answered, "Are you really sure you want to see My glory?" I asked again, "Show me Your glory, please," to which He again responded, "Are you really sure you want to see My glory?"

During this exchange with the Lord I was, with increasing frustration, attempting to turn various lights on with no success. None of the lights would work; there appeared to be no power. As I asked the Lord again, "Please, show me Your glory," I turned and looked out of the dining room window into our dark garden. To my great surprise I saw my daughter Keziah (then six years old) sitting on a bench outside. As she turned around to look back at me from the garden her face suddenly blazed like the sun.

I awoke with a start, not at all convinced that I was ready to see any more of the glory of God than I just had. Praying about this dream afterwards I was struck by the need to live in God's light as well as not seeking to generate any of my own. I also had the very clear sense that God wanted His glory to rest upon children. God wants to reveal his glory in the face of our children.

Keziah had been filled with the Holy Spirit and had spoken in tongues on the same evening as her older sisters back in 2000 when she was three years old. In one of my old journals I have a note of her reporting to her mother that she had had a dream of seeing an angel, wearing what she described as a "golden hat" (was that a halo?) and holding her brother when she was only two years old.

On the morning of the 17th October 2003, just eleven days after my dream, Keziah came into our bedroom dressed and ready for school surprisingly early. She reported that during the night she had been up to heaven. She was not able to recall all that had been said to her but did remember that God had said to her, "Don't be afraid or nervous and be courageous." She reported that she had seen the angels bowing down before the throne of God, saying, "Holy, Holy, Holy." She had seen a rainbow that had appeared solid so that you could walk upon it. She also said that she had seen hell, the "bad place" as she called it. In childish understatement she recalled that the people were not happy there; the food was bad food and it was all dark.

At the end of June 2007, Keziah reported having a number of angelic visitations. One day, coming into her school after playtime when it had just started to rain, she said it appeared to her that the rain became as golden oil falling on the whole school. Looking up she then saw four angels seated on the four corners of the roof of her school. Going into the school itself she said that she saw angels standing at the door to each class room. For several weeks after this she saw angels around our home. Frustratingly, I could not see anything but, particularly when Keziah was seeing something, I was aware of a very strong sense of the presence of God.

On three successive days commencing on Sunday 12th August, 2007, God showed her three linked visions about the coming of revival. In the first of these she said that she was stood in what appeared to be a busy street. People were streaming past her. A tall figure, wearing a blue top with a picture of a dove on it, came and held her hand and told her that revival is coming to Wales. The following day the vision resumed with the same scene. A tall figure, this time with a red top and another picture of a white dove came and held her other hand and told her that revival is coming to England. On the third day the vision concluded. This time a figure dressed entirely in white approached her with a real dove sitting upon his shoulder. He announced to her that revival is coming to the whole world. All three of her visitors, who by this time she took to be angels, disappeared leaving her in the company of the dove who came to rest on her shoulder. What God is able to say to children often surpasses what he is able to reveal to the "mature".

War on children

Children are uniquely special to God. Jesus blessed the children and rebuked his disciples when they tried to turn them away (Mark 10:13-16, Matthew 19:13-15 and Luke 18:15-17). Too often the church has found itself getting between Jesus and the children and has stopped them coming to Him. He said that we are to be like children and to welcome them (Luke 9:46-48, Matthew 18:1-5 and Mark 9:33-37). He also said that we are not to look down upon them, or to cause them to stumble or sin and that their angels always behold the Father's face (Matthew 18:1-10). Revelation is promised to little children but is withheld from the wise and learned (Matthew 11:25-26). From the lips of children and infants God has ordained praise (Psalm 8:2).

The devil hates all that God loves. We have to remember that he is the thief that came to steal and kill and destroy (John 10:10). He hates all that carry the image of God, especially children. Special children are especially hated. God's people are to love what God loves and hate what He hates. We notice that the devil attempted to destroy the infant Moses using Pharaoh (Exodus 1:15-19) and to destroy the infant Jesus using Herod (Matthew 2:16-18). It is striking that there was a co-ordinated, government-led assault on the lives of children as a prelude to the birth of these significant children. In addition we learn that good King Hezekiah's own brother was sacrificed to a pagan god (2 Kings 16:3).

Child sacrifice was something that was never requested or required by the Lord but was the common practice of the nations that surrounded Israel, such as Phoenicia. Abraham was never actually required to sacrifice his son Isaac but did have to be willing to (Genesis 22). It seems that Jephthah might have actually sacrificed his daughter as the result of a foolish and hastily uttered vow (Judges 11:29-40). Elsewhere the scripture was plain that child sacrifice was forbidden (Leviticus 18:21) and was itself a crime punishable by death (Leviticus 20:1-5). The practice was carried out by the apostate kings Ahaz and Manasseh (recorded in 2 Kings 16:3 and 2 Kings 21:5). It may have been previously introduced by King Solomon as it was a requirement of the gods Chemosh and Molech that he worshipped towards the end of his life as he was turned away from following the Lord by his foreign wives (1 Kings 11:7). These sins led directly to God's judgement upon Israel and her being sent into exile.

We live in days when there is an unprecedented onslaught on the lives of children. As a social worker I am aware that in the United Kingdom, on average, a child dies every week at the hands of an adult. However, as the former Deputy Director of Nottingham Social Services Andy Croall once said, "Abortion is the greatest form of child abuse." Ruth Graham, the late wife of the international evangelist Billy Graham, once said that if "God did not judge America for the sin of abortion then he should apologise to Sodom and Gomorrah". It seems to me that Western Europe is no better placed than America in this regard. However, God is full of mercy and compassion, and I believe that he understands and wants to provide for those who find themselves unexpectedly pregnant.

For a number of years I was on the committee of the Firgrove Family Trust, a Christian charity founded in Southampton. The charity had been established by Phil and Sheelagh Clarke as part of the church in the city's response to unplanned crises pregnancies [2]. As such the organisation has sought to provide an alternative to abortion. The emphasis of the work is the kindness and compassion of God. The work has gained huge respect, even with secular agencies, because of its non-judgemental attitude. My own experience of being an 'inconvenient' child gave me a great empathy for unwanted children and fuelled my intercession. I wrote my M.Sc. dissertation on the subject of teenage pregnancy as a result of studying the housing provision that was then supplied by the Firgrove.

Jesus came to grant us abundant life and destroy the devil's works. He has a plan for this generation of children and young people. This was outlined by Peter when he quoted Joel, saying:

Acts 2:17-18

In the last days, God says, I will pour out my Spirit on all people. Your sons and daughters will prophesy, your young men will see visions, your old men will dream dreams. Even on my servants, both men and women, I will pour out my Spirit in those days, and they will prophesy.

The worldwide outpouring of the Holy Spirit that commenced on the day of Pentecost in Jerusalem has continued and increased to this day. It is one of the features of the last days. Logically we are nearer to the Lord's returning now than on the day of Pentecost and so the increased moving of the Holy Spirit is to be anticipated and actively prayed for. In Acts we are told that Paul and Luke, when visiting Caesarea, stayed at the house of Philip the evangelist, one of the Seven. He had four unmarried daughters who prophesied (Acts 21:8-9). We too should expect and ask God to move in our families.

Your Sons and Daughters Will Prophesy

Reading the gospels, the picture that we gain is of Jesus being very comfortable around children and children being very happy to be around Him. In Matthew, the disciples came to Him and asked:

Matthew 18:1-6

"Who is the greatest in the kingdom of heaven?" He called a little child and had him stand among them. And he said: "I tell you the truth,

unless you change and become like little children, you will never enter the kingdom of heaven. Therefore, whoever humbles himself like this child is the greatest in the kingdom of heaven. And whoever welcomes a little child like this in my name welcomes me. But if anyone causes one of these little ones who believe in me to sin, it would be better for him to have a large millstone hung around his neck and to be drowned in the depths of the sea."

When I think of these words of Jesus I tremble for the fate of any who have directly or indirectly caused harm to children. God forbids and condemns every different permutation of incest (Leviticus 18 and 20) and by implication child sexual abuse. I have had to deal with the pain caused by such abuse myself. Lot and his daughters, having escaped the destruction of Sodom, became guilty of incest. They conceived Moab and Ben-Ammi who became the fathers of the Moabite and Ammonite nations - bitter enemies of Israel. Having sown lust through his adultery with Bathsheba (2 Samuel 11), David reaped the consequences in his own family, one of which was incest.

Christians are to grow up to be like children. Too often children have been encouraged to adopt adult attitudes of cynicism and unbelief. The fear of the Lord should guard us from causing children to stumble and sin. Fathers are commanded not to exasperate their children (Ephesians 6:4). The book of Proverbs has much to say about the discipline and training of children (Proverbs 13:24, 19:18, 22:15, 29:15 and 29:17). Not 'sparing the rod' is a figure of speech for all types of discipline and should not be used as a pretext for the physical abuse of children as has been done in the past. Unless a parent has learned to say and mean "no" to their child then their "yes" means nothing.

Later Jesus warned:

Matthew 18:10

See that you do not look down on one of these little ones. For I tell you that their angels in heaven always see the face of my Father in heaven.

The words in Matthew in turn remind us of the encouragement of Paul to Timothy:

1 Timothy 4:12

Don't let anyone look down on you because you are young, but set an example for the believers in speech, in life, in love, in faith and in purity.

Age is not a qualifying requirement for the grace and wisdom of God, nor youth a disqualification. We are told that...

1 Corinthians 1: 27-28

God chose the foolish things of the world to shame the wise; God chose the weak things of the world to shame the strong. He chose the lowly things of this world and the despised things - and the things that are not - to nullify the things that are.

Jesus said:

Matthew 5:8

Blessed are the pure in heart for they will see God.

Perhaps because of this, children can see God much more easily than many adults. Revelation is promised to children and the childlike. In Luke we read that...

Luke 10:21

At that time Jesus, full of joy through the Holy Spirit, said, "I praise you, Father, Lord of heaven and earth, because you have hidden these things from the wise and learned, and revealed them to little children. Yes, Father, for this was your good pleasure."

James and Peter both tell us:

James 4:6, 1 Peter 5:5

God opposes the proud but gives grace to the humble.

We need to receive God's grace rather than remain proud and be opposed. It is our responsibility to humble ourselves and to be like children.

Jesus said:

Matthew 19:14, Mark 10:14
Let the little children come to me, and do not hinder them, for the kingdom of heaven belongs to such as these.

He said this in response to His disciples trying to stop parents bringing their children to him. We see that he took the children in his arms, put his hands on them and blessed them (Mark 10:16).

Earlier in Mark he had said:

Mark 9:37
Whoever welcomes one of these little children in my name welcomes me; and whoever welcomes me does not welcome me but the one who sent me.

In caring for a child we are in some way showing hospitality to Christ. Too often Jesus' disciples have stood between Him and the children that He is wanting to bless.

In highlighting stories about my own children some might be concerned that I am boasting about them. My desire is to glorify God and stir parents with expectancy with regard to what God wants to do and might already be doing in their children. As James says:

James 4:2-3
You do not have, because you do not ask God. When you ask, you do not receive, because you ask with wrong motives, that you may spend what you get on your pleasures.

How many believing parents are open to the possibility of God speaking to them through their children? As I quoted from Isaiah at the beginning of the chapter, "a little child will lead them" (Isaiah 11:6).

The Ministry of Angels

One time when I was at a church meeting I was preoccupied with problems at work with the various families and children that I was trying to help. As I was praying about these situations the words "you have forgotten the angels" came into my mind. Jesus had warned:

Matthew 18:10

See that you do not look down on one of these little ones. For I tell you that their angels in heaven always see the face of my Father in heaven.

God has assigned angels to watch over children and these angels gaze at the face of the Father in heaven. We read:

Hebrews 1:14

Are not all angels ministering spirits sent to serve those who will inherit salvation?

I was recently running along the street with my son. Having been a runner in my youth I have been used to keeping pace with and outrunning him. However, this time was different. He easily outran me. I felt old and out of condition. My prayer has often been that my children would go beyond me in their walk with and experience of the Lord but I had expected to be able to keep pace with them while they were at primary school! I heard Heidi Baker pray for the up-and-coming generation that "our ceiling would be their floor". It appears significant that God is revealing Himself in such power to children. This appears to be preparatory to the call that he has for each of them. This call is in the present and not the future.

So how do children learn? Talking to Abigail and Jemimah in 2001 for a study I was doing at church they told me of four different ways that they learnt things: 1 looking, 2 listening, 3 copying and 4 remembering. Their answers have stuck in my mind. I wrote these things down as I was told them and, as if to emphasise this, my then two-year-old son Daniel picked up my pen when I had finished with it and drew all over the paper.

Look, Listen, Copy and Remember

We learn by looking and so do our children. Jesus said:

John 5:19

...the Son can do nothing by himself; he can do only what he sees his Father doing, because whatever the Father does the Son also does.

Unless we have watched carefully we will not know what we are supposed to do. My son was following this example. Before you can copy you must watch carefully. There is a world of difference between the pre-school child's scribble and adult writing. Before anyone can do the latter they will have spent a long time doing the former. Every loving parent understands this; we just try to discourage scribbling on the walls!

We also learn by listening. Speaking of Himself as the Good Shepherd, Jesus said that his sheep follow him because they know his voice (John 10:5). How then do children listen? Familiarity and training help them and us to distinguish the voice of God from that of a stranger. As adults learning to hear God it is important for us to be still on the inside. We are told to "be still and know that I am God" (Psalm 46:10).

Children need to do the same. Sometimes getting them just to be still on the outside is challenge enough without the stillness within! I have been told that I was a terrible fidget as a child. Parents know that if you don't have a child's attention they will never listen to you however loudly you speak to them. Children have the ability to tune out their voice. We can all be so distracted by worries that we can tune God out.

We need to focus on God and give him our full attention. He will happily give us His. If we allow Him to nourish us with His love and meet our deepest needs then learning will be effortless. We will cease trying to be and simply be. Abigail once asked me, "How do you learn to be a grown up?" I told her that it just takes time. There are no short cuts. It seems to me that many adults need to learn how to be a child.

Children and adults learn by repetition. After we have watched and listened then we can copy. In Hebrews we read that...

Hebrews 8:5

They serve at a sanctuary that is a copy and shadow of what is in heaven. This is why Moses was warned when he was about to build the tabernacle: See to it that you make everything according to the pattern shown you on the mountain.

This verse is itself a quotation from Exodus 25:40.

We see that Moses' tabernacle made on earth was a copy and shadow of the tabernacle in heaven. Moses was not entitled to make things up as he went along. Jesus taught His disciples to pray:

Matthew 6:10

Your kingdom come, your will be done on earth as it is in heaven.

Heaven has the plan that earth is to copy. Unless heaven helps us we are helpless. We read:

Psalm 127:1

Unless the LORD builds the house, its builders labour in vain.

After crossing the Jordan, Joshua, using memorial stones, gave Israel a more permanent reminder of what God had done for them. God has left reminders for you and me too. Following the ending of the First World War, a day of Remembrance was established, "lest we forget" the sacrifices of our forefathers. In Exodus we are told that...

Exodus 2:24

God heard their groaning and he remembered his covenant with Abraham, with Isaac and with Jacob.

Thereafter, the people of God were urged to remember all that God had done for them in liberating them from the bondage of Pharaoh in Egypt. When we remember the Lord He remembers us.

Jeremiah was called as a child. He knew the Lord speaking to him and calling him. He thought that he was too young and that this meant God could not use him. Gideon was the smallest and youngest in his family. God called him and used him to save the nation. Likewise David was the despised youngest son. Jesus has a tremendous heart for children. Every boy and every girl is special to him. Children are not part of the church of tomorrow but, as the worship leader and children's worker Ishmael has said, the church of today.

Paul, writing to Timothy, acknowledged that...

2 Timothy 3:15

...from infancy you have known the holy Scriptures, which are able to make you wise for salvation through faith in Christ Jesus.

Timothy had not arrived 'ready-made' as a pillar of the first century church. Although when he met Paul he was still young, many years had already been invested in his preparation and training. We understand that tuition from Lois, his grandmother, and Eunice, his mother, had prepared Timothy to be able to walk in his calling from a young age (2 Timothy 1:5).

As evidenced by the huge success of the Harry Potter and Twilight novels and films, there has been an explosion of interest in the supernatural among the young. These longings are legitimate and justified. We were made for God, and God is supernatural. If these legitimate longings are not appropriately satisfied then they will find illegitimate expression. At the time of Jesus' triumphal entry to Jerusalem...

Matthew 21:15-16

...when the chief priests and the teachers of the law saw the wonderful things he did and the children shouting in the temple area, "Hosanna to the Son of David," they were indignant. "Do you hear what these children are saying?" they asked him. "Yes," replied Jesus, "have you never read, 'From the lips of children and infants you have ordained praise?'"

As adults we must not hinder the children coming to Jesus but help them to find their way to him. In turn they can lead us closer to him and teach us how to come to God.

Jesus said, "No one can come to me unless the Father who sent me draws him" (John 6:44) or, as he explained, "unless the Father has enabled him." (John 6:65) These words are true whatever our age. It is striking that the Lord had spoken to Samuel three times before his adoptive father, Eli, discerned that God was seeking to gain the child's attention. It was when he understood this that Eli was able to equip the child to receive the revelation the Lord wanted to impart:

1 Samuel 3:9

So Eli told Samuel, "Go and lie down, and if he calls you, say, 'Speak, LORD, for your servant is listening.'"

Listening is an attitude of wanting and expecting to hear. Parents need to encourage their children to listen expectantly. At first Eli did not realise that Samuel was hearing from God.

It is written:

Hebrews 11:6

Without faith it is impossible to please God because anyone who comes to him must believe that he exists and that he rewards those who earnestly seek him.

These words should be applied to every area of our lives, particularly the raising of our children. Faith is more caught than taught; if we do not have it, how can we impart it to our children? If we lack it we must get it. How? We are told:

Romans 10:17

Faith comes from hearing the message, and the message is heard through the word of Christ.

In Luke we are told that in reflecting upon the supernatural experiences around our Saviour's birth "Mary treasured up all these things and pondered them in her heart" (Luke 2:19). This is good advice to parents.

Information about God is not the same as a revelation from him. Parents can give instruction, but only God himself can give a revelation. Our children need a revelation, for without it they cast off restraint and will perish.

Proverbs 29:18

Where there is no revelation, the people cast off restraint.

In these days in which many are throwing off restraint, God wants to reveal himself to the children of this land and also to anyone who will humble themselves and become like them.

Action!

The point of testimony is to provoke us to believe and to reclassify the things that we thought 'impossible' as 'possible with God'. If God has done it once he can do it again. What he has done for others he can do for you. If our faith does not work in our home and for our children then our faith does not work. Perhaps you were expecting that you had to raise your children for God without his help. Think again! Invite God to step into your home and into the lives of your children. I would challenge any parents who expect their children to have to walk through rebellion to change their minds. By and large we get what we expect. Start to live with your children with a greater sense of expectancy.

What can parents do to nurture their children's relationship with God? The most important thing is that we should have a relationship with God ourselves. More than anything we say, our children will study our lives. We should model for our children a profound, dependent and prayerful relationship with God. If something has excited you in the Bible do not keep it to yourself; share it with your children. Moses says:

Deuteronomy 6:6-7

These commandments that I give you today are to be upon your hearts. Impress them on your children. Talk about them when you sit at home and when you walk along the road, when you lie down and when you get up.

Prayer Points

- Pray that we as parents and part of the church would in no way hinder children coming to Jesus.
- Pray that God would pour out his spirit upon the sons and daughters of this generation and that we would recognise when he has begun to answer this prayer.

REFERENCES

1. Burn, Professor John, of the Institute of Human Genetics (Newcastle, 2003).

2. MacNutt, Francis and Judith, *Praying for your Unborn Child;* published by Hodder and Stoughton (1988), reprinted (23 June 2011); ISBN-13 9781444702569.

3. Clarke, Dr Phillip A, *A Heart of Compassion: Grace for the Broken;* published by Authentic Lifestyle (9 Jun 2006); ISBN-13 9781850786634. The story is told in this book.

Blessing or Curse?

Malachi 4:6

Or else I will come and strike the land with a curse.

Wormwood

On 26th April 1986 a Soviet reactor crew turned off the safety systems of the Unit 4 nuclear reactor at Chernobyl to perform what was an unauthorized safety test. Only 36 seconds later the reactor surged out of control, and a steam explosion ripped through the roof. Without any coolant, 150 tons of uranium fuel then melted into the base of the reactor. A second hydrogen explosion ignited blocks of graphite, propelling a plume of radioactive particles a mile into the sky. The explosion was so powerful that it blew the two million pound concrete lid of the reactor into the air. For three weeks the fire spread out of control, sprinkling iodine-131 and other radioactive material as far as Scandinavia, Italy, and Britain. [1]

The history of the Chernobyl disaster may be familiar. It remains the largest manmade disaster in history, the explosion at the centre being estimated to be eight times more powerful than Hiroshima. What is less well-known (but was widely circulated throughout the Soviet Union in the months following the explosion) was that the disaster had been prophesied in the Bible. As evidence supporting this claim, the following passage from the book of Revelation was quoted:

Revelation 8:10-12

The third angel sounded his trumpet, and a great star, blazing like a torch, fell from the sky on a third of the rivers and on the springs of water - the name of the star is Wormwood. A third of the waters turned bitter, and many people died from the waters that had become bitter.

The language appears strange to our modern ears but made more sense to first century Christians familiar with the apocalyptic writing of Daniel and Ezekiel. What chilled Russian readers of this text was that the word that is translated 'Wormwood' in English is 'Chernobyl' in Russian. The city of Chernobyl is named after the Ukrainian word for the plant mugwort or wormwood. I understand that the internal processes of a nuclear reactor bear some resemblance to the workings of a star. I would not rule out other possible fulfilments to these words but have been gripped by this since I first read it in 1986.

The Soviet Union was the first atheist empire in the world. It sought to indoctrinate its entire population into the belief that there is no God. God had been erased from its citizens' vocabulary and painted out of the picture. Overnight the situation was transformed. Only three years after Chernobyl, the Berlin Wall that separated East and West Germany had been torn down and the atheist empire of Communism collapsed.

I wonder, is this what it means for a land to be struck with a curse? The prophet Isaiah said:

Isaiah 26:9
When your judgments come upon the earth, the people of the world learn righteousness.

The truth is, if we live outside of fellowship with God then we live outside of his protection and his blessing. The only safe place to live is close to his heart, but how can we do that?

You Can Choose

In 1990 the international Bible teacher and former Cambridge professor Derek Prince came with his wife Ruth for a week of meetings in Southampton Guildhall. All the churches in the city were invited and the meetings were full. His theme for the whole week was the cross and what Christ accomplished for his people upon it. I felt that it was a privilege to be there. I bought what was Derek's latest book 'Blessing or Curse - you can choose!' which was then on sale for the very first time [2]. Many times since this I have reflected on what a unique 'blessing' it was for me and others in my adopted city to be the first people to be able to read this teaching which has helped people all over the world.

By and large people are comfortable with the word 'blessing'. It is something that is said or done at the end of church services. If at no other time, people will often say, "Bless you!" after another person has sneezed. We tend to feel less comfortable with the word 'curse' which is altogether spookier. It conjures images of superstition and witchcraft.

Although the Western Church finds the concept of cursing difficult to grasp, the Bible takes the subject very seriously. It opens and closes with references to curses (in Genesis 3:14-19 and Revelation 22:2). Furthermore, whole chapters are dedicated to both curses and blessings (Deuteronomy 27-31 and Numbers 22-24). Curses therefore have a biblical basis and 143 times in scripture either God or His servants pronounce them upon nations or individuals. It will serve us well in life to learn to live under God's blessing and avoid living under his curse [3].

When I read Derek Prince's book on the subject I was greatly impacted. I became convinced, as I reviewed my life in the light of its contents, that I had been blighted by a curse. My father and grandfather had been Freemasons, and although my father had left this organisation on principle, the book showed me how unhelpful freemasonry had been to me and my family. This is because of its idolatrous worship but also because of the terrible oaths and curses that the mason speaks over his life, his body and his family as part of his initiation.

At the end of the book there is a chapter entitled 'Seven Steps to Release'. There is a model prayer for release from a curse. As I prayed this prayer I physically felt something leave me. When I sought to identify what changed in me when I prayed, I recognised that a religious spirit had left me. Following this, I was less intense and striving. I was also less legalistic. Of course, with any freedom that we gain we need to retrain our minds. Graham Cooke used to say that it is one battle to break free and another to stay free. I felt more at ease with myself and with God. I also had a much clearer understanding of the cause and the cure of the problems that afflicted the families that I was working with as a social worker. Many were cursed and only the good news about the cleansing blood of Jesus could rescue them.

Even after this breakthrough I needed further deliverance. Through other writers and teachers I have come to see that, given the breadth and depth of the web of masonic entanglement, skilled prayer ministry is necessary to break its victims free. There are 33 levels in freemasonry. It might masquerade as a benign gentleman's club but in fact captures its members in witchcraft. Those who dabble in the lower levels of the organisation are ignorant of the fact that at the very top the worship of Satan is explicitly encouraged. As Freemasons move through the different levels they invoke progressively more serious curses upon themselves. However, even if they fail to proceed through the levels a Freemason and his descendants will remain fully bound until they have been released by the power of the blood of Jesus. He is stronger than the strong man.

Luke 11:21-22

When a strong man, fully armed, guards his own house, his possessions are safe. But when someone stronger attacks and overpowers him, he takes away the armour in which the man trusted and divides up the spoils.

As I reflected on what I learnt it seemed that many in the Church were almost as bound up as those outside. This being the case, how could we expect to deliver others if we had not been delivered? Graham Cooke often said, "We cannot take ground from the enemy if he has ground in us." How can anyone, for example, help a person overcome an addiction if they are controlled by an appetite for alcohol or cigarettes? Their words would ring hollow and appear hypocritical. More importantly, unless the Lord has "restored to us the joy of our salvation" how will we recommend to others the benefits of salvation? (Psalm 51:12)

Too often individuals in the Church have come away from spiritual skirmishes bloodied and bruised like the sons of Sceva. We are told that in Ephesus the seven sons of Sceva found that they were not able to deliver a demon-possessed man despite a previous track record of success. The reason for their failure was because of their lack of relationship with God the Father as demonstrated by their use of the name of Jesus. Unless we are subject to the Father in the name of Jesus we cannot exercise authority in His name. When the sons of Sceva tried to expel the demon, it said to them:

Acts 19:15

Jesus I know and I know about Paul, but who are you?

I have heard Prophet TB Joshua say, "Obedience is the only proof of our faith." We fool only ourselves if we call Jesus Lord but refuse to do as he says. The enemy is entitled to test the validity of our claims to be Christ's followers as he did the sons of Sceva. Even if we enjoy some victories over demons our ultimate success is not guaranteed. Jesus said that at the end of the age...

Matthew 7:22-23

Many will say to me on that day, 'Lord, Lord, did we not prophesy in your name, and in your name drive out demons and perform many miracles'. Then I will tell them plainly, 'I never knew you. Away from me, you evildoers!'

Only those who do the will of the father will be able to enter the kingdom of heaven. Only when we begin to walk under the authority of God the Father, as the centurion recognised that Jesus did, will we be allowed to exercise His authority. In any event, the authority never becomes ours but remains His. For this reason we are told not to "rejoice that the spirits submit to you, but rejoice that your names are written in heaven" (Luke 10:20). Our relationship with the Father is crucial.

What does it mean to see an individual struck with a curse? I shared in the chapter 'A Heart Restored' how I had been freed on another occasion from a 'spirit of death' when I had been falling asleep whilst driving. I had identified that the entry route for this had been the rape that I had suffered as a three-year-old. I would here add that freemasonry can also make a family vulnerable to both sexual abuse and a spirit of death. As our words and those of our ancestors may have imprisoned us so we must make specific renunciation of every curse that holds us. Through the blood that Jesus shed for us on the cross he has done everything that is necessary for our healing, deliverance and salvation. We must learn to apply his blood to our households as the Jewish people did the blood of the Passover lamb to their lintels and doorposts on the night of the Exodus (Exodus 12). Only then will the angel of death pass over families. At the end of this chapter I have suggested some ministries that would be able to help those seeking deliverance.

Many years prior to my first experience of release I had a time of prayer with a group of young people in a house that I shared in Winchester. An older man asked me to lead in praying against the operation of the enemy in the area. With the arrogance of youth I started to do so, and at that moment it felt like a demon jumped on me. I felt an incredible nausea and heaviness and fell over backwards. After further prayer I felt a sense of relief. However, it was some years before I was delivered. I learned a salutary lesson and saw that I had been presumptive. There are different levels of prayer and you have to be adequately prepared to move beyond your usual sphere. You cannot minister freedom if you are held in bondage. There was also an unhelpful emphasis at that time in praying against demons rather than to God the Father in the name of Jesus. Pride can destroy us in such situations whereas humility and falling on God can rescue us [4].

We gain a clearer understanding of how we might live under God's blessing, and what happens when we don't in returning to Malachi. It is here that it says:

Malachi 1:14
Cursed is the cheat who offers a blemished sacrifice to the Lord.

It is also written:

Malachi 2:2
"If you do not listen, and if you do not set your heart to honour my name," says the LORD *Almighty, "I will send a curse upon you, and I will curse your blessings. Yes, I have already cursed them, because you have not set your heart to honour me."*

Although these words tell how the Israelites had incurred the Lord's displeasure they also indicate how to please Him. We are blessed when we are honest in dealings, offer unblemished sacrifices and listen to and set our hearts to honour God. In short we need to cultivate what Bill Johnson calls "a culture of honour".

Mount Gerizim or Mount Ebal?

Moses commanded the Israelites:

Deuteronomy 11:29
When the LORD your God has brought you into the land you are entering to possess, you are to proclaim on Mount Gerizim the blessings, and on Mount Ebal the curses.

Later Joshua organised the people to obey Moses' command (Joshua 8). Having seen these two Mountains in Israel, they are very different in appearance. They are next to each other and subject to almost identical weather conditions but to this day Mount Gerizim looks greener than Mount Ebal. In short Mount Gerizim appears blessed whereas Mount Ebal does not. This is a graphic visual aid to a spiritual principle. After writing this I learned that in modern times Derek Prince was one of the first to make this observation, but having seen it with my own eyes I can confirm that it is true.

Twenty-two years of working in social work in the United Kingdom and the insights afforded me through my own deliverances have convinced me that curses are a real force in the lives of many families of this land. They come from a history of rebellion, disobedience and idolatry. In my view, Christians are not exempt. This is certainly my testimony. An objection that I have heard to the possibility of Christians being subject to a curse is that everything from the person's old life has been dealt with through the cross. Whilst on one level this is true, it does appear from observation of the Church that many of us are yet to appropriate all that Christ died to bring us into.

There is a distinction between a Christian's justification (which is historic fact) and their sanctification (which is an ongoing process). For our own good it appears that we do not receive everything that we are entitled to at the point that we enter God's family. We would not be able to handle it. Solomon tells:

Proverbs 20:21

An inheritance quickly gained at the beginning will not be blessed at the end.

We do not cherish what we have not had to fight to preserve. Again Moses told the people of Israel that...

Deuteronomy 7:22

The LORD your God will drive out those nations before you, little by little. You will not be allowed to eliminate them all at once, or the wild animals will multiply around you.

I believe that the second commandment is still applicable to us. Speaking of idols we are told:

Exodus 20:5-6

You shall not bow down to them or worship them; for I, the LORD your God, am a jealous God, punishing the children for the sin of the fathers to the third and fourth generation of those who hate me, but showing love to a thousand generations of those who love me and keep my commandments.

The great encouragement from this passage is that blessings for obedience have a much longer reach than curses for disobedience and idolatry. You are, given these odds, 250 times more likely to receive a blessing than a curse from your forebears.

However, all of us, me included, are likely to have a mixed heritage of curses and blessings from our ancestors. We need, whilst appropriating the blessings, to cancel curses that continue to overshadow our lives. We have a choice that requires action.

Deuteronomy 30:1

This day I call heaven and earth as witnesses against you that I have set before you life and death, blessings and curses. Now choose life, so that you and your children may live.

Others might object that curses are confined to the Old Testament and Christians lives are governed by the New Testament; that we "are not under law but under grace" (Romans 6:14). The context in which this verse was given makes it clear that the grace of God was given to free us from sin. We are never free to continue to sin. Many remember Jesus' blessings, his beatitudes, given in his Sermon on the Mount (Matthew 5) but forget his curses or woes. Seven times Jesus denounced the scribes and Pharisees as hypocrites and sons of hell (Matthew 23). When Jesus cursed three towns it is noteworthy that none of them remains a living settlement today:

Matthew 11:21

Woe to you, Korazin! Woe to you, Bethsaida!

Jesus cursed a fig tree and it withered and died (Mark 11:21). We are told that it would have been better for Judas Iscariot if he had not been born (Mark 14:21).

If we want to live under the blessing of God, it is helpful to pay attention to the things that Jesus cursed and avoid them. Jesus said woe to those who are rich, well fed, and laughing because they have received their comfort; they would go hungry, and weep and mourn (Luke 6:24-25). He concluded by saying:

Luke 6:26

Woe to you when all men speak well of you, for that is how their fathers treated the false prophets.

From this I do not understand that those who are well-fed, happy, comfortable and possessing a good reputation are cursed, but those who make obtaining these blessings their primary goal are at risk of being cursed. God's approval is the most important thing in our lives.

Careless Words

Blessings and curses are both brought into effect through words. Part of our problem in the West is that we do not understand how powerful words are in general and God's word is in particular. This is unfortunate given that Jesus said:

Matthew 12:36

Men will have to give account on the Day of Judgment for every careless word they have spoken.

The Government slogan used in the Second World War that warned 'Careless talk costs lives' rings true today.

There is still a war on.

Throughout the account of creation in Genesis we are told that God called the world into being by His word. "God said, 'Let there be...'" The world remains dependent upon God's word. We are told:

Hebrews 1:3

The Son ... [sustains] all things by his powerful word.

Men and women are dependent upon God's word whether we understand, believe and appreciate it or not. It is written:

Deuteronomy 8:3

Man does not live on bread alone but on every word that comes from the mouth of the LORD.

These words were Jesus' defence against Satan during His desert temptation. His word is also our defence as we learn to confess it with faith. The reality is that we do need God's word more than our food and drink.

It is because we are made in the image of God that our words imitate the power of His words. Solomon tells us:

Proverbs 18:21

The tongue has the power of life and death, and those who love it will eat its fruit.

A phrase that Carol Ann once found herself using but has had to correct is "shame on you". This was brought home to her when one of our children asked, "Can I take the shame off?" This is quite a mild example compared with the devastating, angry words that can be used in families.

This point is further illustrated by the story of the destruction and rebuilding of Jericho. Following the destruction of the city it is written that...

Joshua 6:26

Joshua pronounced this solemn oath: "Cursed before the LORD is the man who undertakes to rebuild this city, Jericho: At the cost of his firstborn son will he lay its foundations; at the cost of his youngest will he set up its gates."

Many years later, in Ahab's time, foolishly...

1 Kings 16:34

Hiel of Bethel rebuilt Jericho. He laid its foundations at the cost of his firstborn son Abiram, and he set up its gates at the cost of his youngest son Segub, in accordance with the word of the LORD spoken by Joshua son of Nun.

This was a costly rebellion; curses are a force that can and do bring a premature end to people's lives. It would not matter that Hiel was unaware of Joshua's words; ignorance is no defence against such principles. Just in case we thought that this was solely an Old Testament principle we are told that...

1 Corinthians 11:29-30

...those who eat and drink without discerning the body of Christ eat and drink judgment on themselves. That is why many among you are weak and sick, and a number of you have fallen asleep.

Just as there were casualties following the inauguration of the Old Covenant, when Nadab and Abihu died after they offered strange fire (Leviticus 10), so in the New Covenant Ananias and Sapphira died when they lied against the Holy Spirit (Acts 5). Our God is still a holy God.

A curse does require a cause. Solomon tells us:

Proverbs 26:2

Like a fluttering sparrow or a darting swallow, an undeserved curse does not come to rest.

As an aircraft requires a landing strip and permission to land so sin provides the enemy with a green light and runway into our lives. I have heard Prophet TB Joshua graphically teach that Satan rules through sin, whilst God rules through obedience. He also said that no one ever improved their circumstances by speaking negatively about them. Only Jesus was able to say of the 'prince of this world' that "he has no hold on me" (John 14:30).

Our only hope is in the power of the blood that Jesus shed on the cross. Rather than seeking to justify or excuse ourselves this should be our confession. Jesus said:

Matthew 12:37

By your words you will be acquitted, and by your words you will be condemned.

The very mouths that have brought us into bondage can be used of God to bring us freedom.

Witchcraft

At one time I had been working with a family for some years. It seemed that all the professionals involved with them became incredibly bogged down and struggled to make a sensible decision. It was as though we were all walking around in a fog of confusion. At the end of myself one day I asked the Lord what the problem was and why this case seemed so difficult to resolve. I was surprised when He answered me very clearly and quickly saying that "the mother is a witch". No doubt He had wanted to tell me for some time and was waiting for me to ask! When I recovered from my initial alarm I realised of course that the Lord had known all along and that He was in charge of the situation. It was as if suddenly the scales fell from my eyes and it all began to make perfect sense. She had been using the dark spiritual focuses that she was in contact with to manipulate, control and confuse those she perceived to be her enemies. I believe that she and her associates tried to curse me.

I then called upon some friends who were experienced in prayer, and I myself set my face to seek the Lord with fasting for a three day period. It was then as though the fog had cleared and the matter was resolved quickly without further delay. Some curses come from a history of our own disobedience whilst others come through the enemies of the gospel.

Perhaps I ought to give a little more information. Looking at this mother, there were no outward indications of her spiritual problems. I had really warmed to her. Samuel learned that he could not judge by outward appearance but by the Spirit of the Lord who sees the heart (1 Samuel 16:7). Paul tells us that...

Ephesians 6:12

...our struggle is not against flesh and blood, but against the rulers, against the authorities, against the powers of this dark world and against the spiritual forces of evil in the heavenly realms.

It is possible to treat accounts of Satanists praying against Christian marriage as an 'urban myth'. However, to do so is foolish. As a family we have come to a clearer understanding of the dangers and reality of witchcraft through our visits to Africa. At the end of primary school my eldest daughter was given a number of the Harry Potter books as birthday presents and being an avid reader was desperate to find out what the fuss was about. I checked out with one of our church leaders their opinion. It transpired that they were a fan of the books but advised some caution. In the end our daughter read several of the books. We talked and prayed about the contents with her. I also read one of the books, and whilst I found the narrative gripping I felt that it fed my fears rather than developed my faith. During our visit to the Synagogue Church of All Nations we watched a number of dramatic deliverances both live and on video. These were followed up by detailed and sometimes hair-raising testimony of what the freed individuals had been delivered from. As a family we then disposed of the entire Harry Potter collection and many other books we thought unhelpful on our return. We now understand that these books and the power that they possess are derived from witchcraft and it is necessary to cut off all connection with them. Staying ahead of our children's reading is a challenge that we have not always mastered. We have repented of our foolishness. Again our only refuge is in the blood of Jesus and the finished work of Christ and not our ability to get it right. His blood alone brings us near to God (Ephesians 2:13), gives us confidence to enter the Most Holy Place (Hebrews 10:19), purifies us from all sin and enables us to have fellowship with one another (1 John 1:7).

Too many people are concerned with environmental pollution and too few are concerned about moral pollution. A stream cannot rise higher than its source. If we fill our minds with rubbish then it is at this level that we will live our lives. We learn from Solomon:

Proverbs 23:7, New King James Version
As [a man] thinks in his heart, so is he.

We need to change our minds. We are told in Philippians:

Philippians 4:8
Whatever is true, whatever is right, whatever is pure, whatever is lovely, whatever is admirable - if anything is excellent or praiseworthy - think about such things.

This is an active process that requires our full participation and active co-operation. Paul tells us:

Romans 12:2
Do not conform any longer to the pattern of this world, but be transformed by the renewing of your mind. Then you will be able to test and approve what God's will is - his good, pleasing and perfect will.

Guarding my thoughts has provided a personal key to victory over depression.

I understand that many might regard poverty as a curse and up to a point the Bible supports this view. However, the greatest problem for the poor is not their poverty but their sin. This is the same for all of us. Any helping approach that ignores this fundamental issue is doomed to failure.

I learned in Lagos that Jesus Christ died for our sins not our excuses. If we excuse our sins, our sins cannot be excused. God forgives our repentance and not our explanations. Many of the poor do not need someone to tell them that they are sinners; their 'sins' have gained official recognition. They need to be introduced to the 'friend of sinners' who can forgive and take away their sins (Matthew 11:19). God is coming for the poor, and he is coming whether we are ready or not.

Many professing Christians are ignorant of the enemy's devices. The word 'occult' means 'hidden'; God wants that which is hidden in darkness to be brought into the light. In the Western World demons are hidden in smart suits and look respectable. Generally we don't see what is going on. I remember once walking into a family home to speak to a mother and saw her son. As I looked into the child's eyes I saw a demon staring back at me and its name was 'lust'. With professional training and this discernment I understood in a moment what this child must have suffered. I did not have an official licence to offer Jesus to this person but I did pray.

One time when I was walking through a period of professional persecution, I was meeting regularly to pray with a group of experienced intercessors. During one of these times a friend had a strong sense that one of my enemies was going to die. Let me make it clear, we did not pray for the death of any of my persecutors but rather for their forgiveness and salvation. Nevertheless within a week word reached me that the 'witch' that I referred to earlier had died quite suddenly after a short illness. If we walk under God's protection the curses of our enemies will rebound upon them. I have heard similar stories from Christians from other parts of the world.

We need to know that...

Galatians 3:13-14

Christ redeemed us from the curse of the law by becoming a curse for us, for it is written: "Cursed is everyone who is hung on a tree". He redeemed us in order that the blessing given to Abraham might come to the Gentiles through Christ Jesus, so that by faith we might receive the promise of the Spirit.

If we are indeed to live in and offer Abraham's blessing then we must understand that the cross of Jesus and the blood that he shed for us is our only access point to all of this.

Access Points

The enemy however can have many access points into our homes and families. Objects can and do bring a curse. Prior to having children, Carol Ann and I went on a wonderful holiday to Turkey with her parents. Towards the end of our time abroad we wanted to choose a souvenir. In the end we decided it had to be a carpet. We did pray about this, looked around and settled upon a beautiful and rather expensive Turkish rug. Looking at it thoroughly we could see nothing wrong with it, although we did not know what the patterns on it meant. We went ahead with the purchase. However, as the years went by we had misgivings about our acquisition. These increased as our children came. They suffered nightmares and we became conscious of a cold and fearful presence on the landing where the rug was kept.

Reluctant to dispose of the rug I tried praying over it. However, I came to see that it had to go. One November I dumped it on the site of the local bonfire. I have never regretted getting rid of it but did regret acquiring it. Our daughter was no longer bothered by the landing and her night terrors stopped. It is better to lose the world and gain our soul. To enter heaven maimed is preferable to falling whole into hell.

I would counsel parents whose children suffer such terrors to take a prayerful walk around the children's room and their home and throw anything that gives disquiet. I would, for example, stay well away from Pokemon and other similar toys [5]. A guard should also be placed around what we and our children watch on the television and internet. We need to give very careful attention to what we look at, listen to and think about.

Anti-Semitism

A primary reason for a curse coming on individuals and churches is anti-Semitism. God said to Abraham:

Genesis 12:3

*I will bless those who bless you, and whoever curses you I will curse; and
all peoples on earth will be blessed through you.*

This promise was repeated to Abraham's descendants on numerous
occasions. These words remain as potent today as when they were first
spoken.

In the book of Numbers we are told the story of a character who
might be described as a 'spiritual hit man'. His name was Balaam son of
Beor. A text found in 1967 on an ancient collapsed wall in the Deir Alla
region of Jordan provides extra-biblical evidence for the existence of this
cursing prophet. In it he recited curses in the name of other gods [6].
Balaam was sought by Balak son of Zippor who was the King of Moab
because of his formidable reputation. Whoever Balaam blessed was
blessed, and whoever he cursed was cursed (Numbers 22:6). Balak had a
problem; he was frightened of his new neighbours, the people of Israel,
who had just come up from Egypt and wanted them cursed. We get the
impression that, for a fee, Balaam really wanted to help Balak. But for the
angel of the Lord and an argument that he had with his donkey, this is
what might have happened. God warned him:

Numbers 22:12

You must not put a curse on those people, because they are blessed.

The story has its comic moments as the increasingly exasperated
Balak took Balaam to various mountain peaks around the camp of Israel
to see if God would change his mind. God did not because God does not.
It is a huge irony that the line "God is not a man, that he should lie, nor a
son of man, that he should change his mind" (Numbers 23:19) should be
given to Balaam, who is prepared to bend with the wind and whose
character is questioned through the rest of scripture. You are left with the
sense that the bigger miracle was not that Balaam's donkey should speak
but that God should choose to speak through Balaam.

In the climax of the scene God says through Balaam to Israel:

Numbers 24:9

May those who bless you be blessed and those who curse you be cursed!

Balaam, the sorcerer, discovered from experience that there was no sorcery that was effective against Israel. Though he had prayed to "die the death of the righteous" and that his "end be like theirs" (Numbers 23:10), he in fact died at the hands of the Israelites (Numbers 31:8). Forever afterwards Balaam is recalled as the one who, whilst he failed to curse the Israelites, advised the Moabites to entice them into sin so that they might curse themselves (Numbers 31:16). This was because we are told that he loved the wages of wickedness (2 Peter 2:15).

The final reference to Balaam in the Bible is in book of Revelation and Jesus' letter to the Church of Pergamum (Revelations 2:12-17). We are told that this was where Satan had his throne and where Antipas, the faithful witness, had died. Following a few commendations from the Lord he told the church in this city the things that he held against it. Chief among these were that...

Revelation 2:14

There are some among you who hold to the teaching of Balaam, who taught Balak to entice the Israelites to sin so that they ate food sacrificed to idols and committed sexual immorality.

The city of Pergamum was the home of a famous altar housed in the temple of Zeus and a centre of the cult of Emperor Worship. It seems likely that this altar was what was referred to as the "throne of Satan". It was a massive structure built in the 2nd century BC. It was removed by a German archaeological team led by Carl Humann, who began excavating it on 9th September 1878 and later reconstructed it in the Pergamum Museum in the former East Berlin where it can still be seen. Kaiser Wilhelm II celebrated its completion in Berlin in 1902 as the "proudest monument to his reign" with an extravagant festival to pagan gods. It seems significant that within a short time of this, Germany was at the centre of two World Wars that could be attributed to satanic control. In 1933 Adolph Hitler was elected Chancellor of Germany. In 1934 he became dictator and ordered construction of the Tribune at Zeppelin

Field in Nuremberg for his Nazi rallies. The architect, Albert Speer, used the Pergamum Altar as the model for the Zeppelintribüne. The Führer's pulpit was in the centre of the tribune, which was built from 1934 to 1937 [7].

The earlier anti-Semitism of the church reformer Martin Luther was quoted by Hitler as a justification of his Final Solution to exterminate the Jews. Following "Balaam's error" is usually attributed simply to a pursuit of profit (Jude 1:11). However, Balaam's attempt to curse Israel for financial gain was at the root of his downfall. This error contaminated the Church of Pergamum and was later allied to Hitler's attempt to build a throne for Satan in Europe.

We are told:

Psalm 122:6-7

Pray for the peace of Jerusalem: "May those who love you be secure. May there be peace within your walls and security within your citadels."

We are also told the reason that we should do so:

Psalm 122: 8-9

For the sake of my family and friends, I will say, "Peace be within you."
For the sake of the house of the LORD our God, I will seek your prosperity.

I have heard these verses misapplied and reapplied to any and every city. Clearly the church in a region is mandated to seek the peace of its own city (Jeremiah 29:7). However, we must not forget to pray for the peace of Jerusalem. In this context it is presented as enlightened self-interest. If it were not important God would not have told us to do it "for the sake of my friends and family". There has never been a time in history when the peace of Jerusalem has been uncontested; and this has never been more true than today. The peace of Jerusalem is bound up with the peace of our own city. We have to understand that if Jerusalem falls then we all fall.

What does Balaam's error have to do with Western Christianity? For many years I used to subscribe to the Restoration magazine which was first published in 1976. For a time Arthur Wallis was its editor. There was much that I loved and found helpful in its contents. However, one entire edition of the magazine, written after Arthur's death, was devoted to attacking Israel politically and spiritually (Restoration magazine May/June 1991). Christians who believed that the restoration of Israel was a fulfilment of biblical prophecy were accused of accepting Israeli terrorism and supremacy as part of the fulfilment of God's promises [8].

Whilst I have never believed that the Jewish people were faultless, I have always recognised that God has unfinished business with them. I was shocked that so many men that I held in high esteem could sign up to a view that I could see had no basis in scripture. Whilst these teachers were a blessing to the church in many other ways, in this regard they did themselves a disservice. I believe that the doctrine of replacement theology is a heresy. Israel's re-gathering, preservation and continued existence is a testimony to God's faithfulness and a direct fulfilment of his word. The Restoration magazine folded a few months after this issue whilst Israel continues to endure against the odds. Until God's people have learned to agree with the revealed word of God regarding his end time plans for Israel they risk shutting themselves up to error and confusion.

Speaking in the context of the future glory of a restored Israel the prophet Isaiah said:

Isaiah 60:12

For the nation or kingdom that will not serve you will perish; it will be utterly ruined.

Citing this verse Derek Prince said:

...in seeking and praying for the good of Israel, Gentile Christians need to remind themselves that they are serving not merely the interests of Israel, but even more those of their own nation. [9]

Isaiah and Uzziah

In thinking of blessings it has helped me to focus on how Isaiah and Uzziah found their way into the presence of God and left changed, both scarred - one blessed and the other cursed. Uzziah, also known as Azariah, was one of the longest serving Kings of Judah, reigning fifty-two years from the age of sixteen. His name means 'God is my strength' and he gets a good write-up in the book of Kings where we are told:

2 Kings 15:3

He did what was right in the eyes of the LORD, just as his father Amaziah had done.

With this assessment of him we understand that he was a believer; however, considering the whole of his life we can see that having started well he was not 'blessed' at the end.

Isaiah the son of Amoz was a long-serving prophet who lived through the reigns of Uzziah, Jotham, Ahaz and Hezekiah, kings of Judah, and according to Jewish tradition died during the reign of Manasseh (Isaiah 1:1). Isaiah's name means 'the Lord saves'. He is regarded as the most evangelical of the prophets, seeing many details of the life of Jesus some 800 years before his birth. Before considering how Isaiah got it right let us look at how Uzziah got it wrong.

Uzziah started well:

2 Chronicles 26:5

He sought God during the days of Zechariah, who instructed him in the fear of God. As long as he sought the LORD, God gave him success.

Seeking God is the pathway to blessing. There is a valuable lesson in the relationship that existed between the teenage king and the elderly prophet. Uzziah was effectively an orphan king whose own father had been murdered. It appears that Zechariah became something of a spiritual father to him. Some historical sources tell us that Zechariah was well on in years when Uzziah took the throne. The prophet's oversight of the young king provoked Uzziah to continually seek God. As long as he did, God prospered him. God helped him against the Philistines (2 Chronicles 26:7). He began a building programme, constructing towers in Jerusalem and in the desert. He also "made machines designed by skilful men for use on the towers" to "shoot arrows and hurl large stones".

There is a link between the revelations of Zechariah and Uzziah seeking God. The prophet's heavenly access propelled the King towards greatness.

Those same historical sources also inform us that it is believed Zechariah died when Uzziah was in his mid-40s. After this Uzziah's "fame spread far and wide, for he was greatly helped until he became powerful" (2 Chronicles 26:15).

We might think that success would ruin a man's character but rather it reveals it. As long as Zechariah provided understanding to the king through the visions of God, Uzziah continued to do right. Without that vision, error resulted. From the days of the tower of Babel the motivation behind the construction of towers has attracted God's disapproval (Genesis 11). It is not surprising then to discover that "after Uzziah became powerful, his pride led to his downfall" (2 Chronicles 26:16).

How did he sin? He was "unfaithful to the LORD his God, and entered the temple ... to burn incense on the altar of incense" (2 Chronicles 26:16). When he was raging against the priests who tried to restrain him, leprosy broke out on his forehead. He entered God's presence a proud King and left, in disgrace, a poor leper. He was scarred by this disease until his death.

Isaiah also met with God in His temple, in the very year that the leprous King Uzziah died. There he saw the Lord "seated on a throne, high and exalted" (Isaiah 6:1). Years earlier God had told Moses, "You cannot see my face, for no one may see me and live" (Exodus 33:20). So Isaiah would have known that he was in trouble. In fear he cried:

Isaiah 6:5

Woe to me! ... I am ruined! For I am a man of unclean lips, and I live among a people of unclean lips, and my eyes have seen the King, the LORD Almighty.

I am indebted to Borys Greshenko, a Jewish Pastor from the Ukraine, who explained that the phrase translated "woe to me" does not really capture the depth of Isaiah's despair. He said, in effect, "Oi, oi, oi!" He felt that he had been smashed to bits and ruined. There is no room for pride in God's presence. When he saw God as He is, he knew who he was:

"[a] man of unclean lips ... [living] among a people of unclean lips" and what is more "my eyes have seen the King". Then one of the seraphs flew to Isaiah...

Isaiah 6:6-7

...with a live coal in his hand, which he had taken with tongs from the altar. With it he touched [his mouth].

His guilt was removed but his lips would have been scarred.

Uzziah sought to bring fire to God whereas Isaiah was touched by fire from God; both were burned. No one can escape the fire of God; for "the LORD our God is a consuming fire" (Deuteronomy 4:24).

It is better for the fire of God to consume our sin than consume us. With Uzziah we see the truth of the proverb "when pride comes, then comes disgrace". (Proverbs 11:2)

In the case of Isaiah, we see the truth of Jesus' words:

Matthew 5:8

Blessed are the pure in heart, for they will see God.

If we allow God to deal with our heart then our vision will become clear. Uzziah walked tall into God's presence and was laid low whereas Isaiah fell on his face and was raised up. In a moment before God, Uzziah's kingship ended and Isaiah was commissioned for a lifetime of service.

When Isaiah was in the temple the angels cried out, "Holy!", the "doorposts and thresholds shook" (Isaiah 6:4) and his heart trembled. However, there had been a great earthquake a few years earlier during the reign of Uzziah when the whole land had been shaken. We are told that the prophet Amos saw his vision two years before the earthquake, when Uzziah was king of Judah (Amos 1:1).

Hundreds of years later, but recalling this same earthquake and foretelling a future disaster, Zechariah warned:

Zechariah 14:5

You will flee as you fled from the earthquake in the days of Uzziah king of Judah.

Josephus, the Jewish Historian, and the Talmud both record that it was at the moment that Uzziah approached the altar in the Temple to offer incense that this terrible earthquake struck.

On 18th January 749 AD a huge earthquake flattened the cities of the Decapolis including the city of Beth Shan in Israel. The huge columns that had stood for 700 years and supported its pagan temples lay where they landed. On my first visit to Israel in 2006 I witnessed the aftermath of this devastation. None of Uzziah's towers would have withstood such an earthquake; all of them would have fallen. Isaiah anticipated a future...

Isaiah 30:25

.. day of great slaughter .when the towers fall, streams of water will flow on every high mountain and every lofty hill.

Paul Keith Davis, an American prophet, has linked this verse to the destruction of the Twin Towers on 9/11 [10]. Isaiah had seen that...

Isaiah 2:12,14-15,17

The LORD Almighty has a day in store for all the proud and lofty, for all that is exalted (and they will be humbled) ... for all the towering mountains and all the high hills, for every lofty tower and every fortified wall ... The arrogance of man will be brought low and the pride of men humbled; the LORD alone will be exalted in that day.

There is a day when every tower built by man must fall down.

Uzziah was cursed because he trusted in himself rather than in the Lord.

Jeremiah 17:5

Cursed is the one who trusts in man, who depends on flesh for his strength and whose heart turns away from the LORD.

The stories of Uzziah and Isaiah parallel the Pharisee and the Tax Collector in Jesus' parable (Luke 18:9-14). Uzziah might have prayed like the Pharisee: "I thank you that I am not like other men" (Luke 18: 11). By contrast Isaiah prayed like the Tax Collector: "God, have mercy on me, a sinner" (Luke 18:13).

At the end of the parable Jesus said of the tax collector:

Luke 18:14

I tell you that this man, rather than the other, went home justified before God. For everyone who exalts himself will be humbled, and he who humbles himself will be exalted.

Both James and Peter quote the proverb:

James 4:6, 1 Peter 5:5

God opposes the proud but gives grace to the humble.

Pride is opposed or 'cursed' by God whereas humility is 'blessed'. To choose blessing means to humble ourselves.

Of Jotham, Uzziah's son who reigned in his stead, Chronicles records:

2 Chronicles 27:2

[Jotham] did right in the sight of the LORD, according to all that his father Uzziah had done; however he did not enter the temple of the LORD...

Jotham followed his father's positive example in his early life of righteousness and leadership but learned from his mistakes. The Bible says that Jotham did all things right as his father had done but did not enter the Temple to offer incense - that lesson had been learned well. He no doubt saw the agony of his father's leprosy and resolved never to make that mistake in his reign. That is the attitude we must have as we begin follow the example of the men of God that preceded us.

Repentance and Rest

We tend to think of repentance as being something hard and heavy rather than liberating. In the story of the woman caught in adultery Jesus demonstrated his profound wisdom in dealing with sin. He firstly refused to accept the invitation to stone the sinner, challenging those without sin to be the first to pick up a rock. Being without sin himself, judgement was his right, but he would not condemn the woman. Those condemning the woman had been indignant at her sin, but Jesus exposed theirs. They, rather than the woman, all left the scene self-condemned. According to the Law of Moses death was the penalty for adultery. However, having saved her life, Jesus' words to the woman were:

John 8:11

Go now and leave your life of sin.

The New King James Version puts it more bluntly: "Go and sin no more." This is the challenge that we must both live in and offer. Like Jesus we must love the sinner and hate the sin - both our own and others. If we do not care enough to confront sin, we do not care enough.

In the Soviet Union there was once an attempt to abolish the traditional 'six day work, one day rest' pattern and replace it with one based on five or six days. From the autumn of 1929 until the summer of 1931, each year was divided into seventy-two five-day weeks. In an attempt to increase productivity, eighty per cent of each factory's workforce had to work every day (except holidays) while twenty per cent rested. But family and friends could be assigned different rest days and hence might not see each other. Furthermore, machines broke down more frequently because they were never idle and no maintenance could be performed on them [11]. It proved to be a disastrous experiment that had to be abandoned. Yet in Western culture we appear determined to repeat it.

We live in a restless world. We do not know how to repent or to rest. This is truly a curse. Superstores pride themselves in offering a service 24 hours a day. How quickly we have moved from being a society which kept one day special to one that never sleeps.

This is what the Sovereign LORD, the Holy One of Israel, says:

Isaiah 30:15

In repentance and rest is your salvation, in quietness and trust is your strength, but you would have none of it.

Truly a people that do not know how to stop will go nowhere. Unless we have learned to say "no", our "yes" means nothing.

In another age the Poet William Wordsworth wrote:

The world is too much with us; late and soon,
Getting and spending, we lay waste our powers;
Little we see in Nature that is ours. [12]

It has been noticed that the seven day week with one day of rest is universal in all cultures although the day of rest may vary. Rest is a gift from God. I am told that the human metabolism works more slowly on one day in seven. It is hardly surprising because this was how we were designed. We are told that...

Genesis 2:2-3

By the seventh day God had finished the work he had been doing; so on the seventh day he rested from all his work. And God blessed the seventh day and made it holy, because on it he rested from all the work of creating that he had done.

To rest one day in seven is the fourth of the Ten Commandments (Exodus 20:8-11). It was given as a memorial of God's Creation but is also the place where we find God's Presence; there we find the wonderful promise:

Exodus 33:14

My Presence will go with you, and I will give you rest.

To lay hold of it we are told that we must...

Psalm 46:10

Be still, and know that I am God; I will be exalted among the nations, I will be exalted in the earth.

"Be still" is also translated "cease striving".

Ecclesiastes 4:6

Better one handful with tranquillity than two handfuls with toil and chasing after the wind.

Graham Cooke often said that "rest is a weapon". How can this be? The answer is found in Psalm 91 where we are told that...

Psalm 91:1-2, emphasis added

He who dwells in the shelter of the Most High will rest in the shadow of the Almighty. I will say of the LORD, "He is my refuge and my fortress, my God, in whom I trust."

There is one way for people to beat the burnout and that is to come to Jesus. He said:

Matthew 11:28-30

Come to me, all you who are weary and burdened, and I will give you rest. Take my yoke upon you and learn from me, for I am gentle and humble in heart, and you will find rest for your souls. For my yoke is easy and my burden is light.

There are two things that are striking from this passage. The first is that rest is a gift that cannot be earned; it must be received ("I will give you rest"). The second is that rest can be found and, by implication, lost ("you will find rest for your souls"). In both instances a relationship with Christ is the only place where rest has its origin. I understand that the picture of oxen being yoked together that this passage has been thought to convey is mistaken. Jewish rabbis described the revelation or the teaching that they carried as a yoke. Jesus' yoke is light, easy and liberating.

To those who believed that the Sabbath rest was simply the absence of activity Jesus taught:

Mark 2:27-28

The Sabbath was made for man, not man for the Sabbath. So the Son of Man is Lord even of the Sabbath.

The Sabbath or 'Shabbat' is mentioned 62 times in the 4000 years covered by the Old Testament. However, it is mentioned 45 times in the three years of Jesus' ministry [13]. We might think that the Sabbath is something that only has significance in the Old Testament, but it is also for the New Testament. It is also for us; we have a promise of rest.

Hebrews 4:1

Therefore, since the promise of entering his rest still stands, let us be careful that none of you be found to have fallen short of it.

Meditating upon the Sabbath rest, God showed Heidi Baker that to dwell in this rest is to live in continual revival. Jesus, the Lord of the Sabbath, delighted in demonstrating the healing power of his Father on the Sabbath, offending the Pharisees. Across the gospels there are appropriately seven different occasions when it is recorded that Jesus healed on the Sabbath. As we learn to live in a place where we pray continually, we will leave off our own works and enter into the works of God.

Hebrews 4:11

Let us, therefore, make every effort to enter that rest.

We must embrace this paradox and strive to enter into this supernatural rest.

Action!

Even more so than other chapters it has been important to interweave teaching and testimony to provide practical examples of how to apply lessons. If we seek to identify whether we and our families are subject to a curse it is as well to ask if we and they are as blessed as they might be. Whilst to be born again is to be born for battle we are supposed to live victoriously. We are called to fight the good fight of the faith. So let us ask: are we conquerors or do we feel overcome? Graham Cooke has often said, "A good fight is one that you win."

How then can we enter the blessing in daily life that we have access to by the cross? In all of this we need to be guided by the Holy Spirit. At the end of this chapter I have reproduced a model prayer to help those who want to find freedom from curses. This is a prayer used by Mariamma Thampy for breaking generational curses. Mrs Thampy, together her husband, has been used to plant over 2000 churches in India. I suggest that those who want to use the prayer as a tool should do so carefully and thoughtfully. Some parts of it may sound strange, but I would encourage you to stay with it. You and your family may not have knowingly committed all of the sins that are anticipated by this prayer, but you can be sure that you are part of a wider human family that has. I would encourage you to look at this prayer as a starting point in your heart being restored.

It may be that given the depth and persistence of your problems you need others to stand alongside you in prayer. Should you need further help there are many specialist ministries that have developed expertise in assisting God's people to find deliverance from curses and demonic bondage. Amongst these I would endorse Ellel Ministries (www.ellelministries.org) Sozo Ministries International (www.sozo.org) and the Synagogue Church of all Nations (scoan.org).

Prayer Points

Dear Heavenly Father, I come before you today, in Jesus' name, in order to repent of any sins in my life, or in the lives of my ancestors right back to Adam and Eve, that have caused a curse to come upon me or my family.

1. *Lord I specifically repent of all idol worship and occult practices.*

2. *I repent of dishonouring my parents and ancestors.*

3. *I repent of moving the boundary stone and stealing land.*

4. *I repent of leading the blind astray from the way of salvation.*

5. *I repent of withholding justice from the alien, the fatherless and the widow.*

6. *I repent of all lust, fornication and adultery.*

7. *I repent of all drunkenness and drug taking.*

8. *I repent of abortion and shedding innocent blood.*

9. *I repent of sleeping with my father's wife and dishonouring my father's bed.*

10. *I repent of all sexual relations with any animal.*

11. *I repent of all incest in my family line.*

12. *I repent of sleeping with my mother-in-law.*

13. *I repent of all murder and especially secret murder of neighbours.*

14. *I repent of accepting a bribe to kill an innocent person.*

15. *I repent of not being obedient to your Scriptures.*

16. *I repent of anything whatsoever in my family line right back to Adam and Eve that has brought a curse upon us.*

Father, I take authority and I break all these curses over me and my family lines in the name of Jesus Christ of Nazareth. Through faith in Jesus Christ and his finished work on the cross I release us from any and every curse. And by faith I now claim the full blessings of my God for all my people.

1. *We will be blessed in the city.*

2. *We will be blessed in the country.*

3. *The fruit of our womb will be blessed.*

4. *The work of our hands will be blessed.*

5. *Our food and health will be blessed.*

6. *We will be blessed when we come in.*

7. *We will be blessed when we go out.*

8. *The Lord will grant that all enemies who rise up against us will be defeated before us.*

9. *They may come at us from one direction but flee from us by seven.*

10. *The Lord will send a blessing on everything that we put our hands to.*

11. *The Lord will bless us in the land he is giving us.*

12. *The Lord will establish us as his holy people.*

13. *We will keep the commands of the Lord and walk in his ways.*

14. *All the peoples on earth will see we are called by the name of the Lord and they will fear us.*

15. *We shall multiply as a people.*

16. *We shall lend to many nations but borrow from none.*

17. *The Lord will make us the head and not the tail.*

18. *We will be the friends of Jesus Christ who are led by his Holy Spirit.*

19. *We will never turn aside from the way of the Lord.*

20. *We will always be at the top and never at the bottom.*

21. *We will receive every blessing that God has for us even the blessings we don't yet know about.*

And now I command every demon to leave us in Jesus' name. I thank you loving Heavenly Father for releasing us from every curse and every evil spirit that has operated in our lives from the result of curses caused by our disobedience. As for me and my household we shall serve and be led by the Lord. In Jesus' name. Amen. [14]

- Pray that you, your family and your Church would understand how to please the Lord and live accordingly.
- Pray that you and those around you might live under God's blessing and free from His curse.
- Pray for a deeper revelation of the rest of God as the key to true revival and that the Church may enter that rest.

REFERENCES

1. http://www.theforbiddenknowledge.com/hardtruth/ chernobyl_wormwood.htm

2. Prince, Derek, *Blessing or Curse you can choose!;* published by Chosen Books (1990); ISBN-13 978-0800791667.

3. Kitchen, Yvonne, *Freemasonry: Death in the Church;* Fruitful Vine Publishing House (2005); EAN 9780958546409. For more information see this book.

4. Jackson, John Paul, *Needless Casualties of War;* published by Kingsway in 1999. On the subject of praying with wisdom I would strongly recommend this book.

5. On this subject I would recommend John Paul Jackson's book *Buying and Selling the Souls of Our Children*; published by Kingsway in 2000; ISBN-13 9781584830153.

6. http://www.christiananswers.net/q-abr/abr-a014.html

7. Hathaway, David, http://www.formerthings.com/throneofsatan.htm, http://www.thewatcher.co.uk/europe/europe.htm, and *Prophetic Vision,* published by evangelist.

8. Pearce, Tony, *Light for the Last days: Deception in the Church;* http://www.wps6.co.uk/~dev_lfld/view_page.asp?page_id=173&section_id =1&menu_id=226

9. Prince, Derek, *Our Debt to Israel,* Derek Prince Ministries International (1984); ISBN 9657299071

10. Davis, Paul Keith. This insight was shared in a message preached by at Bath City Church in June 2008. I am also indebted to an article shared by Paul Keith Davis entitled *The Generation That Seeks God Will Know His Nature and Power,* published on September 7, 2007.

11. Foss, Clive, *Stalin's topsy-turvy work week,* History Today 54/9 (September 2004) 46–47.

12. Wordsworth, William, *The World is Too Much with Us* (a sonnet written in 1807)

13. Hess, Tom, *Enjoy the Rest of His Presence: Shabbat;* published by Progressive Vision International (2006); ISBN 9657193117; www.jhopfan.org

14. Thampy, Mariamma, *Better than the Weapons of War;* published by Mariamma Thampy, Bethesda Publications, New India Church of God, P.B. No:5, Chingavanam P.O. Kottayam- 686 531, Kerala, South India.

Reclaiming the Land

The Guide

In October 2006, someone gave Carol Ann and I the money to go on an eight day tour of Israel. Carol Ann's parents and some very generous friends shared the care of our four children. It was our first visit to the land. Reflecting on the experience Carol Ann said it was like having your Bible coloured in and becoming three dimensional. You have read the book; now visit the land! Our positive experience was in no small part thanks to our amazing guide Arie Bar-David.

It was through Arie that I gained a profound insight into the importance of restoring the hearts of the Christian children to the Jewish fathers. When I think of him I am reminded of Jesus' words:

Matthew 13:52

Therefore every teacher of the law who has been instructed about the kingdom of heaven is like the owner of a house who brings out of his storeroom new treasures as well as old.

Jewish Bible teachers who can explain the kingdom of heaven are indeed able to bring out the treasures from both the new and old covenants. Someone who is able to read the Bible in its original language is always going to have the edge on those of us forced to read it in translation.

Arie is the son of a Jewish Bulgarian aristocrat named Chaim Bar David. Whilst in Switzerland in the 1920s, Chaim had been handed a booklet containing the Sermon on the Mount by a Salvation Army group. With that, he believed Jesus was the Messiah and in 1928 moved to the land then known as Palestine during the unhappy period of the British Mandate. Today this man's legacy of faith has influenced five generations of Messianic Jews in Israel. His son's full name is Arie Yehuda Bar David and means 'lion of Judah, son of David'. He was born a year before Israel became a state in 1948. As a young man he fought in the army's paratrooper unit in many of Israel's wars since 1967 and once battled alongside the former prime minister Ariel Sharon.

All Israelis have to serve in the Israeli Defence Force (IDF) for two years when they reach eighteen, and for parents it is both a matter of pride and a cause for concern. For Arie's mother it was a particular burden for prayer. Her additional concern was that although she was proud for her sons to serve in the military, she did not want them to kill anyone. Her Messiah's instruction "to love your enemies" weighed on her heart. This made the challenge of military service more difficult. However, taking on board her concern Arie trained as a skilled marksman who was able to disable the enemy without killing them. He also became proficient in ministering first aid. I understand that his mother's prayers were answered, and he never killed anyone.

As Messianic Jews, Arie and his brothers were regarded by both secular and religious Israelis in the IDF with a certain amount of suspicion and distrust. Although extremely able, they discovered that their faith in Jesus was a barrier to promotion. However, the manner and faith with which they served earned them respect. Arie told how he had testified to others of the protection that was afforded to him as a believer. He told our group of a time during the 1973 Yom Kippor War when his platoon were under bombardment and his commanding officer had been injured. He was put in charge of guiding the men to safety. As they followed him he saw a light and knew he had to follow. Again and again he moved the troop from one position to another just before a missile struck. On bringing everyone back safely he discovered that no one else had seen the light.

Arie did not generally like taking 'tourists' on his tours and preferred taking serious Bible students and Christian leaders. This was reflected in his avoidance of the traditional tourist sites and the low priority he gave to taking photographs! In this context his agreeing to take our group of about thirty from various churches in and around Southampton was striking. He was usually booked up about eighteen months in advance but when our tour leader, Ann Hutchinson, had telephoned him less than a year ahead, he had just cleared his diary for the period concerned and to his surprise and ours found himself accepting our booking. Due to the recent conflict most other tours were cancelled.

A subsequent tour for an American group that Arie led was entitled 'Spiritual Warfare and Leadership Lessons' and this title more fully reflected his priorities. After his army service, Arie, who was also a distinguished classically trained musician, played double bass in the Jerusalem Symphony Orchestra for seven years. He had also worked as a carpenter. Following the call of God he laid down his flourishing music career to live on a moshav, or a collective community. Later God restored music to him in a different form: during our tour he was working during the evening translating Handel's Messiah into Hebrew for a concert the following Passover/ Easter in April 2007.

Arie's passionate love of God, His word and His land communicated itself to all who were part of our group and left an indelible mark upon us. Arie is a unique teacher knowing the Bible not through a dry and dusty commentary but, as he told us, through his feet walking the dry and dusty land. He has spent a lifetime studying the scriptures and received a unique revelation and insight. Nowhere was this truer than in the Galilee.

The Galilee

In Northern Israel, Lake Galilee is three hundred metres below sea level and only a hundred metres above the Dead Sea. At its widest point it is seven miles across and fourteen miles from north to south. In the region of Galilee Arie explained that Jesus would have been conscious of standing in his Father's creation. It is a natural amphitheatre bordered by the mountains of the Golan Heights in the North and smaller hills and mountains all around. Contrastingly, in Jerusalem Jesus would have been overshadowed by the creations of Herod the Great. This included Herodian - the mountain that he had had built and where he was buried.

In Galilee crowds could gather freely and would have been able to follow Jesus. In Matthew it is written:

Matthew 4:25
Large crowds from Galilee, the Decapolis, Jerusalem, Judea and the region across the Jordan followed him.

With its many caves and hiding places Galilee was to become the place of resistance to every occupying power. In Jerusalem, which was firmly under Roman control, crowds were not permitted to congregate.

So Galilee became the ministry base of Jesus as had been foretold by the prophet Isaiah. The prophet had written:

Isaiah 9:1-2, quoted in Matthew 4:15-16

Land of Zebulun and land of Naphtali, the way to the sea, along the Jordan, Galilee of the Gentiles - the people living in darkness have seen a great light; on those living in the land of the shadow of death a light has dawned.

Of Jesus' thirty-two beautiful parables, nineteen were spoken in Galilee. Of his thirty-three miracles, twenty-five took place in the province. His first miracle was at the wedding in Cana of Galilee and his last, after his resurrection, was on the shore of Galilee [1].

The region of Galilee was part of the territory of the Northern Israelite Kingdom, the inhabitants of which had been taken into exile by the Assyrians a hundred years before the Kingdom of Judah had been taken into exile by the Babylonians. There had been no widespread return of Jewish exiles from the Northern Kingdom to resettle their territory as there had been for the Southern Kingdom under Ezra and Nehemiah. We notice that although Mary and Joseph were both descended from the tribe of Judah they lived in Nazareth, despite their hometown being Bethlehem, the town of David. The picture that we have from the gospels is that the Jews who were from this region were looked upon almost as second class with a status just above the Samaritans.

Illustrating this prejudice John tells how Jesus' opponents asked:

John 7:42

How can the Christ come from Galilee? Does not the Scripture say that the Christ will come from David's family and from Bethlehem, the town where David lived?

They were plainly ignorant of the fact that Jesus had both been born of David's family and in Bethlehem. They also ignored the implications of Isaiah 9 that the Messiah would live and move in the Galilee region.

Later Nicodemus, who was defending Jesus, asked:

John 7:51
Does our law condemn anyone without first hearing him to find out what he is doing?

The Pharisees retorted scathingly:

John 7:52
Are you from Galilee, too? Look into it, and you will find that a prophet does not come out of Galilee.

However, in Kings we read that Jonah son of Amittai was the prophet from Gath Hepher (2 Kings 14:25). In Joshua we are told that Gath Hepher was part of the land given to Zebulun (Joshua 19:13). So as this town was in the Galilee we must conclude that the Pharisees comments either betray their ignorance of the scriptures and local geography (which is unlikely) or more probably their contempt for Jonah, this famously disobedient prophet, and the region of his birth. Both the man Jonah (because of his disobedience) and his message of repentance to the Gentile city of Nineveh were obnoxious to the patriotic Jew. Jonah's message was no more palatable to him than it was to his countrymen!

This gives a context for Jesus' comment:

Matthew 12:39-40
A wicked and adulterous generation asks for a miraculous sign! But none will be given it except the sign of the prophet Jonah. For as Jonah was three days and three nights in the belly of a huge fish, so the Son of Man will be three days and three nights in the heart of the earth.

Prejudice was not a factor that governed the speech or actions of Jesus. It is written:

Hebrews 13:12-13

Jesus also suffered outside the city gate to make the people holy through his own blood.

We are invited to join him outside the camp, bearing the disgrace he bore.

Matthew tells us that when Jesus heard that John had been put in prison he returned to Galilee. Leaving Nazareth, he went and lived in Capernaum (Matthew 4:12).

Capernaum

Capernaum is a little fishing village beside the Sea of Galilee. It was in existence as a settlement from the second century B.C. to the seventh century A.D and had up to 1500 residents. Jesus is our Emmanuel, 'God with us', coming to live among us.

In Capernaum Jesus did far more recorded miracles than in any other town in the New Testament. When he went to Nazareth where He had grown up, Jesus quoted the people as saying to Him:

Luke 4:23

Do here in your home town what we have heard that you did in Capernaum.

Word spread throughout the region about what was happening in Capernaum. In Nazareth Jesus could "not do many miracles there because of their lack of faith" (Matthew 13:58). By contrast in Capernaum he "healed all the sick" (Matthew 8:16). The truth is that the citizens of Nazareth, in having information about Jesus family and his origins, missed the revelation of His true identity as their Messiah. Being *used to* Jesus, we can tie His hands with our unbelief. Where He is honoured He can be Himself. However, as we shall see, there is yet hope for Nazareth.

In the Western Church we have in many respects become like Nazareth, having had the gospel for over a thousand years – familiar, even safe, with Jesus. Like the citizens of that town we have come to regard

Jesus as a boy who grew up in our midst. In thinking that we have the measure of Him we have merely limited His ability to help and bless us.

Prejudice concerning a person's history can impede them fulfilling their destiny. We can be too preoccupied with where they have come from rather than where they are going. There is a proverbial statement that 'familiarity breeds contempt'.

I am reminded of Lucy's question to Mr Beaver about Aslan, "Then he isn't safe?" to which Mr Beaver replied, "Who said anything about safe? 'Course he isn't safe. But he's good. He's the King, I tell you." [2]. We have attempted to domesticate Jesus, forgetting that he is the "lion of the tribe of Judah" (Revelation 5:5).

Capernaum means quite literally the 'village of the comforter'. Arie told our group that Nahum, the Old Testament prophet, whose name was a root of the town's title, meant 'comforter'. The name of the leader Nehemiah has the same root. The Jewish expectation was that their Messiah would be, amongst other things, a comforter. In Isaiah we read:

Isaiah 40:1

'Comfort, yes comfort my people!' says your God. 'Speak comfort to Jerusalem'.

Jesus, speaking in John said:

John 14:16

And I will ask the Father, and he will give you another Counsellor to be with you forever: the Spirit of Truth.

The word translated here by the New International Version 'Counsellor' and in other versions 'Helper' is the Greek word *paraclyete* which means all of this and more. It means 'helper, counsellor, advisor, friend and *comforter*'. Jesus was the first *comforter* and the Holy Spirit is the second that He promised would come after Him. Jesus coming to live in the town was a demonstration of God coming to the aid of His people.

From Capernaum Jesus called five of his twelve apostles. These include the brothers Simon (Peter) and Andrew and the sons of Zebedee, James and John. It also appears that Levi, the tax collector (also called

Matthew) came from the town. We are told in John that Philip was from the town of Bethsaida *like Andrew and Peter*, but it appears that both Andrew and Peter, through marriage and business, had come to live in Capernaum (John 1:44).

Later Jesus came into Peter's house in Capernaum and healed his mother-in-law. (Matthew 8:14) The town provided a base for Jesus in the region and these people were the building blocks for the future church.

Before Jesus reached the town of Capernaum He had healed the son of the Royal Official, a resident of the town (John 4:46). Mark tells us of Jesus delivering a man in the synagogue of a demon, then literally next door healing Peter's mother-in-law of a fever, before all the sick and demonised in the region were brought to her home to be healed (Mark 1-2). It became a very busy place.

On another visit to the town men broke through the roof of a house to lower their paralytic friend to the feet of Jesus. Close by was the home of the centurion whose servant Jesus healed (Luke 7:1-10). The Mount of the Beatitudes was a short walk away from the centre of the town. Jesus walked across the lake as the disciples were travelling towards the village (John 6:16). Peter also took a four-drachma coin from the mouth of a fish from the sea by the village in order to pay the temple tax (Matthew 17:24). People from Capernaum would have been among the five thousand filled with the miraculous loaves and fish.

We gain an understanding of what attracted Jesus to the town of Capernaum as we look at how two citizens of the town, Peter and the centurion, responded to him. We know that the Lord has no favourites but that faith attracts His attention. He does not keep company with unbelief. Jesus came with a message of repentance:

Matthew 4:17
Repent for the kingdom of heaven is near.

To some this message was welcome if uncomfortable. Peter acknowledged his sin on his first encounter with Jesus. After the miraculous catch of fish, Peter said to Jesus:

Luke 5:8

Go away from me, Lord; I am a sinful man!

When Peter saw Jesus he felt he did not deserve His presence and was convinced that he was a sinner. The centurion also knew that he did not deserve to have Jesus come under his roof (Matthew 8:8). In part this was cultural respect; he was a Gentile and Jesus was a Jew, and Jews were not supposed to go to the homes of Gentiles. This was despite the fact that the centurion had built the synagogue as a demonstration of his love for the Jewish nation and the God of the Jews (Luke 7:5). Love for the Jewish people will move God's heart. He was one of only four Gentiles who were mentioned positively in the gospels and he was praised for having great faith. We have the sense that the centurion was aware of the holiness and purity of Jesus as well as discerning that He was walking under heaven's authority. David Herzog and other men of God have said that the time is coming when churches who refuse to pray for the peace of Jerusalem will themselves not be blessed.

Prophet TB Joshua observed that the centurion was privileged whilst Peter was poor. No one is too poor or too rich to acknowledge his weakness. Today we are less conscious of our sin and weakness. That is why we come and demand healing as if we deserve deliverance or blessing. The reality is that we deserve nothing from God. Jesus knows who we are, where we are coming from and where we are going to. He knows our past, present and future. As we come with our petition or complaint Jesus knows us. Often those who are sick promise heaven and earth but later do nothing when they are well. Jesus knows that it is common for a man to promise much when in need but to do little or nothing when he receives. Fortunately Jesus does not consult our past in order to determine our future.

Unfortunately not everyone in Capernaum had the attitude of Peter and the centurion. The congregation of the synagogue in the town had an issue with Jesus referring to Himself as the "bread of life" and insisting that people must eat His flesh and drink His blood (John 6). Previously some at the town had thought that he had blasphemed by saying to the paralytic that "your sins are forgiven". Here many turned back from following Him at that time and in that place. (John 6:66).

Capernaum was one of the three cities cursed by Jesus for its lack of faith. Jesus said:

Matthew 11:23-24

And you, Capernaum, will you be lifted up to the skies? No, you will go down to the depths. If the miracles that were performed in you had been performed in Sodom, it would have remained to this day. But I tell you that it will be more bearable on the day of judgement than for you.

Miracles are not an end in themselves. They are signs that should take us to God. Miracles should bring us and others to repentance.

Although Capernaum was the 'Village of the Comforter', Christianity is not for those who wish to live a comfortable life. It is often said that Jesus came to comfort the disturbed and to disturb the comfortable. Comfort was never meant to be selfish. We are saved to save others, healed to heal others and comforted to comfort others. Paul said that we are to "comfort those in any trouble with the comfort that we ourselves received from God" (2 Corinthians 1:3). Comfort is not meant to be kept. Freely we have received; freely we are to give.

Jesus' arrival in the town of Capernaum meant that the place could never be the same again. To whom much is given much is also expected. The sense we have was that Jesus greatly inconvenienced Capernaum, bringing crowds of desperate people into the town. He offends the mind to reveal the heart. Today the ruins of the town are owned by two churches. The Franciscans control the western portion with the synagogue and the Greek Orthodox property, built on what was believed to be the site of the centurion's house. The town lies in ruins and is not a functioning community anymore.

The phrase "Blessed are those who mourn, for they will be comforted" is often used at funerals and has an application at such times (Matthew 5:4). Smith Wigglesworth saw that the mourning that Jesus referred to in this passage as a grieving for souls. When we grieve for others, surely a divine and holy comfort follows. Those who sow in tears will reap with joy. Comfort cannot be kept; comfort grows when it is shared. In Psalm 30 it says:

Psalm 30:5

Weeping may remain for a night, but rejoicing comes in the morning.

I returned to Capernaum on subsequent visits to Israel in 2007 and 2008 by which time I thought that I had seen everything there was to see in that ruined town. I had 'been there and done that'. It was an archaeological site where nothing lived. However, God is a God of surprises. When I visited in 2008 I stood again in Capernaum.

On this occasion Pastor David Muyiwa Adeola, one of the leaders of Kensington Temple in London, England, said that that those visiting the town and seeing just archaeology were missing the point. He told us that wherever Jesus had walked there was an open heaven. Nowhere had the heaven been more open than in Capernaum. Its destruction as a settlement had guaranteed the preservation of this open heaven. He told us to pray. This place was a place of impartation. So in the ruins of the synagogue that had been built over the synagogue where Jesus had worked so many of his miracles, we prayed. Those in their twenties were invited to pray for any in the group who needed healing. As we prayed the power of God was present to heal and many needs were met. People were laid out on the stone pavement as God ministered to them. Then as they saw what was happening other tourists from other buses started to ask for prayer, and the Lord ministered to them as well. It was only with great difficulty that our group was persuaded to return to their bus and leave this place.

We cannot live in Capernaum; there is no longer a settlement there. However, we are commissioned to turn our communities into Capernaum by inviting Jesus to live in our midst. He is after all Emmanuel, God with us. Jesus said:

John 14:12

I tell you the truth, anyone who has faith in me will do what I have been doing. He will do even greater things than these, because I am going to the Father.

We must look for and expect the greater works. This will only come to pass through persistent, prevailing prayer. Indeed I would go further and say that it is only 24/7 prayer that will establish the presence of God amongst the people of God and within our communities.

Nazareth

On the same visit to Israel whilst worshipping God in a large tent in the grounds of a Nazareth hotel I was overwhelmed by the pungent scent of lilies. I turned around sure that someone had carried a bouquet of flowers into the meeting but I saw none. I asked a friend if they could smell anything, but they could not. Slightly puzzled I continued to worship the Lord. Later when returning to my hotel room the only odour I noticed was that of rotting food waste from the kitchen bins. This indicated that there was no natural explanation for the aroma of lilies. Then, still in Nazareth, I awoke in the middle of the night and the room was filled with the most delicious fragrance - this time not of flowers but of sweet oil. The fragrance was accompanied by a powerful sense of the presence of God and the phrase "the balm of Gilead" came into my mind.

Jeremiah had asked:

Jeremiah 8:22
Is there no balm in Gilead? Is there no physician there? Why then is there no healing for the wound of my people?

Balm is made of natural aromatic substances that are used for healing and soothing. They are obtained from plant resin. The word balm came from balsam, a shortening of the Greek word 'balsamon', which in turn represented the Hebrew words 'baal shemen' and meant 'lord of oils'. Gilead was a well-known exporter of balm from the earliest of times. Joseph was sold by his brothers to a caravan of Ishmaelite traders who were transporting a cargo that included balm. Jeremiah's question was rhetorical; there was a great deal of balm in Gilead. The Lord himself wants to be the doctor for the wounds of his people. He is the 'Lord of oils' and he wants to reveal himself as 'the balm of Gilead'.

There is still hope for Nazareth. Although Jesus chose to live in Capernaum as an adult, the town was destroyed; Nazareth where he had lived as a child remains a vibrant community. The sin of Nazareth's unbelief, although terrible, was not as severely judged as the unbelief of the citizens of Capernaum. Jesus had said that it will be more bearable for Sodom on the day of Judgement than Capernaum. I heard an Egyptian man of God called Nabil Attala bring a clear prophetic word to the church leaders of Nazareth in October 2008. He prophesied that if they repented of the town's sin of unbelief that still gripped people then the power of the Lord would be released not just in Nazareth but the whole region. This also applies to the church in the west. Morning by morning the Muslim call to prayer rings out across the town of Nazareth as it does increasingly loudly across Western Europe. The sleeping church needs to awake, arise and answer this call to prayer. If we fail to pray, the prayers of others will prevail.

Many times we do not see unbelief as sin but dress it up as a reasonable intellectual position. If we are to see the heart of our church restored we must agree with God's assessment. Where there is a culture of honouring Jesus, the heart of God is turned towards us. In Hebrews we are told that "without faith it is impossible to please God" (Hebrews 11:6) whilst in Romans it says more starkly that "everything that does not come from faith is sin" (Romans 14:23). Unbelief is sin. When we see unbelief for what it is then we are in a position to confess, repent and receive forgiveness. In a passage where Jesus encourages us to "have faith in God" (Mark 11:22) I understand that he is not telling us to pull ourselves up by our bootstraps but to receive faith from God. We are not expected to work faith up. He is in effect inviting us to have the faith of God.

Reclaiming the Land

Is our land healed? If not, then why not? The responsibility is with us. The days are desperate, and desperate days require desperate measures. If the land is lost it can be reclaimed.

On 10th November 2002, when visiting London, I heard Les Isaac say:

Christians are embarrassed to be themselves. If what you have is real why aren't you prepared to talk about it? The church is the answer to crime. The church may not be relevant but it is still credible. We are the ecclesia, the called out ones. God has forgiven us. He wants to forgive thousands of others. We need to provoke the nation. Many people are nocturnal. Go where they are. We are too busy. There are many people who are searching for Jesus. God creates opportunities. He that is wise wins souls. Be overtly Christian; we are here for a purpose. For God so loved the world that he gave his only son. Everything that God wants to do in this world is through us. We need to be radical and available.

I was impressed with this direct, practical and radical message. God had spoken to Les Isaac and he was seeking to obey. In January 2003, two months later, he set up the first Street Pastor's team. There are now over a hundred teams of Street Pastors around the United Kingdom, including in my adopted town of Southampton. They have seen some remarkable results including a drop in the crime rate in areas where teams have been operating.

To reclaim our land then, the church needs to follow this example. God does want to reveal his prophetic strategy to recapture the hearts of the people of the land, but I believe that it will be in the prayer room rather than the committee room. The ideas will come from God, and the glory must go to Him. We have been called to make disciples of all nations. It is His initiatives and not ours that will win the day.

We need to search our hearts and ask whether our sins are confessed and forgiven. Let me repeat that Christ died for our sins and not our excuses. If we excuse ours sins, our sins cannot be excused. Are we confident that our prayers are being heard and answered? If they are not and if we are praying right then they should be; otherwise the promises of Jesus concerning prayer are meaningless.

The word of God to the people of Israel at the time of the dedication of Solomon's Temple comes to mind:

2 Chronicles 7:14

If my people, who are called by my name, will humble themselves and pray and seek my face and turn from their wicked ways, then will I hear from heaven and will forgive their sin and will heal their land.

Judgement begins in the house of God. It is a very big 'if'. "If *my people*", not "if the Government" or "if the politicians". We, the people of God, have the responsibility, and we will be held to account. A radical root-and-branch repentance is called for to avert the disaster that hovers over the whole of the Western World. We need to awake and return. There is also the promise of revival to be claimed.

It is imperative that we begin to learn the distinction between praying and seeking the face of God. Praying can imply mere talk on our part without a careful listening for God's answer. Talk is cheap. Seeking the face of God suggests a steady, determined pursuit that is not something that we do at meetings and then forget when the mood is no longer upon us. We will need his grace and stamina, and remember that the Father is seeking true worshippers. God requires our obedience and not our advice. Too often it is easy to be offended at the 'wicked ways' of others and content with our own. We must acknowledge and turn from our own wicked ways.

Have we, as the "my people" mentioned in 2 Chronicles 7:14, really humbled ourselves? Pride and self-sufficiency are the blight of Western Christianity. Cynicism is one of the "wicked ways" we must leave behind. If we take all of these steps as thoroughly and consistently as is implied here then I believe that the Lord will not be able to resist us. If we truly fulfil our part then he will not be slow in fulfilling his part. He will hear from heaven and will forgive our sin and heal our land. God's word has lost none of its power. He is waiting for us to prove his word in our experience and plead his promises. If we want to move from Nazareth to Capernaum then this is the map that we have to follow.

God's desire and intention is that the church should become a house of prayer for all nations and that his people should find joy in this house of prayer (Isaiah 56). This requires a change of attitude on behalf of the whole church. Paul's injunction to "pray continually" (1 Thessalonians 5:17) is not an impossible dream but a practical instruction. There are, across the globe, a growing number of 24/7 Houses of Prayer that are living in the good of this command. Amongst these are the International House of Prayer for all Nations (IHOP), based in Kansas, which has been established for over ten years, and the Jerusalem House of Prayer for all Nations (JHOPFAN) situated on the Mount of Olives and established in

1987. The church prospers where prayer is a priority. We are to seek first the Kingdom of God and not as an afterthought.

As Western Christians we are running out of alternatives. For too long we have felt that we can run the church without Christ. In coming to the end of our resources we can begin to avail ourselves of God's. It is in dying to ourselves that we can begin to live in the resurrection life of God. Continual prayer is the door to the presence and power of God that we so desperately need. It is no longer optional but essential. We must restore the church to the command and control of her Lord and master.

Hosea 6:1

Come, let us return to the LORD. He has torn us to pieces but he will heal us; he has injured us but he will bind up our wounds.

It is only when we return to God that He can begin to restore our hearts. To do this our hearts must not only be turned to God the Father but also to the God of our fathers. We have to recognise where we have come from to know where we are going. If we acknowledge our inheritance, we will be able to fulfil our destiny.

In AD 325 the first Christian Roman Emperor, Constantine the Great, summoned the Council of Nicaea, principally to deal with the heresy of Arianism. However, through this council he enforced a prohibition against celebrating the Lord's Supper on the day before the Jewish Passover which had been the habit of the Church in the previous centuries [3]. So the widening gulf between Christianity and Judaism became a formal divorce. It was at this point that the Church became disconnected from its Jewish roots. God will restore all things. This is why he is raising up an Elijah people.

Action!

Firstly I would encourage the reader to pray and ask for the provision to visit the Promised Land of Israel. If your own church is not arranging a tour you might consider joining a tour arranged by a Christian media organisation such as GOD TV, Premier Radio or United Christian Broadcasters who have all taken people to the land. If this prospect appeals to you I would encourage you to connect with the believers from the Arab and Jewish communities in the land. You might also consider visiting one or two of the four prayer houses that surround Jerusalem and stay a while to pray in them. If you love the Bible you will find no difficulty in loving the land of the Bible.

Meditate on the message of Capernaum and Nazareth. Consider what these towns have to say to the Western Church. How can we move from an over-familiarity with the basic tenets of Christianity to a living relationship with the risen Christ?

How should we be looking to increase the role and value of fatherhood in the church?

Prayer Points

- Begin to humble yourself; pray and seek the face of God for your land to be healed.
- Pray that God would establish prayer houses all over Western Europe and that we would see a prayer explosion around the globe.
- Pray that hearts should be turned around and restored.

REFERENCES

1. Hoffman, Carl, *Who were the Galileans in the Days of Jesus,* http://www.crosswalk.com/news/israel-insights/who-were-the-galileans-in-the-days-of-jesus.html

2. Lewis, C.S., *The Lion, the Witch and the Wardrobe;* published by Harper Collins (1950); ISBN-13 9780060764890.

3. Eusebius, *Life of Constantine* Vol. III Ch. XVIII; The Epistle of the Emperor Constantine, concerning the matters transacted at the Council, addressed to those Bishops who were not present.

Restored to the Fathers

Malachi 4:5

...he will restore the hearts.

Destination in sight

Reading this book you might think that the writer has arrived with his heart restored. If I had any illusions about this before, the Lord has disabused me of this notion during the process of writing. I have been the recipient of many wonderful miracles but remain a work in progress. God is after our hearts - both mine and yours.

God's desire is to restore the hearts of the children back to the hearts of their fathers. In this journey he wants to place the passionate heart of the fathers inside the hearts of the children. To do so he wants to restore individual hearts back to himself by correcting the lies and half-truths that we have believed about him. These lies may have been sown into our lives through society, education, our upbringing or experience. No matter how these lies arrived they must depart. The Lord wants to restore the family to the heart of society and the word of God to the heart of the family. We must rebuild our family altars, for families that pray together stay together. Society will not work without working families and families cannot work without God.

For some time a prayerful friend had been telling me that I needed more healing than I had received. I knew enough of myself to agree but knew enough of God to trust that he would reveal what was hidden in the darkness. I prayed about it and did not seek to work it out myself.

On 17th July 2011, well after the latest deadline I had set for finishing this book had passed, I awoke from a bad dream. Mercifully the details were lost to me, but I knew that it had something to do with the abuse. I shared this thought with Carol Ann, and later in the day she had an insight. She understood that the abuse I had suffered as a child had taken place more than once. I was appalled but knew what she had told me was true. I could see that this had profound implications. It explained a trait I had of returning to or persevering with difficult situations that I should walk away from. Often God's dealings with his people are gradual, and his healing is progressive. It was significant that God should have revealed this when I was just being promoted at work.

I asked God for healing. It took me a while to see the significance of the date when I had this dream - it would have been my father's 91st birthday. When I realised this I had a profound sense of my heavenly Father's love. I turned to Psalm 91 and read the following words:

Psalm 91:1-2, 9-10

He who dwells in the shelter of the Most High will rest in the shadow of the Almighty. I will say of the LORD, "He is my refuge and my fortress, my God, in whom I trust." And later, If you make the Most High your dwelling - even the LORD, who is my refuge - then no harm will befall you, no disaster will come near your tent.

God wants us to live in him. He wants to be our refuge, fortress, and our dwelling. In these days when disaster is breaking upon the nations, living in God is the only safe place. I remembered that the Dutch saint Corrie ten Boon had died on her 91st birthday; she had been born in Amsterdam on 15th April 1892 and died in Orange, California on 15th April 1983. The title of her biography 'The Hiding Place' comes from a psalm:

Psalm 119:114, New King James Version

You are my hiding place and my shield; I hope in Your word.

As Moses was once hidden in the cleft of a rock so God wants to hide us in him. If you are hidden in Christ no enemy will find you.

A few weeks later, I had a day when I felt dreadful for no obvious reason. I was at the New Wine Summer Conference and during the evening worship felt worse rather than better. I found myself draped over a chair sobbing, feeling such pain in my heart. Much of what the speaker said that evening was lost on me, but I do remember him saying how Jesus was able to walk through locked doors and say to frightened disciples, "Peace be with you!" (John 20:19) As he spoke the pain in my heart was eased. These words brought me relief, and I realised that this was exactly what Jesus had done for me. He had just walked into a locked room and spoken peace. Although we may be some way from our hearts being restored we can be sure that what God has started he will finish and that this destination is in sight.

Rumours of revival

Jesus said:

Matthew 5:6
Blessed are those who hunger and thirst for righteousness, for they will be filled.

Many times the church has looked at those discontented with 'business as usual' as a bother rather than a blessing. Yet the author of Psalm 42 opened by saying:

As the deer pants for streams of water, so my soul pants for you, O God.

We are not meant to live without God. Though many do so, it is madness to try. God has placed within us intense longings for himself that he alone can satisfy. We are told that he has placed eternity in the hearts of men (Ecclesiastes 3:11). If God is everything to us we should not be surprised by intense feelings of desperation when his presence is absent. These feelings could be as strong as homesickness, hunger or thirst. When such desires are supernaturally stirred it is certain that God intends to answer them.

Revelation 22:17
Whoever is thirsty, let him come; and whoever wishes, let him take the free gift of the water of life.

By implication if we are not thirsty then we will not come.

From the end of January through to the beginning of March 2012 I felt it impressed on me that I should seek God through a forty day period of prayer and fasting. To be honest I did not know why I had to but I knew that I did. Revival was a recurring theme running through my prayers over this time.

In the middle of this period my then fourteen-year-old daughter Keziah and some of her friends from The King's School travelled to Rwanda. She had been looking forward to this two week trip for four years. I and many others prayed a great deal for them. Moved by both the needs and the aspirations of the country after the genocide of 1994, her head teacher, Paul Johnson, had been taking groups out to Rwanda since 2008. This enabled pupils to experience Christian mission in Africa first hand.

A few days before she left Carol Ann and I went to a prayer meeting for the trip. During the meeting I quoted Isaiah:

Isaiah 43:18-19

Forget the former things; do not dwell on the past.
See, I am doing a new thing! Now it springs up; do you not perceive it?
I am making a way in the desert and streams in the wasteland.

Summarising what I felt for the group, I shared with the leaders that this trip would be different. I emailed them:

It will be marked by a new measure of freedom and of the power and the joy of the Holy Spirit. Don't let past programmes or events, even good ones, limit the new thing that God wants to do in and through you. As I have been praying it is like I have been seeing the cloud of God's presence coming down on the group. There will be a new freedom for the whole group to move in the power of the Holy Spirit.

God wants to breathe a breath of revival across the whole group. The young people are going to find that they have a great freedom to pray and prophesy and will be astonished at how the little that they bring is exactly what is needed by the African Christians that they meet. It will be like the boy bringing his packed lunch to Jesus, only to see it multiplied, and what had been his food, feed the multitudes. This link with Rwanda has already had a transforming impact upon the school but my sense is that this is going to be accelerated. It is like God wants to plant a real African

revival in the hearts of the children, in their families, in the school, and
indeed in the regional church. Get ready for God's surprises.

Although I wrote these words in faith no one was more surprised than me at the extent to which they were fulfilled. The night before the group set off I was in another prayer meeting with some friends. One of them had grown up as the son of missionaries in Africa. He knew many of those who had been used of God in the Rwandan revival that began in 1936 and continued in waves through the 1950's. By 'coincidence' he had a copy of HH Osborn's book 'Fire in the Hills' (describing the revival which spread from Rwanda) in his car and loaned it to us. Keziah carried it in her luggage as we took her to the airport the following day [1].

On Monday 6th February 2012, just a few days into the trip, I awoke from a dream in which I had been watching a prayer meeting.

In the dream I heard a voice say, "You are in revival."

I was excited by the implications but unsure of the application; who was in revival? My nation, my church or my family? The answer to my questions became clear in the following days.

That day in Rwanda proved to be a significant one for the team. Unexpectedly, their bus broke down, and their itinerary (including a radio show and visit to a school) was cancelled. This allowed a further time of preparation. That evening a teacher led a time of worship, prayer and sharing. Keziah read Isaiah 64 and asked God to rend the heavens and come down, and there was a real sense of freedom and anointing on the lives of the whole team, children and adults alike. A young woman led the worship, releasing the group into a deeper level of encounter with God. One teacher wrote that it was as if they were in "the throne room of the Almighty".

The following day they saw the beginning of large numbers responding to the young people's testimonies and the preaching of the gospel when sixty two committed their lives to Christ. The Wednesday was a rest day but on the Thursday they took the morning assembly at a primary school that had opened in 2011. They performed songs and sketches to an assembly of seven- to twelve-year-olds. 'Jonah and the Whale' and 'David and Goliath' dramas were followed by a short message from Keziah who shared how you never need to be afraid of circumstances when God is on your side. The teacher who recorded the occasion wrote:

When Keziah made the appeal, asking the children whether they wanted Jesus to forgive their sins and live in their hearts, all 301 children present raised their hands. It was a very solemn moment. Who knows its significance in God's scheme of things? [2]

When I received this account I was sitting at my desk at work. I lost all composure. As I read, tears coursed down my cheeks, and I needed to step outside for a walk and to worship God. In all of my Christian life I had never seen anything like my daughter just had. Keziah later wrote:

God was the hero in it all, my words were small. I felt like I had no idea what I was talking about; the words just flowed out of my mouth. I prayed right before I got up to speak that God would put his words in my mouth so it wasn't me talking to or touching their hearts - it was God.

As the trip went on we read with wonder the accounts of what the Lord was doing through the children. By the end of the trip some 1500 people had responded to the gospel. Teachers who were veterans of previous trips had never seen a response like this. God had broken in.

At the end of the trip Keziah wrote:

Rwanda is a country of healing. God uses the broken to mend the broken, and love seeps through the hard times. I am amazed by what I have seen. God has done so much in and through us. I feel like a changed person. I love Rwanda.

After this she had to return to school and resume her studies, but had been ruined for what might be termed 'normal' Christianity. A seed had been sown in both of our hearts.

A few days before the end of my fast I had a further prophetic dream. In this dream I and a friend of mine were in what appeared to be a revival meeting in a Western setting. I saw many people worshipping God. My friend told me that the Lord had given him the ability to prophesy to people who had no relationship with God in such a way that they came into a relationship with him. I found that I could do the same. We took turns sharing and kept on returning the meeting to worship. One of us spoke to a woman who we understood had sustained a gunshot injury, and as we did so God began to heal her. No human being was the focus of this meeting; God was. Walking past me as he left this room, a man filled my pockets with money. The only limits to God's power and provision are man's ability to trust him and take him at his word.

Clearly what God has been doing for many years in Africa he is able to do again in the West. Indeed it is essential that he does. The church needs to give him no rest until we begin to see it happen. God wants to touch and change our hearts. More than that, he wants to give us his heart.

A Heart like David

If our hearts are restored, what will they look like? In all of scripture the heart of one man is held up as an example to us. The prophet Samuel told the apostate King Saul when the kingdom was being removed from him that...

1 Samuel 13:14

...the LORD has sought out a man after his own heart and appointed him leader of his people.

God wants a regime change or a heart transplant amongst his people. Either way he is removing the kingdom from Saul and placing it under the care of David. He wants leaders in the coming revival to have a heart like David.

From the account of scripture it seems remarkable that David could have been so well beloved. In human terms there would appear to be little to choose between him and Saul. Plainly David did not find favour with the Lord because he did everything right. He was an adulterer, a ruthless murderer and on one occasion offended God as he numbered his fighting men. Yet we know that God has a different perspective from us:

1 Samuel 16:7

...the LORD looks at the heart.

Considering what we learn of David's heart in his Psalms we see why he was favoured by God. David's musical skill first brought him into Saul's service; when he worshiped, the king's demons were subdued. King David was Israel's greatest warrior but was also (as Mike Bickle has said) a lovesick worshipper. He composed many songs and even made musical instruments (2 Chronicles 7:6).

David said:

Psalm 9:1

I will praise you, O LORD, with all my heart.

As a result his heart was full of joy, and he could say:

Psalm 4:7

You have filled my heart with greater joy than when their grain and new wine abound.

He could say:

Psalm 16:9

My heart is glad.

This found expression when he was found leaping and dancing before the Lord (2 Samuel 6:16). He cared nothing for his dignity but was passionate about the honour of God. Answering his wife Michal's reproof at his abandoned display in worship, he said:

2 Samuel 6:22

I will become even more undignified than this, and I will be humiliated in my own eyes.

David was concerned about the condition of his heart knowing that only those with "clean hands and a pure heart" could ascend the hill of Lord and stand in his holy place (Psalm 24:4). When he knew he was wrong he was determined to put it right. When confronted by the prophet Nathan concerning his adultery he prayed:

Psalm 51:10

Create in me a pure heart, O God, and renew a steadfast spirit within me.

He pleaded that the Holy Spirit should not be removed from him. David knew that...

Psalm 51:17

The sacrifices of God are a broken spirit; a broken and contrite heart, O God, you will not despise.

When David became aware of having grieved God's heart, his own heart was broken.

All of this reveals that David's heart's desire was to come into and remain in the presence of God. It is no coincidence that the Israelite Kingdom reached its zenith during his forty year reign. This preoccupation with the presence of God was the key to David's success. It is evident in his words:

Psalm 27:4

One thing I ask of the LORD, this is what I seek: that I may dwell in the house of the LORD all the days of my life, to gaze upon the beauty of the LORD and to seek him in his temple.

Like Martha in the New Testament the church can be distracted with many preparations; like Mary and David we need to discover that only one thing is necessary (Luke 10:42).

David's passion for God's presence was all consuming. He said:

Psalm 132:3-5

I will not enter my house or go to my bed - I will allow no sleep to my eyes, no slumber to my eyelids, till I find a place for the LORD, a dwelling for the Mighty One of Jacob.

David's priority is revealed when we look at his relationship with the Ark of the Covenant. After this holy box had been built by Moses and carried into the Promised Land by the Levites under Joshua's guidance it was housed in the Holy of Holies within the Tabernacle. The tent came to rest at Shiloh where it remained for three hundred years from the days of Joshua through to the time of Samuel. Jewish tradition has it that during these years the tent was replaced by a solid structure. On one visit to Israel I was taken to the settlement of Shiloh and to a rectangular outline on a bare hillside where it is believed the Tabernacle had been built. In this wild and beautiful setting there was a fearful sense of the holiness of the Lord. The Ark of the Covenant was taken out of the Tabernacle at Shiloh onto the battlefield by the wicked sons of Eli, Hophni and Phineas. It was captured and these priests were killed. God allowed the Tabernacle which had housed the Ark to be destroyed (see Psalm 78:60 and Jeremiah 7:12-14). After a brief excursion into Philistine territory as a result of which these enemies of Israel suffered fearful plagues it was returned to the land but found no permanent resting place, staying first in Beth Shemesh and then in Kiriath Jearim in the house of Abinadab. Eleazar, Abinadab's son was then consecrated to guard the ark (2 Samuel 6:3).

During the forty year reign of Saul the Ark was neglected and received little mention. It was used once to consult the Lord during Jonathan's victory over the Philistines (1 Samuel 14:18-19). David was convinced that the Ark of the Covenant should be brought to Jerusalem. His first attempt to carry the Ark to his capital city was a failure. He did not obey Moses' rules for transporting it but used a cart as the Philistines, who knew no better, had done. In the process Uzzah reached out his hand to steady the Ark when the oxen pulling the cart stumbled; the Lord's anger burned against him and he perished (2 Samuel 6:7). In this respect God was not "Uzzah friendly"!

Uzzah and Ahio, like Eleazar, were recorded as being the sons of Abinadab; however they were not consecrated. We do not know whether Uzzah had not been well taught by his father or had not listened to his instruction. Uzzah (whose name means 'strength') would have grown up with the Ark of the Covenant in his home and became over-familiar with the presence of God. We must not rely on our strength:

Zechariah 4:6

'Not by might nor by power, but by my Spirit,' says the LORD Almighty.

I have wondered whether he had dusted the Ark and in some way, having lived with it, thought that it belonged to him. This is a warning to us all. No one can seek to control, contain or help God.

David was understandably much more reverent and careful when he next tried to move the Ark. During those three months David gained courage to move it because he learned that the Lord had blessed the "entire household" of Obed-Edom where it rested at that time (2 Samuel 6:12). This Jewish king was provoked to jealousy by this Gentile man; Obed-Edom was a Gittite and not one of God's chosen people. He brought the Ark to Jerusalem and "set it in its place inside the tent that [he] had pitched for it" (2 Samuel 6:17). David's real desire was to build a house for the Lord, but because he had been a man of blood he was forbidden (2 Samuel 7:4-6). The Lord promised that his son would build him a house and that God would build a lasting dynasty for David.

One of the first things that he did when he became King over Jerusalem was to establish 24/7 worship (1 Chronicles 15-16). Although David did not build the temple he who wrote down the plan that he had received from for his son Solomon (1 Chronicles 28:19). He personally financed 4,000 musicians, 288 singers and 4,000 gatekeepers to minister continually to the Lord (1 Chronicles 23:5 and 25:7). Within David's Tabernacle, worship and prayer continued night and day (1 Chronicles 25). In the same way we live in days when the sons must build in fulfilment of the fathers' vision.

The prophet Amos foretold that in the last days God will "restore David's fallen tent" (Amos 9:11). The phrase "David's fallen tent" is thought to be a figure of speech for a restoration of the fallen dynasty of David. It is surely no coincidence that this passage was part of the selected readings for the Jewish people on 14th May 1948, the day that Israel was reborn. It is being fulfilled through his greatest descendant Jesus Christ.

This prophecy was quoted in the account of the Council of Jerusalem in the book of Acts with a reason added:

Acts 15:17

...that the remnant of men may seek the Lord, and all the Gentiles who bear my name.

Jesus had told the woman at the well that the Father seeks "true worshipers [who] will worship [him] in spirit and truth" (John 4:23). He is looking for a company of people who will have a heart to honour and worship God like David.

For this reason when it was recorded in the book of Acts that the Lord said, "I have found David son of Jesse a man after my own heart; he will do everything I want him to do" (Acts 13:22), King David was commended as one who "served the purpose of God in his own generation" (Acts 13:36). With these words in mind Arthur Wallis urged, "Find out what God is doing in your generation and fling yourself into it." God has a purpose in this generation. We have only one life. Let us commit to fulfil the purpose of God through our lives in this generation.

Return

For many years the church has been praying:

Isaiah 64:1
Oh, that you would rend the heavens and come down, that the mountains would tremble before you!

It is good to pray this way, but it can leave the impression that the problem is unwillingness in heaven rather than on earth. This is not true. Heaven is willing; are we?

Joel 2:12-14
"Even now," declares the LORD, "return to me with all your heart, with fasting and weeping and mourning." Rend your heart and not your garments. Return to the LORD your God, for he is gracious and compassionate, slow to anger and abounding in love, and he relents from sending calamity. Who knows? He may turn and relent and leave behind a blessing.

If we desire to see God rend the heavens we must be prepared to rend our hearts. Revival has to start somewhere. It must begin in our hearts. It is in this rending of our hearts that they can ultimately be restored to our fathers.

On 14th May 1988 I had reached the end of a Bible class on teaching and preaching that had been led by Arthur. The climax of the course was to preach a five minute trial sermon before Arthur and Tony Morton (who was leading the church). I was terrified but became more so as I prepared my message. The verse I had been given to prepare from was:

Zechariah 1:14

I am very jealous for Jerusalem and Zion.

It seemed obvious to me what I had to say - reiterated by the fact that the day I would be speaking was the fortieth anniversary of the rebirth of the state of Israel! Given that the church has generally been silent about this significant event, it felt that I was being very controversial in stating that the rebirth of Israel was a miracle and a fulfilment of scripture. I knew that my message was a good one but felt that my delivery left much to be desired. Arthur, seeing my nervousness, was kind enough to tell me that I had said nothing wrong. Many in the church believe that God's hand is on Israel but have not spoken out to that effect. It is now time to stand up and speak out.

God says to us through Isaiah:

Isaiah 62:6-7

I have posted watchmen on your walls, O Jerusalem; they will never be silent day or night. You who call on the LORD, give yourselves no rest, and give him no rest till he establishes Jerusalem and makes her the praise of the earth.

At a time when no nation is standing with Israel God is calling the body of Christ to stand with and pray for the peace of Jerusalem. Unless the church does this she will not fulfil her end time call. No one will have peace unless Jerusalem is at peace.

It is striking that the church has rarely equalled and has yet to surpass the power and impact that it possessed in the first century when it was led by Jewish Apostles and connected to its Jewish root. It was then claimed that the Christians had "turned the world upside down" (Acts 17:6); in truth these disciples up-righted an upside-down world. The hearts of the children must turn back to the fathers if they are to do the same again. The promise through Haggai remains good:

Haggai 2:8
The glory of this present house will be greater than the glory of the former house.

Our best as well as our most challenging days are ahead of us. Jesus is coming soon and will come suddenly. Even if this were not true we only have one life and we should live it for God. All must appear before him. When He returns, will He find faith on the earth? The call of God is to rise up and become an Elijah people who will prepare the way for the coming of the Lord. To do this we must impact society in every sphere but most particularly in family life.

To conclude let us return to Malachi:

Malachi 4:5-6, NIV, 2011
See, I will send the prophet Elijah to you before that great and dreadful day of the LORD comes. He will turn the hearts of the parents to their children, and the hearts of the children to their parents; or else I will come and strike the land with total destruction.

These words provide both a promise and a warning. God will most certainly intervene in human history. He has done so before and will do so again. How we meet him depends upon us. Will we encounter him as our father or our judge?

Many have taught of the danger of complacency in this last, Laodicean age of the church. Jesus warned:

Matthew 24:12
Because of the increase of wickedness, the love of most will grow cold.

A lukewarm church makes Christ sick. We must return to our first love. God is looking for passionate people who will carry his fiery heart of love for the world that He gave his Son for. If our restored hearts have a destination, it is this: to fulfil both the great commandments and the great commission. We are to love the Lord our God with all of our heart, mind, soul and strength and in expression of our obedience to His command to love our neighbour as ourselves. We are commanded to go into the whole world and preach the good news to all creation.

Action!

You have reached the end of this book but I would encourage you not to simply take my word for what has been written. Check it out against the scriptures. In the days in which we live we all need to cultivate the attitude of the Bereans. We are told:

Acts 17:11

...the Bereans were of more noble character than the Thessalonians, for they received the message with great eagerness and examined the Scriptures every day to see if what Paul said was true.

I would encourage Christians to read their Bibles not as a document to study but as a manual for life. We need the word of God more than our breath or daily bread for it brings us to life. We are not really alive unless we hear God through his word. Derek Prince described how when he began studying the Bible he initially thought that he was reading it - only to discover that it was reading him! Many are familiar with this experience. Mark Twain is reported to have said:

It ain't those parts of the Bible that I can't understand that bother me, it is the parts that I do understand. [2]

Something that I learned from the African church that I visited with my family was that we need to read the Bible not with an open commentary but with an attitude of devotion. For many years I had a battle with feeling that I was not praying enough. It was with a great sense of relief and liberation that I heard TB Joshua say that to read the Bible with devotion is to pray. Prayer is a two-way conversation in which what

God has to say to us is far more important than what we have to say to him. When we read the Bible with a reverent heart we will hear God. The Bible is the best commentary upon itself. God said through Isaiah:

> **Isaiah 66:2**
> *This is the one I esteem: he who is humble and contrite in spirit, and trembles at my word.*

To read the Bible with devotion means to tremble at God's word. This means trembling with a thrill, with the fear of the Lord and with love. The best way to do this is to read the Bible as it was written. Peter tells us that the Bible came into being when men spoke from God as they were carried along by the Holy Spirit (2 Peter 1:20). If we tremble at God's word when we read it then we will be carried along by the Holy Spirit. This cannot but change our hearts.

Prayer Points

- Ask the Lord to restore your heart and to give you a passionate heart like David.
- Pray that people everywhere would take God at his word and claim his promises.
- Ask him to restore his word to the heart of the family and to the heart of the Church.

REFERENCES

1. Osborn, HH, *Fire in the Hills: the revival which spread from Rwanda;* published by Highland books (1991). ISBN 0946616795.
2. http://www.equipuk.org/
3. Twain, Mark, http://thinkexist.com/quotation/it_aint_those_parts_of_the_ bible_that_i_can-t/262060.htmlas

From the Publisher

Other titles in the **Timeless Teaching** series:

Books available from the publisher:
www.onwardsandupwards.org